Design & Development of the
INDY CAR

by Roger Huntington

THANKS

I would like to express my deepest appreciation to those who provided pictures and drawings that are such a vital part of this book. To the historical files of the Indianapolis Speedway, Jerry Gebby, Griff Borgeson and CAR & DRIVER Magazine. To Speedway photographers Ron McQueeney and Dan Francis, and to Milo Rowell for access to his voluminous private color collecton. And my great thanks to artists Vic Berris of AUTOCAR Magazine, C.O. La Tourette and Dave Kimble for their brilliant technical cutaways. Words are a dime a dozen, guys—but it takes pictures to tell a story!

Thanks to those who helped make sure those dime-a-dozen words are right: Gordon Schroeder and Myron Stevens with the period covering the '30s and '40s, and Ralph Payne with the '50s, '60s and the '70s; Hugh MacInnes and Duke Hallock looked over turbocharging; Dick Ronzi reviewed the '63 and '64 Ford Indy-engine development; Don Bartos helped with the Cosworth engine.

Co-Publishers: Bill & Helen Fisher; Executive Editor: Carl Shipman
Editorial Director: Tom Monroe; Art Director: Don Burton; Book Design: Tom Jakeway
Typography: Cindy Coatsworth, Joanne Nociti, Michelle Claridge
Front Cover Illustrations: Penske PC6 drawing by Tony Matthews
Stutz Team Photo courtesy of IMS
Back Cover Illustrations: Duesenberg & Offy engine drawings by Dave Kimble
Chaparral photo by Ed Ingalls

Published by H.P. Books, P.O. Box 5367, Tucson, AZ 85703   602/888-2150
ISBN 0-89586-103-8 Library of Congress Catalog Card No. 81-80683
©1981 Fisher Publishing, Inc. Printed in U S A

TABLE OF CONTENTS

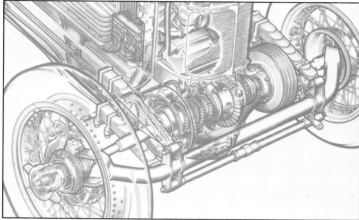

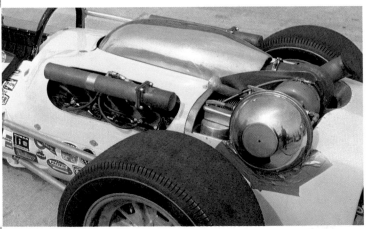

INDY 500
THE CARS

The Indianapolis 500-mile race is unique if for no other reason than all the books that have been written about it. It's the best-documented race in the world. Most of the books are about the men involved—the drivers, mechanics, car designers, car owners, race officials. Or about the color and glamour and excitement of great races down through the years. A lot of drama has unfolded on the famous bricks in some 70 years of auto-racing history. Lots of fodder here for the writer with a personal touch.

This book is different. We're going to be looking at the machines that made the 500. The cars, not so much the men. This type of documentation is sadly lacking in every type of motor racing. How often have you read that Joe Blow won such-and-such a race by so many seconds—how he battled it out wheel-to-wheel for the last ten laps, to outsmart his opponents on the last turn? You could imagine he beat them in a foot race. More often than not, the type of car he was driving isn't mentioned. Whether a Chaparral or Wildcat, or a Miller or Duesenberg. The driver has always been the big story.

But these same men would be the first to tell you they never could have won without the right car under them. A car with competitive acceleration, braking, cornering, steering response, durability. I've talked to hundreds of professional race drivers. Not one ever downgraded the importance of his car in the elusive "winning combination." Not one ever hinted he could win with a poor car by "driving over" a serious lack of horsepower or handling response or durability. Some have even admitted, in a special moment of candor, that the car might be most of the winning combination!

You can read this from the way a driver's confidence focus changes as he gains experience. "Give me a chance and I'll show you," says the rookie. The veteran is on much safer ground when he says, "Give me a decent 'ride' and I'll show you." The veteran has learned the hard way that *it's the combination that wins.* The right car, the right driver, the right crew chief, a smart car designer—even a car owner who has plenty of money and is willing to spend it!

But the "combination" can be pretty elusive sometimes. How many times have you seen last year's Indy winner not even in contention this year? Even though he may be part of the same team—the same mechanics, car designer, car owner. Maybe they're even running the same car. But it's been modified from last year. Suddenly last year's winning driver can't seem to get through the corners as fast, can't pass everybody on the straights like last year. He tries every driving trick he knows. The speed just isn't there. But does the driver say he's lost some skill in 12 months? That he's losing his touch? Hey! The classic racetrack explanation has been the same for 70 years: "We can't seem to find the combination." What he's really saying: "There's something wrong with the car. If the mechanics don't find the problem soon, I'll be lucky to qualify."

So I think maybe it's high time for a book on the cars that have made Indianapolis history. How were they designed? Why were some faster than others? Why didn't the fastest car always win? How did rule changes affect the design of cars? Which were the "milestone" cars that started important trends? Who were the men responsible for these breakthroughs? How much did Indy-car development influence passenger-car progress, and vice versa? And, very important, what were the effects on race cars of developments in the related industrial technologies—tires, fuels, metallurgy, machining techniques, synthetic materials, electronics? Some say race-car development is like a Buck Rogers island in a Medieval world. Don't believe it. Sometimes it's the other way around. We might even explode a few myths about famous Indianapolis cars when we dig behind the people and the color and the glamour.

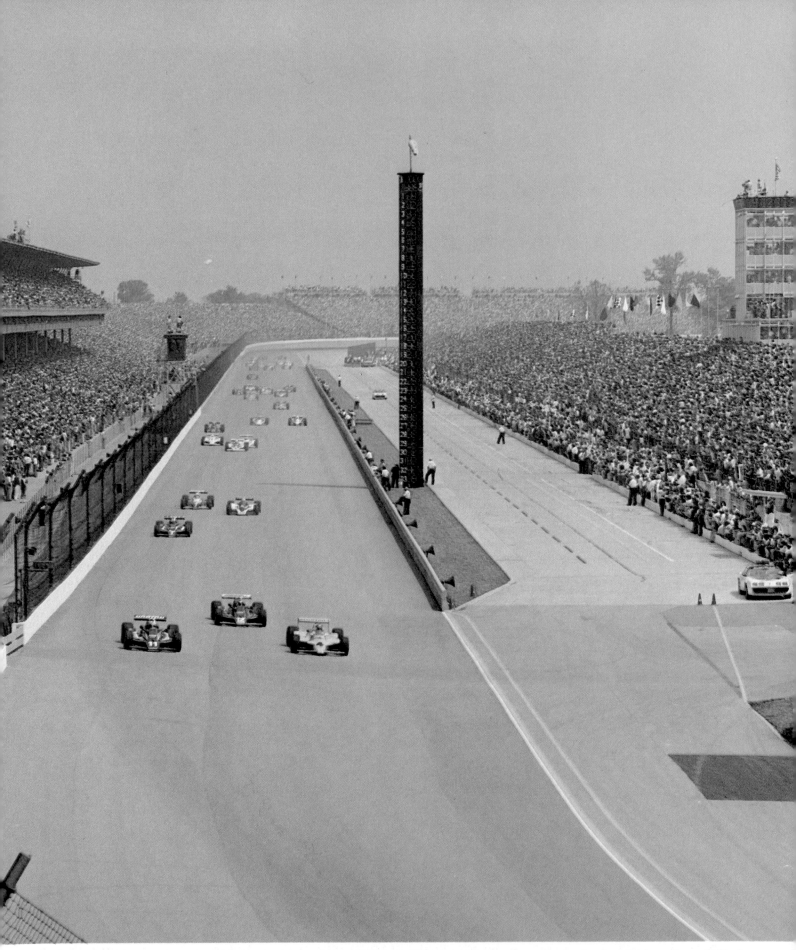

Johnny Rutherford leading the pack for the start of the 1980 Indy 500. Looking north up the main straight from turn-1. Truly the single "greatest spectacle in racing"—or in sports for that matter. This book looks beneath the skin of the cars that have run the Indy 500 why they were or were not successful. Photo courtesy of Indianapolis Motor Speedway.

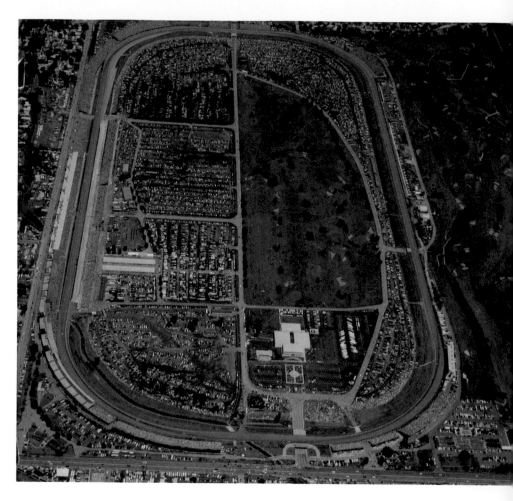

A NEW KIND OF RACETRACK

The Indianapolis 500 could never have become the world-famous race it is without a very special, unique track to run on. In fact, when the track was originally conceived in 1908, there wasn't an auto-race or test course anywhere in the world even remotely resembling it. High-banked oval speedways like Brooklands in England, Montlhery in France and Monza in Italy were years in the future. The idea of a closed, oval-like track that could handle lap averages of 80 and 90 mph *and* be mostly visible from one big grandstand was quite radical in the early 1900's.

Why build it in Indianapolis? Why not in Detroit, the cradle of the automobile industry? Simple: Detroit *wasn't* the cradle of the auto industry. Indianapolis was! Some 250 makes of passenger cars and trucks have come out of Indianapolis. And up until 1905,

more cars were manufactured there than in Detroit. In the early years of the century there wasn't any more logical place in the world to build a great auto speedway than Indianapolis.

Actually the original purpose of the speedway was to publicize the new "horseless-carriage" type of transportation, and to promote technical development of the automobile. The original founders, headed by Carl Fisher, were all automotive men. None expected to take the last dollar of profit out of the track. It was to be a service to the industry that had already made them wealthy.

Distance around — Physically the track has always been impressive when compared with other great auto racetracks of the world. Lap distance on the inside line is just 2.5 miles, laid out roughly in a rectangle — two long straightaways on the sides and short "chutes" on each end connected by four corners struck on a radius of 840 feet.

This gives a distance of 1/4 mile (1,320 ft.) through each corner, with 3,301 ft. for the two long straights and 660 ft. for the two short chutes. Obviously the four corners make up more than one-third of the total lap length. The original track width was 50 ft. on the straights and 60 ft. in the turns.

Banking—Selecting the degree of banking for the turns was a problem. There was no way the designers could have anticipated future cars with the potential for 200-mph lap averages. They calculated the banking for cars of their day. The major bank angle selected was 16.6°, with the outer 10 ft. of the turns increased to 36°. When calculated with the turn radius of 840 ft., the main part of the banking would give a neutral "hands-off" speed of about 60 mph. In other words, this is the speed that a car could corner with no side force—that is, the resultant of the centrifugal force and car weight would be perpendicular to the track surface. Neutral speed on the outer 36° portion of the banking would figure to about 100 mph. It wasn't intended that cars would run out that far. The reason for the sudden increase in banking was to deflect cars back to the inside if they should spin out toward the wall. This reinforced-concrete retaining wall was originally 9-inches thick and 33-inches high.

From another standpoint you could say the Indy turns were banked for speeds of 80 to 90 mph. This would be the maximum theoretical speed on the 16° banking before tire traction would be lost on the original tar-and-crushed-stone surface. Cars could exceed this theoretical speed by drifting and broadsliding, like you see on dirt tracks. But it seems obvious that the track designers had lap speeds in mind of well under 100 mph when they calculated Indy's corners.

Track surface—It's interesting how the track surface turned out to be brick. In fact the original surface, was a carefully graded and rolled mixture of tar and crushed stone. It was entirely unsuitable. The first race in 1909 turned out to be a literal blood bath from a series of crashes caused by punctured tires, flying stones and uncertain traction. The whole Indianapolis idea almost died right there. There was no choice but to either abandon the track or hard-pave it. It boiled down to a choice between bricks and concrete. Concrete was cheaper, but bricks lasted longer. Bricks it was. It's to Carl Fisher's credit that he didn't count pennies at this critical time. If the paving choice had been concrete—like they used for most of the great autodromes of Europe, and which have now crumbled to dust—our beloved Indianapolis 500 might never have survived for 70 years.

We should call it the "brickyard" only with a note of reverence!

1
AGE OF THE MONSTERS
1911—1919

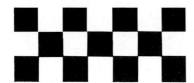

The Marmon Wasp that won the first Indy 500 in 1911 was essentially a hopped-up, stripped-down production sports model powered by a huge 477-CID 6-cylinder, T-head engine. It developed about 110 HP at 2,400 rpm, and propelled the car to a top speed of nearly 100 mph. Note the first rearview mirror mounted high on the cowl. Photo courtesy of IMS.

THE FIRST INDY RACERS

The first cars to compete in the 500-mile race, both domestic and foreign, were essentially stripped production sports models with relatively minor modifications. Many, in fact, were entered by the companies which produced them. It was pretty much a matter of picking your fastest model, stripping off unnecessary body parts, and doing a little minor "tuning" to get maximum straightaway speed, decent handling in the turns, and enough durability to run 500 miles flat-out.

These first Indy racers, then, had all the good and bad points of production passenger cars in that period around 1912. Most of the engines were huge 4- and 6-cylinder monsters of 400- to 600-CID, T-head valve layout—valves on opposite sides of the cylinder bore—and typically producing *maybe* 100 HP at 2,000 rpm. High revs were out of the question

because the heavy cast-iron pistons and unbalanced crankshafts made for tremendous inertia loads on the bearings. And these bearings were a soft babbitt, or lead-base metal, poured or cast into a bronze shell. Lubrication was usually by the hit-and-miss "splash" system. Connecting rods scooped their oil out of troughs and the mains got theirs by gravity drip feed. The oil pump only needed 2—4 pounds per square inch (psi) pressure to do its job.

Perhaps the most reliable components on those early engines were the carburetors and ignition magnetos. Carburetors were generally a single-jet updraft type, often with a barrel-type throttle. Fuel feed was by gravity or hand air pump, so there wasn't much to go wrong. Ignition reliability was assured by using two spark magnetos and two spark plugs per cylinder. In fact, combustion chambers were so huge that the fuel mixture wouldn't burn com-

pletely when one plug was used!

A typical chassis used a channel-section ladder-type frame, semi-elliptic leaf springs all around, Hartford friction shock absorbers, and external-contracting brakes on rear wheels only. Many used transmission brakes. Tires were usually of fabric carcass construction with smooth or simple grooved treads. They were inflated to 80—100 psi and mounted on clincher-type rims. Drivelines consisted of a cone-type clutch, 3-speed crash-type transmission, with shaft drive to a bevel-geared axle. A few cars used chain drive.

Probably the most notable characteristic of those early Indy chassis was the tremendous twisting and bending of the frame. This prevented any degree of precise suspension tuning. You couldn't predict what path a wheel would follow when rising over a bump. And this, of course, also affected steering geometry. The best you could hope for was to get a car that

Joe Dawson won the 1912 race in a 4-cylinder, 491-CID National—another hopped-up sports car. It developed 120 HP at 2,200 rpm, and could lap the brick track 4 or 5 mph faster than the 1911 Marmon. Photo courtesy of IMS.

could stay on the course and avoid other traffic. Following a precise "groove" lap after lap hardly seemed possible.

How about performance? With car weights of 2,000—2,500 lbs. and 100 HP or so from the engine, top speeds were around 90 mph—maybe 100 mph from the fastest cars. And average lap speeds were around 80 mph. This would imply turn speeds of 70—75 mph.

Remember, they were just stripped, mildly modified production sports cars, not genuine built-from-the-ground-up racing cars.

WERE THE EUROPEAN RACERS REALLY BETTER?

It took the French and Germans to show us how to build "genuine" racing cars. And, yes, they were better cars—in those early days anyway.

The French Peugeot racers, winners in 1913 and front-row qualifiers up to World War I, were probably the most significant and progressive race-car designs of all time. They were certainly the most copied. In fact the 4-cylinder "Offy" had its roots in that primitive Peugeot engine.

Its pattern is as familiar today as it was radical then: Four cylinders in-line; dual-overhead camshafts operating four valves per cylinder through cup-type followers; pent-roof-type combustion chambers with a centrally located spark plug; cylinder block and head cast integral; barrel-type crankcase with crankshaft and main-bearing bulkheads inserted from one end. Sound like an Offy? Peugeot introduced these features nearly 70 years ago!

And the engines really did give superior performance. The 7.3-liter version that won the 1913 Indy race developed 162 HP at 2,250 rpm, giving the car a top speed of 115 mph. Winner Jules Goux never used more than 1,700 rpm in the race. Later, smaller-displacement versions delivered even

more HP per cubic inch—and the cars were even faster on lap speed, if not top speed. It was immediately obvious to many automotive people that this was the right way to build a deep-breathing, high-revving race engine. Copies began springing up all over the world. In fact Indianapolis Speedway management was so intrigued by the glamour of that early Peugeot-type performance that they commissioned the Premier Motor Co. to build a three-car team of replicas when the French company announced they would stop building racing cars in 1914. These "speedway team cars" helped fill out a lively field for the 1916 Indy race.

If there was one flaw in that early Peugeot performance equation, it was the use of extremely long strokes in all their engines. This boosted piston speeds, which in turn increased internal friction and inertia forces, severely limiting rpm. The 1913 Indy winner, for in-

9

Joe Dawson winning the 1912 race in his No. 8 National. In those days it was a major feat to finish the 500 miles at anywhere near the top speed potential of the car. Many cars were barely running at the finish—if at all.

Earliest cars had tires mounted on demountable rims that had to be slipped off the wheel during a tire change. This required more time than with later demountable wheels—and there were plenty of tire changes. Photo courtesy of Jerry Gebby.

Wheel-spindle and axle breakage was common in the early days, causing many crashes. Metallurgy and heat-treating were in their infancy, and designers didn't know how to design and build components to handle the loads experienced by "high-speed" race cars. Consequently there were many fatigue failures. Photo courtesy of Jerry Gebby.

French Peugeot that won the 1913 race was far advanced beyond American cars. It featured a dual-overhead-camshaft engine, demountable wire wheels, adjustable friction shock absorbers, and an unprecedented top speed of 115 mph. Driver Jules Goux never used full speed in the race. Photo courtesy of IMS.

When Peugeot stopped building race cars prior to World War I, Indianapolis Speedway officials contracted with the Premier Motor Co. to construct Peugeot duplicates for the 1916 race. Peugeots were so popular with the fans that track officials thought they'd better find another source of supply! But the Premiers didn't go as fast! Photo courtesy of IMS.

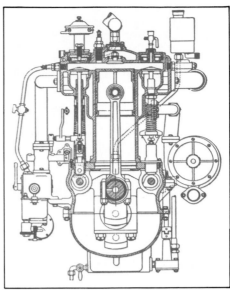

Very early American Indy racers used basically stock engines. The "T-head" configuration was popular, with a broad, flat combustion chamber, valves on both sides of the cylinder, and dual camshafts in the crankcase. Very simple. Screw-in plugs above each valve allowed the valves to be removed, ground and replaced with the integrally-cast cylinder-head/block.

stance, had a stroke length of almost 8 in. It was limited to a modest 2,250 rpm. Even the later 3-liter versions were limited to 2,800 rpm—a crying shame. With the breathing potential of the advanced valve and porting layout, even considering the primitive bottom-end setups and lubrication systems, those vintage Peugeots could just as well have been developing 20% more HP at 3,500 rpm.

Admittedly there was a valid excuse for the extreme stroke/bore ratios of the period. European Grand Prix rules then limited bore diameter, rather than total displacement like in America. Thus, it behooved the engine designer to use the longest possible stroke to get maximum dis-placement. Peugeot just went further than anyone else.

Perhaps we should pause here and establish proper credit for the brilliant ideas that went into those early French racing cars.

Actually Peugeot had little to do with the design of the cars. They just financed their construction and campaigning. The concepts and development came from three previous Peugeot Grand Prix drivers—Paolo Zuccarelli, Jules Goux and Georges Boillot. These men wanted to build a G.P. car that would beat the world, and they were able to talk the Peugeot management into backing the project. They hired a young Swiss draftsman, Ernest Henri, to put their ideas on paper. It has become popular legend that Henri designed the cars. This is not true. Henri was a very capable draftsman-engineer, and he had a knack for detailing mental images on paper. But he was not creative in his own right. In fact they say Zuccarelli was responsible for 80% of the ideas that went into those early Peugeots.

11

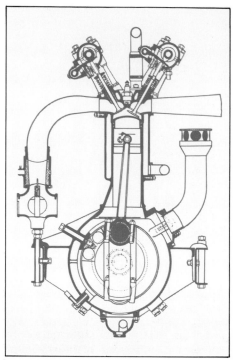

Dual-overhead-cam Peugeot engine has been the pattern for most of the world's racing engines ever since, including the venerable Offy. It featured a 60° angle between valves, four valves per cylinder, central spark plug, and integral cylinder-head and block casting. Look like an Offy? Worst feature was the long stroke, which increased friction, limited rpm and reduced power. The Indy version used cup-type cam followers rather than the finger type on this early model.

French Delage racer that won the 1914 race gave away some 70 CID to the bigger American engines. It developed a modest 105 HP at 3,100 rpm from 380 cubes. Relatively light 2,300 lbs. and streamlined body nose gave it the speed to do the job. Photo courtesy of IMS.

This is further substantiated by studying the French Ballot racing cars that were so competitive at Indianapolis in the period before the war, Ernest Henri went over to Ballot—and he singlehandedly designed those first postwar racers. And, sure enough, they were little more than 8-cylinder versions of the prewar 4-cylinder Peugeots. There were few significant differences. Henri even continued to use long strokes when there was no longer any need under European rules. The effect on usable rpm was the same. His 4.9-liter Ballot designed for the 1919 Indy race was limited to 3,000 rpm. It was a fast car, but it could have been faster.

THE AMERICANS FIGHT BACK

I've been singing the praises of the French racing cars around the World War I period. But actually there were several American-built-from-the-ground-up cars that were quite competitive in these years. Like Stutz, Duesenberg, Miller, Frontenac, Maxwell. No American car won the 500 between 1913 and 1919; but some of them were always very competitive on lap speed, and they had a good finishing record. They just didn't quite have the spark to win.

It's interesting that none of these above-mentioned American makes copied the Peugeot dual-overhead-cam layout. All but Duesenberg used a single-overhead cam, operating four valves per cylinder through roller rocker arms. Spark plugs were located on each side of the combustion chamber. This was the layout of the very successful 1914 Grand Prix Mercedes which won the following year with Ralph DePalma driving. How much the American designers were influenced by the German car we don't know. But it's certain the single-overhead-cam 4-cylinder engine was the racing style in this country prior to 1920. European designers were actually much quicker to copy the Peugeot theme than our people.

Admittedly there wasn't a big difference in performance between well-executed examples of the two layouts. All the above American engines were built to the 300-CID limit that started in 1915. And they all developed somewhere between 120 and 135 HP at about 3,000 rpm. The Peugeot and Mercedes engines were built to a 4.5-liter—274 CID limit in effect in Europe at that time. They gave 110—120 HP at 2,800 rpm. So actually all were quite equal on a basis of HP per cu.in. If you calculate the "brake mean effective pressure" (BMEP), or the average combustion pressure on the pistons during the power stroke, you find all these engines fall in the narrow 115—120 psi range.

You would think there should be greater differences in perfor-

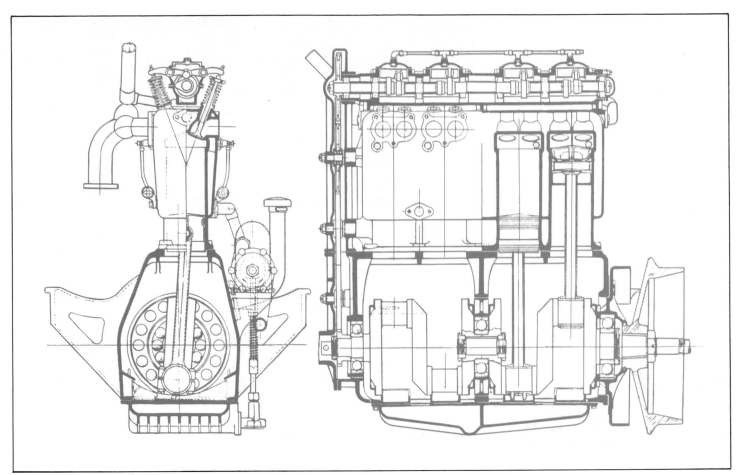

1915 Stutz 4-cylinder made by the Wisconsin Engine Co. Earliest American "full-race" engines had single overhead camshafts, usually with four valves per cylinder and spark plugs on each side of the combustion chamber. Note the very long stroke and ball bearings on the crankshaft mains. This engine had pressure lubrication to the sleeve-type rod bearings—an advanced feature then. Drawing courtesy of Jerry Gebby.

mance with these two valve, port and combustion-chamber layouts. Evidently any differences in the breathing of the various engines was offset by their high internal friction due to the long strokes on all the engines. All were literally bogged down by friction.

It's also interesting to compare average lap speeds for the American and European cars in the 300-CID period (1915—'19). Howdy Wilcox sat on the pole in 1915 with a Stutz at a speed of 98.90 mph. Ralph DePalma was right beside him in the Mercedes at 98.58 mph. And a Peugeot was

Many early Indy cars were produced and sponsored by automobile companies. Here are the smartly outfitted drivers and mechanics of the 1915 Stutz team. Cars were painted a brilliant white with red numbers. The three cars finished 3rd, 4th and 7th. Photo courtesy of Jerry Gebby.

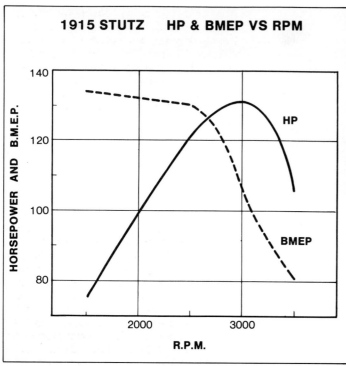

1915 STUTZ   HP & BMEP VS RPM

1915 Stutz engine developed 131 HP at 3,000 rpm from 296 CID. But note the radical drop-off of power and BMEP (cylinder pressure) at higher speeds. This was primarily to excessive internal friction, inadequate carburetion, and poor intake and exhaust flow from bad valve timing. With modern valve timing and carburetion, this engine could develop half again as much power!

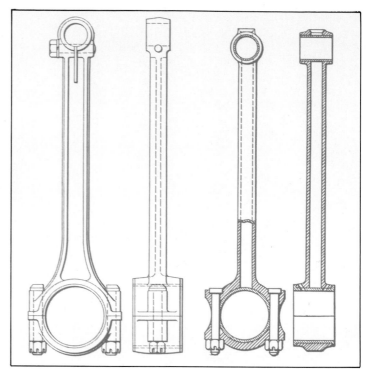

Fred Duesenberg used both tubular and H-section connecting rods in his early engines. Tubular rods had a better strength-to-weight ratio, but were more costly to manufacture. They were usually forged, then drilled to get the hollow shank.

third at 98.47. What could be closer? In 1916 there were two Peugeots, a Maxwell and a Premier in the front row—they started four abreast in those days. In 1919 Frenchman Rene Thomas astonished everybody with a lap record of 104.78 mph in the new straight-8 Ballot. They claimed 140 HP for that car. But the Americans were right in there. Louis Chevrolet qualified his Frontenac at 103.10 mph, and the third and fourth highest qualifying speeds were American cars.

What I'm saying is, the American racers were just about as fast as the European cars on a lap-average basis during the 300-CID period. Their engines produced as much HP per cubic inch, but they just didn't seem to have the ruggedness and durability to win the race.

THE BIG PROBLEM: DURABILITY

Yes, the toughest problem faced by the race-car designer in those days was how to run 500 miles at lap speeds anywhere near the true potential of his car. His second problem was how to raise his average race speed by reducing time lost during pit stops.

Consider the durability problem. I've mentioned the primitive splash-lubrication systems in the early years. It's a wonder the engines could run more than a few minutes with these. Many mechanics used castor-based oils in those days, as it was reputed to have more film strength and "oiliness" than mineral oils of the day. Some claimed 250 rpm more engine speed with castor. Additives were unknown, so you couldn't modify

the original characteristics of your oil to do a special job. Splash-lubrication systems eventually gave way to full-pressure systems by the end of the decade. Ball bearings replaced plain babbitt bearings in some critical areas. By 1919 lubrication wasn't a limiting factor on engine output.

Another phase of the lubrication problem gave everybody fits in those early days. This was the matter of oil leakage out of engines due to primitive and inefficient oil seals and gaskets. Do you have any idea how much oil all those cars dumped on the track in 500 miles? The record was 104 gallons. That's gallons, not quarts! It was common for one car to consume 20 or 30 gallons during the course of the race—cars that used only 10 or 15 gallons were considered real "tight!"

Ace American driver, Ralph DePalma, chose German Mercedes race cars in the early years. He won the 1915 race in this 4.5-liter (274 CID) 4-cylinder powered Mercedes. Although not the fastest, they were very rugged and durable. Note the chain drive and "streamlining" on the front frame horns.

Cutaway of the 4.5-liter (274 CID) 4-cylinder Mercedes engine that powered the 1915 winner. It featured their unique aircraft-type fabricated cylinder-block/head construction. In fact the whole design was basically aircraft, including the tower-driven single overhead camshaft and four valves per cylinder. It developed 115 HP at 2,800 rpm. Courtesy of AUTOCAR.

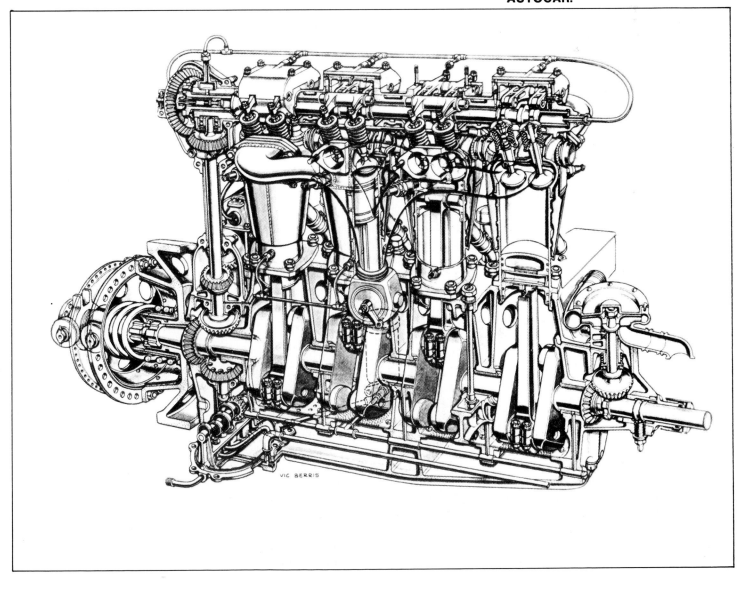

VIC BERRIS

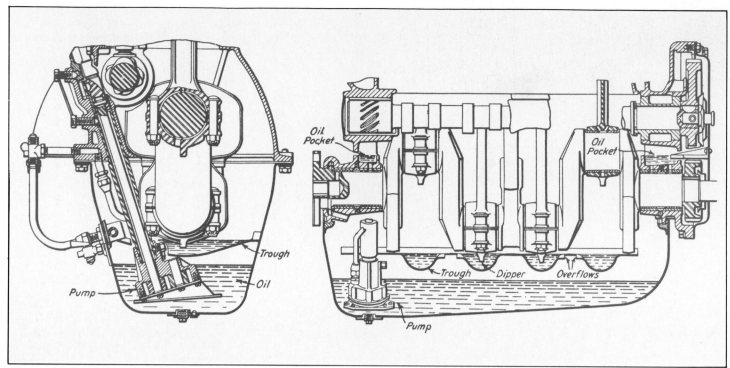

Many of the very early American Indy engines—specifically those based on production passenger cars—used primitive splash lubrication of crankshaft and rod bearings. The oil pump supplied oil at 2—3 psi to troughs and oil pockets, from where it could be dribbled or scooped into the bearing friction surfaces. Very hit and miss. A lot of oil was thrown around inside the crankcase, contributing to oil loss past the piston rings and through seals—horsepower losses were high.

But can you imagine what would happen to the track with 20 or 30 cars dumping that much oil? After a couple of hundred miles the bricks were just like ice. And, to top it, when a car would blow an engine and dump a lot of oil in one spot, course workers would throw sand over it. No such thing as absorbent "oil-dry" in those days. Sand mixed with oil produced a slippery dust film almost as bad as the oil. Excessive oil on the track made wheel-to-wheel racing real hazardous in the late laps. You didn't have much control of your car. A lot of crashes were caused by the oil—it's a wonder there weren't more.

This situation continued for many years at Indy. In fact, the mid '30's came before rules were passed to limit the amount of oil used by a car.

Metallurgy and fabrication techniques limited durability in the early days, both in the engine and chassis. Not much was known about alloy steels and heat treating. Chrome-nickel and chrome-vanadium steels were the strongest known steels, but they had only about half the strength of modern commercial alloys. Forging techniques were also not developed, so often the race-car builders had to hand-forge many of their parts. Of course nodular-cast-iron alloys were not known, so iron castings had little fatigue strength. They were brittle and cracked easily. Designers had no choice but to put a lot of "beef" into their parts, then hope the stresses wouldn't break them. This added unnecessary weight in many cases. Some builders tried to save weight with aluminum castings even before World War I. Louis Chevrolet's 1915 Frontenac engine was mostly aluminum. But the light alloys never caught on in racing until much later when metallurgy and fabrication tech-

niques were better developed.

Can you guess which components were the most prone to breakage in these early days? How about valve springs, connecting rods and steering arms? That's it. They caused more race dropouts than any other pieces.

BOOSTING THE AVERAGE

Time lost changing tires in the pits was the worst enemy of average speed in the early days. The first cars used fabric-carcass tires on clincher rims. These assemblies were clamped on wood-spoke wheels so the whole rim/tire assembly could be readily demounted. A tire could be changed in about 60 seconds with this arrangement, maybe 40 seconds with a top crew. A lot of tire changes were necessary as the race progressed. Most cars used at least 8 or 10 tires in 500 miles, requiring four or five pit stops. Fabric tires had so much internal

Early Duesenberg engines, circa 1915, were of the "walking-beam" type. A camshaft in the crankcase operated horizontal overhead valves through long pivoted rocker arms on the side. This layout gave a tight, fast-burning combustion chamber. Note dual plugs in top of chamber. Photo courtesy of IMS.

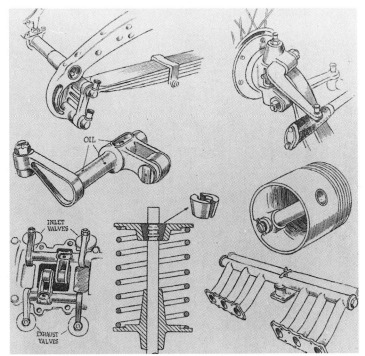

Typical engine and chassis details seen around the Indy garage area in the World War I period. You have to creep before you can walk! Drawing courtesy of Jerry Gebby.

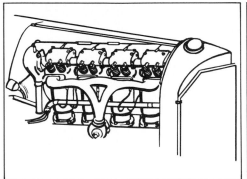

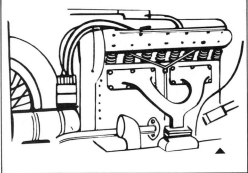

Much attention was paid to smooth, streamlined intake-manifold design in the early days. Some of the piping was beautifully constructed, but restrictive carburetors killed much of the performance potential.

friction as they rolled that a great deal of heat was generated. Nobody checked tread temperatures, but a hint of how much heat was produced is given by the inflation-pressure buildup: The tires started out cold with maybe 50 psi, but within a few laps you were riding on 85 to 100 psi! No wonder failures and blowouts were common.

European cars introduced wire-spoke wheels and slip-off hubs to the speedway in 1913. They said the wire wheels would reduce tire wear by being more flexible and cushioning shocks. Also the com-plete wheel-and-tire assembly could be pulled after the hub nuts were spun off with a special wrench. Actually the wire wheels didn't seem to make that much difference. The Peugeots used as many tires as our cars, and their tire changes averaged over 60 seconds. That race was won on the track, not in the pits. Remember that was the race when winner Jules Goux was said to sip champagne on every stop!

The real breakthrough came in the 1914—'15 period. This was the switch to the cord-carcass tire with knock-off-hub nuts on the wire wheels. These nuts had ears that could be struck one blow with a hammer and they would spin all the way off. No wrench was needed. Tires could be changed in 20—30 seconds, using lever-type jacks to lift one end of a car in a split second. Also the cross-ply-cord carcass of the tire developed much less internal friction so there was less destructive heat buildup. Tire life was doubled. But it was still pretty poor by standards of a few years later. You have to remember that these were not special racing tires. They were tires normally used on high-speed road

Louis Chevrolet's 1916 Frontenacs were a breakthrough in compact, light, streamlined construction. Much aluminum was used in the engine and chassis. Unfortunately their performance was not outstanding—so no one paid much attention.

cars. It wasn't until the mid-'20s that Firestone took over the Indy scene with specially made speedway tires.

AT THE END OF THE DECADE

It's interesting that, in this first decade of Indy development, the cars gained 20 mph in lap speed—from around 80 mph to 100 mph—with very little increase in horsepower. That is, the 300-CID engines of 1919 developed only maybe 20 HP more than the 400—

600-CID engines of 1911. And yet the cars were much faster around the track. How come?

Lighter weight was one factor. The specially built race cars of 1919 were 300 to 400 lbs. lighter than the stripped touring cars of 1911. They could accelerate quicker on the same amount of power. No doubt tires were a factor. The later tires ran less pressure and the cord carcasses combined with the more flexible wire wheels to give more bite in the turns—especially on an oily

track. There had been some chassis development, too, but no big breakthroughs. Most of the cars still had beam axles, leaf springs and friction shocks. Progress had been in frame stiffness and better matching of spring stiffness and shock control. Mechanics were just beginning to realize there was speed to be gained in suspension "tuning."

Indianapolis cars had begun to gain just a small degree of sophistication as we swing into the Roaring Twenties . . .

1916 Frontenac engine featured an aluminum crankcase, pistons, water pump and other accessories. The cars were more than 200 lbs. lighter than most of the competition. Apparently power output was deficient. Note the Mercedes-like exposed camshaft tower-drive, rocker arms and valve stems and springs.

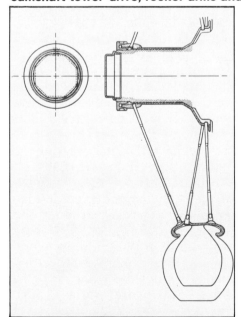

Rudge-Whitworth slip-off wire-spoke wheel, introduced on the French cars, was a vital breakthrough at Indy. The wheel mounted on a splined hub, retained by a spin-off nut that could be removed in seconds for quick tire changes. Note clincher-type rim.

The first straight-8 Duesenberg race car was finished so late that it was driven from the shop to the track the morning of the 1919 race. It was fast in the hands of driver Tommy Milton; but he was eliminated early by a broken rod. Photo by Jerry Gebby.

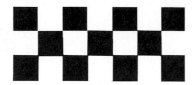

2
ALL-AMERICAN RACERS
1920—1929

Duesenberg race-car shop was in one corner of the passenger-car factory in the early '20s. It was not nearly as well equipped as the Miller shop in Los Angeles. Unlike the Miller setup, much of the specialty work was farmed out. Photo by Jerry Gebby.

AMERICA VS. EUROPE, WHEEL-TO-WHEEL

Except for the first couple of Indy 500's, all the races in the first decade were contested by almost as many European cars as domestics. Indy in those days was truly a melting pot of the world's finest racing cars. Admittedly the foreign cars won probably more than their share of the prize money. It wasn't necessarily because they were faster—as we learned in the previous chapter—but you could probably mark it down to better durability, maybe better pre-race preparation, and certainly racing luck. It was consistent domination simply because the foreign cars were just as successful on the board speedways and other tracks as on the AAA Championship circuit.

And they added a lot to the show. American race fans loved

them because they went fast and were noisy. Many American professional racers bought them and raced them because they were fast and durable. Track operators, including the Indianapolis management, liked them because they packed in the crowds. Perhaps the only ones who were less enthusiastic about the European cars were American car manufacturers who had to compete against them. They even seemed quite philosophical about it all. The international character of auto-speed competition was an accepted fact in those days.

Thus it came as no surprise when our AAA Contest Board adopted the same 3-liter (183-cubic inch) displacement limit in 1920 that was adopted for European Grand Prix road racing. Up to that time we had used even cubic-inch limits for Champion-

ship racing—like 450 CID in 1913, 300 CID in 1915—and we hadn't paid much attention to existing European rules at the time. It's fortunate that the European cars were able to remain competitive when they went down to 4.5 liters (274 CID) in 1914. They had to spot us 26 CID after we went to 300 cubes the following year.

But American race officials wanted to promote, not discourage, overseas competition when they adopted the European 3-liter limit in 1920. Almost everybody, officials and racers together, felt it would be good for the American professional sport. There was very little opposition to the decision to go to smaller odd-cube, even-metric displacement engines in general. There was even much feeling that the 300-CID cars were too fast in 1919!

Anyway, with America and

Murphy's No.12 Duesenberg that won the 1921 French G.P. has been restored to original condition by the Speedway museum. Fred Duesenberg used long, tapered tails on many of his early racers to get some streamlining effect. This car's top speed was well over 100 mph. Photo courtesy of IMS.

Duesenberg brothers, August and Fred, taken in 1925. Fred was the idea man, an intuitive engineer with little formal schooling. August was the builder who turned Fred's ideas into iron, steel and aluminum parts. Photo by Jerry Gebby.

Miscellaneous race-car and engine parts in the Duesenberg shop in the early '20s. Many of these parts were hand-forged and fully machined. Chrome-vanadium steel was the toughest material then known. Photo by Jerry Gebby.

More parts for the 1920 and '21 3-liter straight-8 Duesenberg engine. The large ball bearing supported the center main. Use of aluminum pistons was just starting. Photo by Jerry Gebby.

Europe starting out on a new formula at the same time with the same displacement limit, the racing world watched eagerly to see how the new cars would compare at Indianapolis in May. Two French companies, Ballot and Peugeot, sent teams over. Duesenberg and Frontenac represented the U. S. with new 3-liter cars.

It's interesting to note differences and similarities in the new engines. Actually the French engines were virtual scale-downs of the larger engines they had used in the World War I period. Ballot had a Henri-designed straight-8, with the usual dual overhead cams, 4 valves per cylinder with cup followers, barrel-type

crankcase, etc. The Peugeot was a 4-cylinder copy of the "Henri-designed" Grand Prix engine of the 1913 period. Both had the usual long strokes. But more sophisticated bearings and lubrication systems allowed higher revs.

The new 3-liter Duesenberg was also a scale-down of the 300-CID straight-8 of 1919. It retained the single-overhead camshaft, operating two exhaust valves and one inlet per cylinder through finger followers—with the spark plug on the inlet-valve side of the combustion chamber. Delco distributor-type ignition was used. The overhead cam was driven by a vertical shaft, the block/crankcase was a single iron casting and a separate cylinder head was used. Full-

pressure lubrication was a feature. The engine was said to be safe to 3,800 rpm.

Louis Chevrolet's Frontenac engine, designed by young engineer Cornelius Van Ranst, showed the greatest deviation from earlier practice. It was also an in-line 4-cylinder; but the single overhead cam was replaced by twin overheads—in the Peugeot tradition—with 4 valves per cylinder and cup followers. An interesting feature was the relatively narrow 38° angle between the valves—most other dual overhead engines of the period had around 60°. Van Ranst felt the narrower angle would help breathing by reducing port curvature. The same trick was used to

1922 Duesenberg racing team posing on the Beverly Hills boards. Drivers (L to R) Ernie Olsen, Roscoe Sarles, Eddie Miller and Jimmy Murphy. Duesenberg's most successful days were in the early '20s. Millers dominated in the late '20s. Photo courtesy Griffith Borgeson.

improve the Offy 55 years later! Van Ranst also followed the Peugeot lead with an integral head/block casting and aluminum barrel-type crankcase. Dry-sump lubrication was another feature, and ball bearings supported the crank to improve durability in long races. It was quite rugged and reliable for its time.

The new 183-CID cars were not expected to be as fast as the 300-CID cars in 1919. And they weren't. Horsepower was pretty much the name of the game in those days. That is, chassis design and tuning were not developed to a point where they had any big effect on lap times. All the chassis were similar in design, and none of the cars were getting through the corners substantially faster than any others. Acceleration and peak straightaway speed were the big factors in lap average. And these, of course, depended heavily on available horsepower.

You can see this dramatically by comparing reported maximum horsepower figures for the four new 3-liter engines against their highest qualifying speeds for the 1920 race:

Engine	Power	Speed
Ballot	107 HP @ 3,800 rpm	99.15 mph
Frontenac	98 HP @ 3,200 rpm	96.90 mph
Duesenberg	92 HP @ 3,600 rpm	90.20 mph
Peugeot	90 HP @ 3,000 rpm	88.82 mph

See what I mean??

Actually the power-vs.-speed situation under the 3-liter formula was much the same as it had been under the 300-CID formula in the 1915—'19 period. With one important difference: American cars started winning the races. After years of frustration, when American cars that were usually just as fast as their European rivals were repeatedly nosed out of the winner's circle, Americans started to show what they had. Van Ranst-designed Frontenacs won the 1920 and '21 races, and Jimmy Murphy closed out the 3-liter formula in 1922 with a win in his hybrid Miller-engined Duesenberg. The

European cars were by no means uncompetitive in these years, of course. They had at least one car in the first 5 places each year. They qualified well. And one-third to one-half of the cars entered during the 3-liter formula were French or British cars. They had as much chance at the gold as the American machines.

But American cars won the races in the early '20s—and the bulk of the Indy prize money. The situation turned right around from the frustrating European domination of the World War I period.

And that wasn't all . . .

THE SWEET TASTE OF REVENGE

Two months after the 1921 Indianapolis race, Fred Duesenberg sent a four-car team to

Early 122-CID Duesenberg straight-8 engine of 1922. A single vertical shaft at the front drove the dual overhead cams. Ignition was by Delco distributor. Note the Omac carburetors. Duesenberg refused to use the superior Miller carburetors. Photo courtesy of Griffth Borgeson.

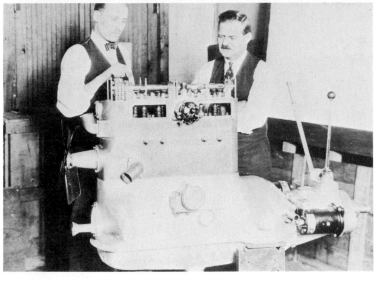

Cornelius Van Ranst and Louis Chevrolet inspect an experimental engine they built for Stutz in the early '20s. This team fielded some very competitive Frontenac race cars during that period. They were pioneers in the use of aluminum. Photo courtesy of IMS.

France to compete in the prestigious French Grand Prix road race—against strong opposition from Ballot, Fiat in Italy, and a team of Sunbeams from England. The Duesenberg entry was financed by a wealthy French sportsman, Albert Champion, who had made his money in America years before in the spark-plug business. Champion was dying to see what an American speedway car could do against the best European road-racers, but in the Europeans' backyard and at the Europeans' own game. Champion had noted the foreign domination at Indy in the World War I period and the sudden turn-

around under the 3-liter formula. The logical match-up was to drop some American speedway cars into the European road-race setting, and see what they could do.

Jimmy Murphy made history as he drove his Duesenberg to a magnificent 15-minute victory over the second-place Ballot, averaging 78.1 mph for 321 miles over a crushed-rock surface that was murder on tires—and downright dangerous from flying stones. Murphy finished with a punctured radiator and flat tire, in one of the toughest, most grueling races he was ever in. The French officials were so shocked and disappointed at the American win

that they practically snubbed the Duesenberg team at the victory banquet. Ernest Ballot said his second-place car won the "moral victory" because Murphy couldn't have gone another mile in his Duesenberg. It was a bad scene. Albert Champion was so disgusted that he left France and never returned.

But wasn't it sweet revenge for all those European wins at Indianapolis in the World War I period?

How did an American speedway car beat the best European road racers in their own backyard? And on the first try? Certainly a big factor was the unique 4-wheel

Jimmy Murphy winning the 1921 French Grand Prix road race with a 3-liter Duesenberg. He defeated the best European cars in a head-to-head race over a tough, long course. This was sweet revenge for the Indy races won by European cars in the World War I period. Photo courtesy of Griffith Borgeson.

Jimmy Murphy points out the unique hydraulic brakes that helped him win the French G.P. When they were properly balanced, he could go deeper into the corners than the mechanically braked European cars—which gained him a lot of time. Photo courtesy of Griffith Borgeson.

hydraulic-brake system on the 1921 Duesenberg. It was a byproduct of Fred Duesenberg's Model-A passenger car that had been introduced a few months earlier. The idea was to utilize hydraulic pressure to increase the maximum shoe pressure against the drum, and to provide a more precise balance of braking forces between the four wheels. The original system was crude by today's standards: Fluid passages drilled in the front axle and steering spindles; toggle actuation of the two shoes from a single piston; a mixture of water and alcohol as the fluid; leather seals.

But the brakes worked. Standard passenger-car brakes were installed on the race cars when they were shipped to France, as Fred Duesenberg knew the braking demands in a road race were far tougher than on a speedway. In early practice the front wheels would tend to lock up, causing violent fishtailing. Murphy ran off the road and wrecked one of the cars in one of these episodes. In a panic, Augie Duesenberg—Fred's brother, and right hand man, who had gone over with the team as crew chief—started trimming lining off the front-brake shoes, hoping to get a better balance between front and rear braking. After a little chopping and testing they got the balance just about right. After that the Duesenberg drivers could slide all four wheels with a minimum of pedal force—even after the linings had heated up and faded some. The European drivers could barely slow down with hot linings. Consequently, the Duesenbergs could go deeper into the corners.

It might also be mentioned that the American cars were not defi-cient on horsepower, as they had been in the 1920 season. Fred Duesenberg had boosted his engine's peak to a reported 114 HP for 1921, mostly through camshaft design. The French Ballots had a little more power, too—but there didn't seem to be any big difference in speed or acceleration.

It was a combination of brakes, teamwork and just plain guts that won for the Americans in France in 1921.

THE GOSPEL ACCORDING TO MILLER AND DUESENBERG

It's ironic that the builder/designer team that won the first two Indy races under the 3-liter formula—Louis Chevrolet and Cornelius Van Ranst—had relatively little influence on the evolution of the American speedway car in the 1920's. After their

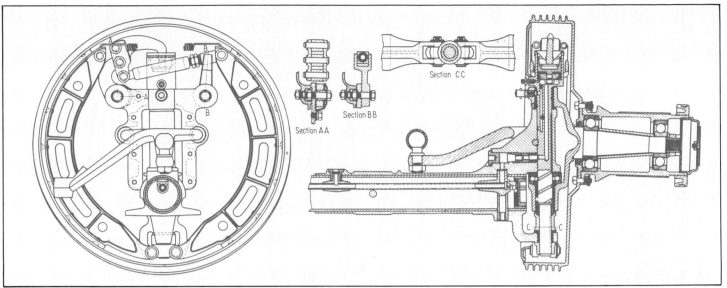

Internal details of the early Duesenberg hydraulic brake. Note fluid passages drilled in front spindle and kingpin. A single piston operated the leading brake shoe through a bellcrank, then the trailing shoe by a link from the bellcrank. Hydraulic fluid was a mixture of alcohol, water and glycerin. Same basic brakes were used on the Duesenberg Model A passenger car.

successes of '20—'21, economic pressures obliged Chevrolet to convert his shop to the manufacture of overhead-valve cylinder-head conversions for Model T Fords. Van Ranst designed them. And they worked. Frontenac-Ford conversions caught on immediately, and the business boomed. An 80-HP "Fronty" Ford finished fifth at Indy in 1923! The heads sold for years for Ford "hot rods" and dirt-track racers all over the country.

But this wasn't influencing the exotic speedway cars of that day. Both men eventually drifted into the automobile industry and out of racing. Perhaps their most important contributions were Chevrolet's experiments with aluminum in 1915, and Van Ranst's narrow-valve-angle head in 1920. This setup was used on the straight-8 Frontenac that won the '21 Indy race.

Meanwhile Harry Miller and Fred Duesenberg were coming to the fore as top builders of American Championship cars. Actually both men had been on the Indy scene since before World War I. Fred built only engines at first, but complete cars later.

Engine in Murphy's Duesenberg was fitted with Miller carburetors for the French G.P.—the other Duesy team cars had trouble with their French Claudel carbs. Despite its long 4-5/8-in. stroke, this engine was said to be safe to 4,200 rpm. It was seldom revved above 3,600 rpm in the race. Photo courtesy of IMS.

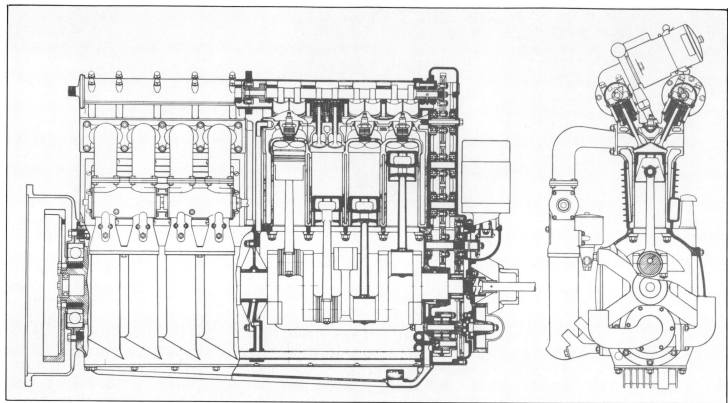

First Miller straight-8 displaced 3-liters (183 cu.in.) for the 1920—'21 formula. This was designed by Leo Goosen—and you can see design features he used later in the Offy: four valves per cylinder, cam-drive gear train at front, tubular rods, oil pump at front, diaphragm main-bearing supports, integral head/block casting, cup-type cam followers, dual valve springs, separate aluminum crankcase, clean porting, etc. Ignition was by Bosch cam-driven magneto. All in the best Goossen tradition! Drawing courtesy of Car & Driver.

Miller learned the benefits of ample carburetion in the early '20s. He designed a duplex version of his popular single-throat racing carb, so four could be used side-by-side on a straight-8 engine. He was also the first to use long velocity stacks for a ram effect.

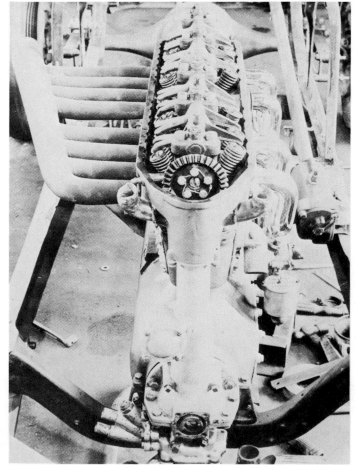

Overhead valve gear of the 3-liter Duesenberg race engine of the 1920—'21 period. A single overhead cam, driven by vertical shaft at front, operated inclined valves through rocker arms. They claimed 114 HP. Photo by Jerry Gebby.

Miller originally manufactured pistons and carburetors for racing, high-performance cars and aircraft. He gradually slid into complete engines and cars when various racing professionals bugged him to make special parts for them in his well-equipped machine shops. By the early '20s both men were deeply involved in the Indy scene, and were making most of their income from the racing sport.

It's amazing that these two men, who had such a tremendous influence on the development of the American racing car, were so opposite in temperament and engineering ability. Fred Duesenberg was not a trained engineer. But he had an uncanny "mechanical intuition," if you will. He seemed able to sense when a part was beefy enough, or of the proper shape, to absorb operating loads without breaking. He could quote dimensions to a draftsman to 1/64 of an inch—and usually the part would work without modifications. Fred did employ draftsmen. But only to put his own ideas on paper. They had to do very little detailing on their own. In fact, Cornelius Van Ranst did drafting for Duesenberg on aircraft engines during World War I.

Then there was August Duesenberg, Fred's brother and confidant. He was vital to the overall Big-D operation. Augie was as good making things as Fred was designing them. He was an expert welder, machinist and fabricator—with a tenacious get-it-done, make-it-work attitude. If Fred could design it right, the thing was as good as made when Augie took 'hold of the project.

Harry Miller was neither a trained engineer or designer. But he literally bubbled with ideas. You could call him a master innovator. He was willing to spend time and money on meticulous workmanship and testing to get the durability required of an Indy car. He needed only a good draftsman and shop foreman to have a

winning combination in those golden years of the 1920's. He found these men early in Leo Goossen and Fred Offenhauser.

These two men turned Miller's ideas into immaculately-finished cars that could win races against the best in the world. Under Miller's inspiration and guidance, Goossen became perhaps the most capable race-car designer in the world for the next 50 years. He could start from just a rough sketch, or even a word description, and turn out a complete design on paper—including stress analysis, tolerance dimensions, selection of materials, heat treats, machining methods, the whole bit. And the thing would usually work without major modifications.

It's not true that Goossen was the real brains behind the Miller operation. Goossen was not an idea man, never even went to the racetrack. He just had the knack for putting another man's ideas into workable designs. So Harry Miller supplied the ideas and Leo Goosen put them on paper.

Fred Offenhauser was a vital cog in the Miller empire, too. He was to Harry Miller what Augie Duesenberg was to Fred: a brilliant shop foreman who could turn Goossen's blueprints into hard parts. Offenhauser had all the mechanical skills. Just as important, he had a passion for cars and cleanliness in machining and fabricating race-car parts. No cobbling or get-a-bigger-hammer work from Offenhauser. Everything was clean and neat. And Miller fully supported Fred in this. No shortcuts. Both Miller and Duesenberg race cars were beautifully constructed in the 1920's. But if you had to choose between them on overall workmanship, the Millers would get the nod.

So these were the teams that were to shape the American Championship Car for at least another 10 or 15 years. And not only did they shape the technology, the fierce competition be-

tween them pushed both companies to heights they would never have reached otherwise. This made big-time U. S. racing better for both the racers and the fans.

MEASURING THEM UP

It's interesting to compare the Miller and Duesenberg design philosophies as competition picked up under the 3- and 2-liter (183- and 122-CID) formulas in the early '20s . . .

After the good showing of the in-line 8-cylinder Ballots and Duesenbergs in 1919, it was inevitable that this would be the dominant engine layout for at least the next few years. On paper it was right. Where total piston displacement is limited, potential horsepower is increased by using more cylinders with shorter strokes—the engine can be wound tighter and burn more fuel per unit of time. It's that simple. It's not an unmixed blessing, because more cylinders bring more inertia loads and internal friction. But with the technology of the '20s, 8 cylinders proved a better deal than 4 or 6. Today we're doing more with 12 cylinders than with 8, because of more sophisticated bottom-end and valve-gear technology.

So Harry Miller went the same route as Duesenberg, and everybody was using 8 cylinders in the early '20s.

And both of them followed the early Peugeot dual-overhead-camshaft, center-spark-plug arrangement for optimum breathing and clean combustion. From here, there were significant differences in the Miller and Duesenberg straight-8 engines in the '20s. Duesenberg used a conventional cast-iron block/crankcase casting with detachable cylinder head, with conventional main-bearing bulkheads cast in the crankcase. Miller cast his block and cylinder head in one piece, and bolted this casting to an aluminum barrel-type crankcase with bolt-in diaphragm-type main-bearing supports. The same layout

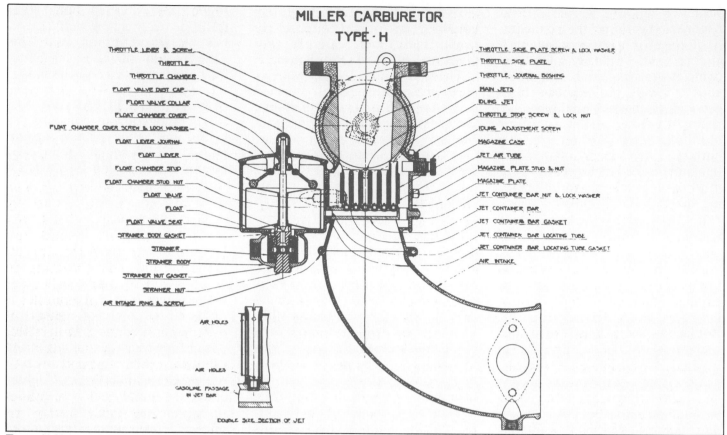

MILLER CARBURETOR
TYPE · H

THROTTLE LEVER & SCREW
THROTTLE
THROTTLE CHAMBER
FLOAT VALVE DUST CAP
FLOAT VALVE COLLAR
FLOAT CHAMBER COVER
FLOAT CHAMBER COVER SCREW & LOCK WASHER
FLOAT LEVER JOURNAL
FLOAT LEVER
FLOAT CHAMBER STUD
FLOAT CHAMBER STUD NUT
FLOAT VALVE
FLOAT
FLOAT VALVE SEAT
STRAINER BODY GASKET
STRAINER
STRAINER BODY
STRAINER NUT GASKET
STRAINER NUT
AIR INTAKE RING & SCREW

THROTTLE SIDE PLATE SCREW & LOCK WASHER
THROTTLE SIDE PLATE
THROTTLE JOURNAL BUSHING
MAIN JETS
IDLING JET
THROTTLE STOP SCREW & LOCK NUT
IDLING ADJUSTMENT SCREW
MAGAZINE CASE
JET AIR TUBE
MAGAZINE PLATE STUD & NUT
MAGAZINE PLATE
JET CONTAINER BAR NUT & LOCK WASHER
JET CONTAINER BAR
JET CONTAINER BAR GASKET
JET CONTAINER BAR LOCATING TUBE
JET CONTAINER BAR LOCATING TUBE GASKET
AIR INTAKE

AIR HOLES

AIR HOLES

GASOLINE PASSAGE
IN JET BAR

DOUBLE SIZE SECTION OF JET

Type-H Miller carburetor was widely used for racing in the World War I period and in the '20s. Its barrel-type throttle valve uncovered a battery of jets in sequence as it opened, progressively richening the air/fuel mixture. Very crude, but simple and effective.

carried to the later Offy. It was felt that eliminating the cylinder-head-gasket joint, and distributing main-bearing loads more evenly around the full perimeter of the crankcase would make the engine more reliable under high-rev conditions.

The Miller layout must have been more "right," because Duesenberg copied it in his 91-CID engine in 1926.

Crankshaft design was an interesting paradox. Duesenberg originally used the 4-4-throw arrangement—two flat 4-throw sections rotated 90° to each other—simply because he was forging his shafts. The one 90° twist was about all they could manage with the crude technology of the day. Otherwise it was a lousy crank design for a straight-8 because it left an unbalanced dynamic couple that shook the engine. But here comes Miller, using the same 4-4 arrangement. But he didn't need to. With his full

machine-shop facilities, they were machining their crankshafts out of solid-steel billets. They could have machined them any way they wanted. Admittedly the 4-4 arrangement gave even 180° firing intervals at each end of the engine, which assisted in ram tuning the carburetion. But it has always been debatable whether the carburetion benefit offset the harmful effects of the high-speed vibration.

One of Fred Duesenberg's great contributions to general engine development was the thinwall babbitt bearing, developed for his 300-CID Indy engine in 1919. Up until then the guys were casting soft babbitt onto thick bronze shells, then inserting these in the main-bearing bulkheads or rods. Fred reasoned that he could improve heat transfer and reduce babbitt cracking by casting a much thinner layer directly on the rod or main bearing support—without the bronze shell between. Nobody thought it would work. They

expected the thin babbitt would pound right out. But it did work and bearing life was multiplied many times. Within a few years all the racers—and many auto companies—started using "thinwall" babbitt bearings in their engines. Ball and roller bearings pretty much phased out within a few years.

It should be noted that both Miller and Duesenberg used tubular connecting rods during this whole period. They were forged from bar stock, then drilled through the center shank for lightening. They theorized that a hollow versus solid cylindrical column has maximum stiffness in relation to weight.

This was a legitimate argument in the early '20s when chrome-nickel and chrome-vanadium were the strongest known steel alloys. But Harry Miller had discovered chrome-molybdenum (chrome-moly) steels for race cars about 1924. These alloys could have been forged in the familiar H-section for a fraction of the cost with very little difference in weight and they would undoubtedly have worked just as well. Racers weren't looking for any easy way out in those days. The more exotic the better, seemingly. And, believe it or not, essentially the same type of forged tubular rod was used in the later Offy's, so Goossen must have liked it too!

There were also interesting differences between Miller and Duesenberg chassis construction. Duesenberg was a stickler for cutting weight. His frame side rails, for instance, were aluminum channel section with hard-oak filler planks for reinforcement. Weight was substantially less than an all-steel frame of equivalent stiffness. Duesenberg also eliminated spring shackles and saddles by carrying the main leaf between sliding rubber blocks at front and rear, arching the spring leaves up over the axle in a near semicircle. He even cast his rear-axle center sections from aluminum, and used thinwall chrome-nickel steel for the housings.

Fred justified his fanatic weight-shaving efforts in a special technical paper for the Society of Automotive Engineers (SAE) in 1923. One striking example he cited was: they were able to increase average lap speeds by 12 mph on the very rough Sheepshead Bay board speedway by merely reducing the unsprung weight of the rear axle 35 lbs. The same gear ratio was used and the peak engine speed actually went down 300 rpm. The heavier axle bounced so much that the tires spent as much time in the air as they did on the track! Fred's point was that weight saving was bound to help you in many ways—and in every area of the car.

Harry Miller was more interested in strength and durability than weight. His cars were exquisitely constructed of the most exotic alloys, by the most advanced fabrication and machining

techniques. Then everything was hand-assembled and fitted. The smallest parts were carefully surface-finished. Miller race cars were literal works of art—even more so than the fabled Bugattis.

Examples: The de Dion tubes for the front-drives were not commercial steel tubing. They were machined from steel-alloy forgings, then bent to shape by filling them with sand, heating, and forming them slowly over a jig. Many other highly stressed chassis parts were machined from forgings—wheel hubs, steering knuckles, spring perches, steering arms, etc. Practically all components were either bolted, pressed or shrunk together. Miller used very little welding. He didn't trust the gas-welding techniques of the day. And he didn't like the looks of a gas-welded seam!

Another example of exotic hand work was the radiator shell. Steel shells were hand-formed, with each grille wire bent over a form, then hand-soldered to the shell. Finally, the assembly was gun-blued to give it the special finish Miller liked. Brake levers were machined from bar stock, then fitted with cored aluminum castings for the handles. Hand-formed sheet-steel fuel tanks were supported on steel tubes attached to bronze brackets riveted to the tank, with a bronze ball-and-socket joint at the frame. All bronze hardware was cast and hand-finished.

Perhaps the most remarkable thing about the Miller race cars of the '20s is that they were made almost entirely in the Miller shops. Very little of the work was farmed out. This gave Miller tight control of the quality and workmanship. In contrast, Fred Duesenberg didn't have the facilities and personnel Miller did, so much of his work was farmed out. This didn't necessarily mean poor workmanship in that day, but it did limit the techniques Duesenberg could use. He sometimes had to accept what the supplier could deliver.

MORE HORSEPOWER PER CUBE

With the trend to smaller engine-displacement limits in the '20s, progress picked up in squeezing more power out of each cubic inch. I've already discussed the switch to 8 cylinders. This allowed higher engine speeds, a big factor in the power-per-cube race. So was the general switch to dual overhead camshafts, domed combustion chambers and centrally located spark plugs. This layout helped combustion and the inclined valves gave a cleaner porting layout for better breathing. In some cases they used 4 valves per cylinder, which was even better.

Three other vital areas of development contributed mightily to performance in the '20s: (1) Cam timing, (2) carburetion, and (3) compression ratio.

The potential of longer valve-timing durations and overlap was gradually realized over a period of years. The first engines had more or less "square" timing—valves opening and closing very near top and bottom centers of the intake and exhaust strokes. Gradually the designers realized that volumetric efficiency was increased by using the momentum of gases flowing in and out of the valves to pack or scavenge the cylinder. Exhaust valves were opened earlier to let combustion pressure "blow down" before the piston started back up. They closed inlet valves later to allow the ram effect of incoming gases to pack the cylinder. And they helped scavenging by giving a few degrees of overlap between the exhaust and intake strokes.

By the late '20s it was common to open the inlet valve 5—10° BTC, and close it 30—40° ABC. Exhaust timing was just the reverse: 30—40° BBC and 5—10° ATC. This was a huge improvement over the square timing of the early racers.

Carburetion progressed swiftly once it was realized how restrictive one carburetor throat could be.

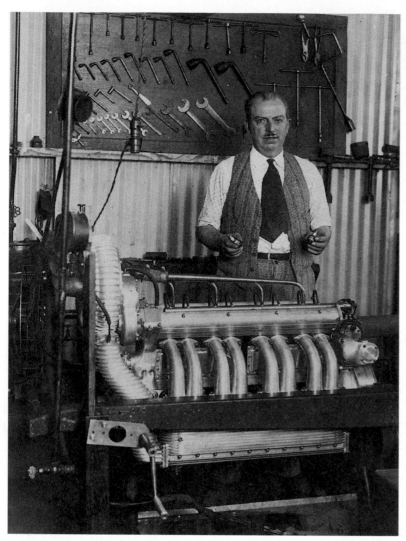

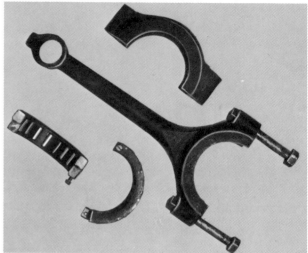

Harry Miller in his race shop in the mid '20s. His shop was equipped to do almost any type of machine work or fabrication, including sheet-metal fabrication and painting. He also had one of the only dynamometers on the West Coast at that time—an Italian Ranzi electric type. This helped enormously with detail engine work and tuning. Photo courtesy of Car & Driver.

Typical tubular-type roller-bearing connecting rod used for racing in the early '20s. Roller and ball bearings were widely used in engines at that time. Sleeve-bearing technology was still pretty crude. Photo by Jerry Gebby.

Most early engines used single-throat carburetors. Straight-8's of 1919 used two single-throats, each serving four cylinders through separate manifolds. The 4-4 crankshaft arrangement made this logical, as four cylinders at each end fired at even 180° intervals of crank rotation. By the end of the 3-liter formula (1922) the 8's were running four single-throats, each serving two cylinders through simple branch pipes.

Miller carburetors were generally used. This design used a spiral-shaped rotary throttle that uncovered a battery of jets as it turned, so progressively more fuel was supplied as the throttle opened. A conventional float bowl maintained a fixed fuel level for the jets. It made a good racing carb—but it wasn't flexible enough for the street.

Anyway, Miller designed a dual-throat version of this carb in the early '20s, using a single float bowl. By the mid-'20s, most straight-8's were running four of these—with each throat serving a single cylinder through a straight pipe. And this layout, in turn, led Miller to early experiments with "ram tuning" of the intake pipes. He found that adding a specific length of pipe on the inlet side of the carb throat caused a hump in the torque curve in certain RPM ranges as if there was a definite ramming of the air on the intake stroke. He never went very far with these experiments—like using telescoping ram tubes in dyno tests. But he did recommend short ram pipes for engines using a separate carb throat for each cylinder. Some of Miller's carburetion systems of the mid-'20s look

pretty hairy even today!

Engine designers were well aware of the benefits of a high compression ratio from the earliest days of the automobile. But they were always frustrated by the poor anti-knock quality of straight-run distilled gasoline. The octane rating method hadn't been devised then. If you were to test those early gasolines by a modern compression comparison you would come up with an octane equivalent of somewhere around 55—about like kerosene. Engines would ping and rattle and shake with any compression ratio above 4.5 or 5.0-to-1.

It was known before World War I that benzol—an aromatic compound made from coal—was effective in suppressing knock at higher compression pressures. It wasn't volatile enough to make a good

2-liter (122 cu.in.) Miller in Fengler's Durant Spl. in 1923, showing four duplex Miller carburetors. These engines developed about 120 HP at 5,000 rpm, or 1 HP per cubic inch. This was on a gas-benzol fuel mixture with a modest octane quality. Photo courtesy of IMS.

L.L. Corum surprised everyone by finishing 5th in the 1923 Indy race in a hopped-up Model T Ford speedster. A special "Fronty" cylinder head gave 80 HP at 3,600 rpm from 121 CID—top speed was less than 100 mph. He finished with one pit stop and no tire changes. Photo courtesy of IMS.

In 1924 Duesenberg became the first to install a centrifugal-type supercharger on an Indy racer. He fitted it to the left side of the engine, driven by bevel gears off an accessory shaft running along the crankcase. Early superchargers generated only about 3.5-psi boost pressure, and increased engine power only 10—15 HP. Pete DePaolo won the 1925 race at over 100 mph average speed with this one. Photo courtesy of IMS.

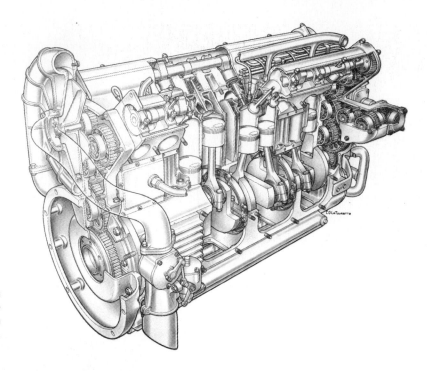

1926 8-cylinder Miller 91. To get an appreciation for the sound design of the Miller engine, compare this drawing with that of the last-design Offy on page 85. Drawing by C.O. La Tourette.

motor fuel when run pure. But it mixed readily with gasoline to make fuel blends that could take much higher compression than the straight-run gas. By 1920 most of the racers were running various gas/benzol blends with compression ratios around 6.0-to-1.

Another breakthrough came in 1922 when Thomas Midgley, an obscure scientist working at GM Research in Detroit, discovered tetraethyl-lead—a compound that could be added to gasoline in tiny quantities to greatly improve its knock resistance. The story is told that GM's "Boss" Kettering, an avid race fan, took a bottle of the secret fluid to the speedway in 1922, and offered it to Tommy Milton—telling him he could raise his compression to 7.5-to-1 by adding just 2cc (cubic centimeters) per gallon to his gas/benzol fuel. Milton used the stuff, but was forced out of the race early with mechanical problems. But he came back again in 1923, using high compression and "Ethyl fluid," and won the race. He credited that victory to his superior engine performance with the lead.

Within two years everybody was running leaded fuel with 7 and 8-to-1 compression ratios.

SUPERCHARGING: PROBLEMS AND PROMISES

The idea of supercharging an internal-combustion engine—forcing the air/fuel mixture into the cylinders under pressure—was kicked around from the earliest days of tne automobile. In 1908 an American, Lee Chadwick, built some race cars with crude belt-driven centrifugal "blowers." It's questionable whether the device was efficient enough to develop any positive pressure in the inlet manifold. But the cars would go 100 mph, and made quite an impression.

Superchargers were first seen at Indianapolis in 1923, when the German Mercedes company sent over a team of 2-liter cars with gear-driven Roots-type blowers. These had interlocking lobed rotors that pushed air into the manifold, much like a gear-type oil pump works. The engines didn't seem to develop any more power than our naturally aspirated 2-liters; but they attracted a lot of interest among our mechanics and designers.

It's hard to pinpoint the origin of the centrifugal supercharger on the Duesenberg that Joe Boyer drove to victory in the 1923 Indy race. We know Fred Duesenberg was exposed to aircraft supercharging concepts during World War I when testing the world's top aircraft engines in his New Jersey shop. During these years he became acquainted with Dr. Sanford Moss, head of General Electric's turbo-machinery division and the father of aircraft turbosupercharging in this country. Fred was also a frequent visitor at the Army's McCook Field in Dayton, Ohio where they were experimenting with supercharging during the war and immediately afterwards. During these visits he came in contact with a young civilian engineer, David Gregg, who was almost fanatically interested in the future of supercharging for both aircraft and automobiles. Gregg knew as much about the infant science as anyone else in the country at that time. It has been said that Fred began experimenting with crude centrifugal blowers even before 1920.

Apparently it was the team of supercharged Mercedes in the 1923 Indy race that really got him going. The story goes that he contacted David Gregg shortly after that race, and asked him to design

By 1926 Miller was driving his superchargers through a sophisticated cushioned gear train off the cams at the back of the block. The drive gear had a two-piece hub cushioned by rubber blocks or coil springs to absorb shock loads. Overall ratio step-up was 5.35-to-1. Here driver/mechanic Tony Gulotta installs the blower and gear-drive unit. Photo courtesy of IMS.

...re brought to Indy under the ...disadvantage because their ...-range torque than top-end ...e scourge of the European ...rican cars. It finished 7th in ...esy of IMS.

some sort of engine-driven centrifugal compressor for his 1924 Indianapolis cars. The two engineers hassled back and forth quite a bit in the next few months, trying to design something on paper they thought would work. Fred wanted to use ball bearings. Gregg said they would never last at 40,000 rpm. Fred wanted to flood the bearings with oil. Gregg insisted: just plain bronze bushings and a fine oil mist would be best. The two men finally worked things out, and came to Indy with three supercharged cars they felt would run fast and hold up.

A centrifugal-type supercharger uses a bladed rotor—a fan-like device enclosed in a housing—that scoops air in at the hub and hurls it off the ends of the blades at high velocity into the intake manifold. It depends on the momentum of the fast-moving air mass to increase the pressure in the manifold. On the Duesenberg they mounted the blower on the left side of the crankcase. It was driven at 8-times engine speed through bevel gears and shaft from the auxiliary-shaft that ran along the right side of the crankcase to drive the oil pump and distributor. These long shafts twisted

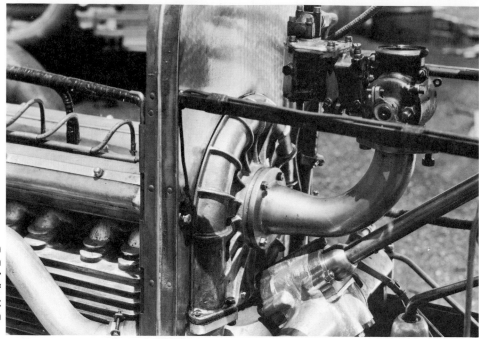

Miller made a large single carburetor with a 2-inch-diameter barrel. Used with supercharged engines developing over 200 HP, it could be jetted for a variety of fuels, including straight methanol. But one wonders what the airflow restriction was. Photo courtesy of IMS.

enough—like a torsion bar—to cushion the gears from shock loads during quick engine-speed changes. The carburetor was mounted on the suction side of the blower—so fuel vaporization could help cool the mixture—and the outlet was directed to dual manifold sections.

We have to realize that these first Duesenberg superchargers were incredibly crude and inefficient, despite Gregg's background. Rotor-tip speeds were way above sonic velocity, so shock-wave effects set in. There was no spiral diffuser path to smooth the air flow off the rotor tips. The device was little more than a fan in a closed housing. Fred admitted later in an SAE paper that those first blowers generated only 3.5 psi boost pressure at 5,000 rpm engine speed, or 40,000 rpm blower speed. Worse than that, the inefficient air flow absorbed more than 20 HP just to drive the blower. The compression efficiency—"adiabatic" efficiency, as engineers say—was only 10—14%. The blower couldn't have added more than 10 or 15 HP to the engine's output.

Result: The new supercharged Duesenbergs were not a bit faster than the unblown Millers in the 1924 Indy. In fact Boyer's winning car qualified 14 mph slower than the pole-setting Miller, and the fastest blown Duesy started in the second row. The Duesenberg won by good preparation, fast pit work and, yes, luck!

But all the racing world saw was that a revolutionary supercharged car had won the 500. That's all it took. The future of supercharging in American speedway racing was assured.

To be very objective, Harry Miller and Leo Goossen did a better job of developing the supercharging concept in the next few years than Fred Duesenberg. Duesenberg had the idea first, but Miller did more with it. One reason is that Miller had some extremely sharp racer-engineers in his camp that provided a lot of valuable technical input—they included Frank Lockhart, Leon Duray, Tommy Milton, Zenas and John Weisel and C. W. Van Ranst. Miller could sit back and let the ideas flow in. With Leo Goossen to draw them up . . . it was an unbeatable combination. For some reason, these kind of brains didn't seem to cluster around Fred Duesenberg. It might have been a personality thing. Miller was a joker, a back-slapper. His shop in

Los Angeles was always a mecca for the top racing pros.

Supercharger design progressed very rapidly after 1924. Miller's first superchargers in late '24 and '25 were located at the back of his 122-CID engine, driven through a train of gears off one of the camshafts, and developed 8—10-psi boost pressure. For the smaller 91-CID engine introduced in 1926, they designed a more efficient 5.35-to-1 gear-drive off the back of the crankshaft, with the blower mounted on the bell housing. The main drive gear on the crank had a two-piece hub with spring cushioning—like a clutch-disc hub—to isolate the gears from shock loads. This new drive arrangement proved very reliable, at least for high-rev speedway racing. Aerodynamic refinements inside the blower increased boost-pressures 12—13 psi at peak engine speed.

The real breakthrough came in 1927 when the Miller team developed *inducer vanes* for the impeller hub, and *diffuser vanes* in the outlet scroll of the supercharger. These tricks were being tried in aircraft superchargers at the time, and they smoothed the air flow through the impeller and housing.

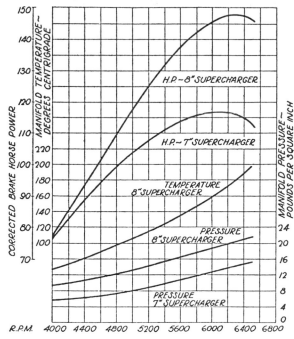

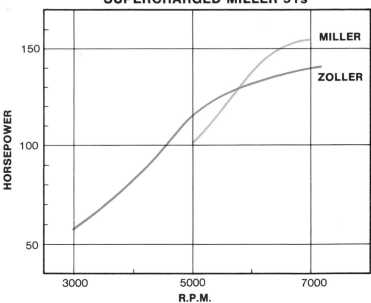

SUPERCHARGED MILLER 91s

How much horsepower did a 91-CID Miller supercharged engine really develop? These are curves from AC Spark Plug laboratories' test of the 1926 engine equipped with a 7-in. blower, and the 1927 version with the improved 8-in. unit. Both used a gas-benzol fuel. These are facts!

More power curves for a supercharged Miller 91 using gas-benzol fuel. Top curve (154 HP) was taken in the Miller shop on the Ranzi dyno. Lower curve was run by the Zoller Engineering Co. in England, in the process of developing a positive-displacement supercharger for road racing. Zoller wanted more power in the 3,000—5,000 rpm range. Engine was tested with the standard centrifugal blower and special "mid-range" camshafts.

Boost pressures immediately jumped to 20 psi with no appreciable increase in rotor-tip speeds—indicating adiabatic efficiencies in excess of 60%. Quite an improvement over the 10—15% efficiency of the first Duesenberg blowers.

A dramatic example of the effect of these supercharger efficiency improvements on overall engine performance was seen in a test in the laboratories of the AC Spark Plug Co. Side-by-side dyno tests of standard 1926 and 1927 Miller 91-CID engines were run on leaded gasoline. The '26 version developed a peak of 117 HP at 6,100 rpm with 13-psi boost. The '27-type peaked 148 HP at 6,300 rpm and 20 psi—with no change other than the supercharger. You can imagine what that difference would mean in track speed.

Actually these outputs were increased dramatically by later intercooler developments and alcohol fuel. I'll get to that later.

FRONT-WHEEL-DRIVE: MILLER'S BETTER IDEA

Well, maybe it wasn't really Miller's idea. Actually Jimmy

Miller front-drive layout was unusual in having the change-speed gears on the output side of the differential as this subjected them to full wheel torque. It was convenient from a packaging standpoint; but it made for high gear loading and hard shifting—only factors when accelerating out of the pits. Photo courtesy of Car & Driver.

35

Drive train and front suspension assembled. Miller front-drive layout used inboard drum brakes and forward-facing quarter-elliptic springs. A de Dion tube tied the wheels together. Conventional outboard brakes would have added to the unsprung weight. The de Dion tube was heavy, too, but they didn't know much about independent suspensions in those days. Regardless, it was lighter than the bouncing axles the rear-drive cars were using. Cord later purchased the Miller patents and adapted this same suspension and drive layout to their L-29 passenger car. Photo courtesy of Car & Driver.

First front-wheel-drive Miller at the Speedway was driven by Dave Lewis in 1925. He finished 2nd, which impressed everyone. The new drive layout and lowered CG seemed to get through corners faster, plus the cars were easy to drive and not hard on tires. They were the cars to beat in the late '20s. Photo courtesy of IMS.

Murphy, 1922 Indy winner, gave Miller an order for a front-drive race car shortly after that race. He was flush with money and felt the pull-instead-of-push effect would get him through the corners faster, giving him an advantage over the rest of the field in the '23 race. He gave no directions as to the engine-transmission-drive layout, but left it up to Miller and Goossen. Murphy just wanted a car that would go fast and corner fast.

What emerged was a masterpiece of simplicity, efficiency and durability. The key to the whole thing was the transmission. They wanted three forward speeds, with direct-drive in high gear. They could have put a conventional transmission between the engine and front-axle differential, but this would shove the engine too far back. Putting the gearbox ahead of the differential would have precluded direct-drive in high. They ended up by placing the transmission crosswise on the front-axle center-line, with the differential in unit with the gears inside the main gearcase. Front-wheel spindles were carried on forward-facing quarter-elliptic springs, and a de

Dion tube bent around in front of the gearbox to tie the two front wheels together. Double Cardan-type U-joints gave constant-velocity rotation, and the front drum brakes were carried inboard on the gearbox to eliminate their unsprung weight.

The transmission worked better than it had any theoretical right to. Due to space limitations, the gears had to be on the output side of the ring and pinion—meaning they were subjected to output torque—engine torque multiplied by the ring-pinion ratio. Also the gears had to be very narrow because of these space limitations. And to top it, the rotating inertia of the clutch discs, ring and pinion gears, and the differential had to be coped with when shifting gears. Shifting had to be done very slowly and gingerly. It's a wonder the gearbox ever stood up in speedway racing. It never could have in European road racing, where constant up-and-down shifting was necessary. Somehow these Miller front-drives worked very efficiently for many years at Indianapolis.

The cars were fast. Murphy never got to drive his car—he was killed in a dirt-track race at

Syracuse before Miller delivered it—but Dave Lewis qualified the car in the second row for the 1925 Indy race. Lewis and Bennett Hill teamed to drive it to second place that year. After that Miller was swamped with orders for duplicates of the Murphy design. And by the late '20s these front-drive Millers were the cars to beat on the fast board speedways as well as at Indianapolis.

Students of U. S. racing history have always speculated as to why those front-drives seemed to be faster with a given amount of horsepower on fast banked speedways. There were several possible reasons:

They were 100—150 lbs. lighter than equivalent rear-drive cars, due to elimination of the heavy rear axle.

By using a special dropped rear-axle tube, and seating the driver low on the low floorpan, they got the body cowl height down to 36 in. This reduced the car's frontal area dramatically so there was less wind resistance at straightaway speeds. Also the center of gravity was lowered considerably, so theoretically they could corner faster.

LOUIS MEYER'S CAR

1920-vintage Millers showed as much exquisite workmanship under the skin as on the surface. Truly they were built like a fine watch. Miller craftsmen built practically every component in the car—frames, brakes, radiator shells, gas tanks, steering parts, gearboxes, springs. Very little was farmed out. Photo courtesy of IMS.

Louie Meyer won the 1928 race in this "classic" rear-drive Miller 91. Note how much higher the car sets than the front-drive Millers. Turn speeds were slightly slower, and Meyer's qualifying speed was 11 mph slower than the Miller front-drive on the pole. But the fastest car doesn't always win. Photo courtesy of IMS.

Then of course there was the age-old argument that it's better for driving force to pull the car through a corner, rather than push it through. No one has ever proved this axiom scientifically. But Indianapolis railbirds have always believed it. We know from modern suspension engineering that moving the driving force to the front wheels increases the front-tire slip angles in a turn—assumedly making a car more stable and less apt to spin out. Whether this would allow the driver to hold his car closer to the "ragged edge" is debatable.

At any rate, front-drive cars were very successful at Indianapolis for many years after Miller introduced the concept in the mid '20s. Thanks to Jimmy Murphy, it was one of *his* better ideas.

SOMETHING NEW IN TIRES

Up through the early 20's, the various tire companies did not make special racing tires. Race cars used high-speed tires of the type that would be used on high-performance sports cars. They pretty much followed the basic tire technology of the day. The cord-type

ERNIE TRIPLETT-BUCKEYE DUESENBERG
INDIANAPOLIS MOTOR SPEEDWAY 1929

Duesenberg race cars of the late '20s didn't show the fine detail workmanship of the Millers. But they were lighter and many drivers said they handled better in the turns. Unfortunately engine power was barely competitive—victories were few and far between. Note the lever-type hydraulic shocks and Firestone Balloon tires. Car builders and mechanics were realizing it took more than just power to get around the Speedway quickly. Photo courtesy of IMS.

Early 91-CID supercharged Millers were sold without intercoolers. Most teams fabricated their own. What you see here cost $5,000, produced 154 HP at 7,000 rpm, and weighed 330 lbs. ready to race. Photo courtesy of IMS.

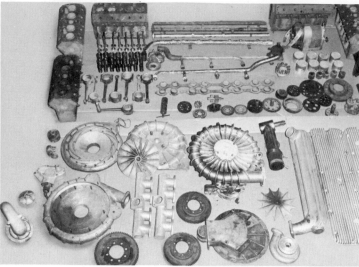

Internal parts for a Miller 91 were tiny, built with watch-like precision. The engines were not delicate, but were very expensive to race. Parts in the foreground are supercharger, supercharger-drive, manifold and intercooler components. Impeller speeds up to 40,000 rpm required high precision. Photo courtesy of Car & Driver.

carcass came along before World War I. The straight-side tire on a drop-center rim arrived shortly after the war. Inflation pressures were generally 50—60 psi. Cord carcasses and straight-side construction improved tire wear dramatically. By the early '20s it was common to go 500 miles at Indy with only one or two tire changes.

The first real breakthrough in specific race-tire design came in 1925 with Firestone's original "Balloon" tire. The new design offered two important advantages: One, the casing was fatter and wider than any previous tire, so it put more square inches of rubber on the track for better traction. Just as important, inflation pressure was dropped from 50 psi to 30 psi. The result was a tire that could conform to the track surface and absorb bumps more readily, thus keeping the tire against the track for a continuous "side bite." Earlier 50-psi tires would bounce so much—especially with the stiff springs and shocks of the day— that the cars tended to be very skittish in the turns. Cars became much more stable and controllable with the softer Firestone Balloons.

Practically all the cars used the new Firestone tires in the 1925

race—qualifying speeds were up 2—3 mph for comparable cars. That marked the beginning of Firestone domination of the Indy scene. They prepared special tires for American speedway and dirt-track cars every year after that. They had the Indy-car business pretty much to themselves for the next 40 years.

PEAK PERFORMANCE

Up to now I've been talking mostly about "standard" racing equipment developed by major commercial suppliers in the '20s— Duesenberg, Miller, Firestone, etc. The ultimate performances achieved by this equipment in the late '20s, just before the end of the 91-CID formula, were the result of private car owners trying new tricks on the standard hardware in their own garages. They achieved performances far beyond what you could get out of a "stock" Miller or Duesenberg.

The two major areas of development were supercharger intercoolers and alcohol fuels . . .

The intercooling idea is generally credited to Frank Lockhart, in the '26—'27 period. Because compressing air in a supercharger inevitably raises its temperature, reducing its density in the process,

the objective was to cool the air/fuel mixture in some type of radiator or heat exchanger between the blower and cylinders. This increases mixture density, and gives even more power by introducing more air/fuel mass into the cylinders.

Many different types and shapes of intercoolers were tried in the late '20s. Most were essentially air-to-air heat exchangers—finned tubes or plates forming narrow passages for the hot fuel mixture to flow through to the cylinders. The idea was to expose the fuel mixture to a cool surface having a large area to absorb its heat quickly, without excessively restricting the air flow. The principle wasn't a whole lot different than that of the evaporator in a modern car air-conditioning system, except the air-flow mass was greater.

I have never been able to find any test figures on the efficiency of these early Indianapolis intercoolers. I do have figures showing supercharger outlet temperatures of 300—350°F with 15—20 psi boost pressure. If the intercoolers were even 50% efficient, this would drop the mixture temperature going into the cylinders to around 200°F—and this would

The most unusual supercharged Miller 91 appeared in Tommy Milton's Detroit Special in 1927. It had a special two-stage supercharger, said to pump over 40-psi boost and produce 300 HP at 7,000 rpm. With its own hand-built front-drive unit, the car cost a reported $250,000 to build. It was the Novi of its day—only it never went very fast! Photo courtesy of IMS.

account for a theoretical horsepower increase of 20%, based on the increased mixture density.

Maybe the intercoolers were only 30 or 40% efficient. I don't know. They were pretty crude. But at any rate there was apparently enough power increase to be well worth the bother. All the top racers used them in the late '20s. And the cars seemed to be faster than non-intercooled cars with similar equipment.

The first extensive experiments with alcohol fuels at Indianapolis are usually credited to Leon Duray, around 1927. He liked alcohol for two reasons. It had a very high "latent heat of evaporation," making it very effective in cooling the air/fuel mixture going into the cylinders. It even cooled internal engine parts like pistons and valves. It was very difficult to overheat any alky-burning engine unless the air/fuel mixture was too lean. Another good feature of alcohol was the great resistance to combustion knock or detonation. The octane rating is 'way over 100 by modern tests. Duray quickly learned that he could run a higher volumetric compression ratio with a given supercharger boost pressure when burning alcohol. Its

Supercharger intercoolers came in all shapes and sizes in the late '20s. The idea was to cool the hot air/fuel mixture coming from the blower. This gave a denser mixture in the cylinders, and thus more power. This typical layout with the Duesenberg "sidewinder" supercharger was said to add 20—30 HP. Photo courtesy of IMS.

knock resistance appeared to be much greater than the leaded gasoline-benzol blends used at the time. He experimented with both methyl (wood) alcohol and ethyl, or grain alcohol, but found the methyl type more effective for cooling and knock resistance. We call this "methanol" today.

There was only one bug: Much higher fuel consumption. Methyl alcohol contains less heat value per pound than gasoline, so you have to run a richer air/fuel mixture, and only get 1/3 to 1/2 the miles per gallon. This meant more pit stops for fuel. It was a tradeoff. Higher lap speeds vs. more pit stops. Duray experimented with blends of alcohol, gasoline, benzol, and even acetone—trying to get the best compromise be-

It took big money to race in the '20s, too. Cliff Durant (left), heir to a GM stock fortune, provided much of the money that Leon Duray (right) converted into going fast. Duray had a million ideas—most of them expensive. Durant got his kicks from an occasional stint behind the wheel. Everybody had fun. Photo courtesy of IMS.

In 1928 Leon Duray drove this front-drive Miller to a lap record of 124.02 mph. It stood for nine years. This was a once-in-a-lifetime run when everything worked exactly right. But a lot of credit should go to Duray's engineering. He was a pioneer with intercooling and alcohol fuel, among other things. Photo courtesy of IMS.

tween performance and fuel consumption. I can find no reliable records of some of the fuel formulas he may have used in the 500-mile races.

The story is that he was running pure methyl alcohol when he drove his front-drive Miller to the Indy lap record of 124.02 mph in 1928—a record that stood for nine years, longer than any Indy lap record before or since. It was a once-in-a-lifetime lap that Duray couldn't duplicate.

One specially interesting variant on the supercharging theme was a modified front-drive Miller, known as the Detroit Special, first driven by Tommy Milton in the 1927 race. It was financed by two wealthy GM stockholders, and was actually constructed in the basement of the GM Building in Detroit. Milton and Van Ranst were the chief designers, and Dr. Sanford Moss was brought in to design a unique two-stage centrifugal supercharger. Two conventional centrifugal impellers were mounted back-to-back on a common shaft driven at 3.9 times crankshaft speed. Their housings and ductwork were laid out so the outlet of one impeller fed into the inlet of the other. In this way the compression effect of the two was multiplied—giving what was

reported to be over 40-psi boost pressure at a modest engine speed of 6,800 rpm! The engine was never run on a dyno; but the designers estimated it developed over 300 HP on a highly leaded gas-benzol fuel.

Apparently that estimate was highly optimistic. The car was not fast or responsive in any sense of the terms. In Indy races in the late '20s it always qualified 10—15 mph slower than the fastest Millers and always dropped out of the races with supercharger or engine troubles. Two-stage supercharging was apparently an idea whose time had not yet come. There was something radically wrong with the way it was applied on the Detroit Special.

So how much horsepower did those supercharged 91-CID engines develop in the late '20s? This is hard to pinpoint, as the hottest ones were never run on dynamometers. Harry Miller always quoted the figure of 154 HP at 7,000 rpm for a late 91 with the advanced 8-inch supercharger, using leaded gas-benzol fuel. I've already referred to the independent test on this same engine by the AC company, which showed 148 HP at 6,300 rpm. There's good agreement there. And Fred Duesenberg quoted the power of

his "standard" 91-CID engines as 145 HP at 6,500 rpm. Still good agreement.

Consider modifications like intercoolers, higher compression, special camshafts, alcohol fuels, supercharger improvement, etc. that the racers were doing in their own garages. These effects could certainly account for a 50% power increase over the Miller and Duesenberg factory figures. That would suggest around 225 HP. Then there was the International Class F speed record Frank Lockhart set with his 91-CID Miller at Muroc Dry Lake—a two-way average of 164 mph. Some estimate that would have required 280 HP at the flywheel. I doubt it. I believe 225 HP could have done it easily.

So let's say the hotter Miller 91's of the late '20s—with all the goodies—produced 210—230 HP at 7,000 rpm with a maximum rev limit around 8,000 rpm. Probably the average one was down around 160—180 HP. There is every reason to believe the 91-CID Duesenbergs were at least 20—30 HP below equivalent Millers. They were several MPH slower on lap speeds and they won only an occasional Championship race after George Souders' Indy win in 1927. Most of the top teams were run-

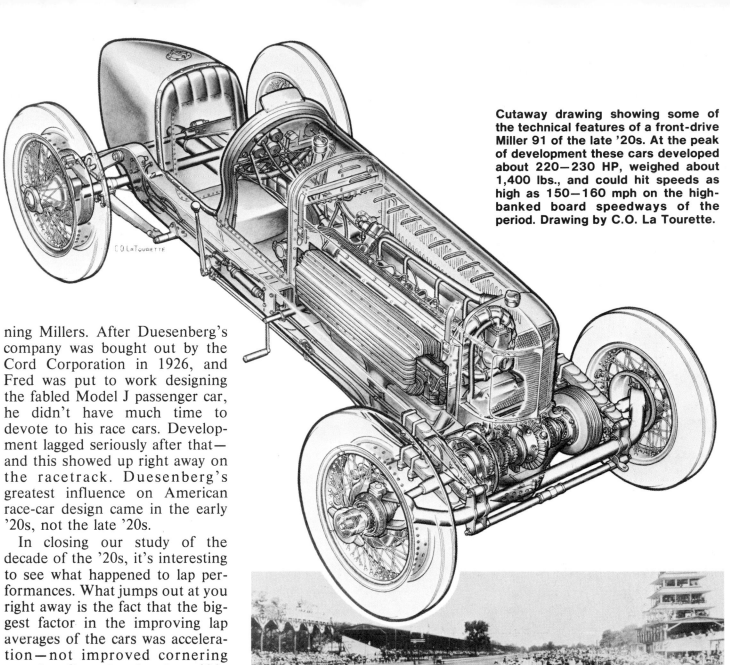

Cutaway drawing showing some of the technical features of a front-drive Miller 91 of the late '20s. At the peak of development these cars developed about 220—230 HP, weighed about 1,400 lbs., and could hit speeds as high as 150—160 mph on the high-banked board speedways of the period. Drawing by C.O. La Tourette.

ning Millers. After Duesenberg's company was bought out by the Cord Corporation in 1926, and Fred was put to work designing the fabled Model J passenger car, he didn't have much time to devote to his race cars. Development lagged seriously after that—and this showed up right away on the racetrack. Duesenberg's greatest influence on American race-car design came in the early '20s, not the late '20s.

In closing our study of the decade of the '20s, it's interesting to see what happened to lap performances. What jumps out at you right away is the fact that the biggest factor in the improving lap averages of the cars was acceleration—not improved cornering speeds. Cars in the late '20s weighed 500 lbs. less and had 100 horsepower more than the first 3-liter cars of the early '20s. This gave them much superior acceleration off the turns. You can see it by comparing lap averages, turn speeds and peak straightaway speeds:

MAXIMUM SPEED (mph)			
	Avg.	Turn	Straight
Early '20s	100	80	120
Late '20s	120	90	150

Firestone Balloon tires increased turn speeds at least 5 mph when they were introduced in 1925. It's obvious from these figures that the Indy racers hadn't yet scratched the chassis-development surface to get faster cornering. They were still literally feeling their way through the turns.

Challenges ahead for the '30's . .

Indy pit scene during the 1928 500. These were really "the pits" in those days—sawdust-filled cubicles with low wood partitions. Speedy pit work was still far in the future. Photo courtesy of IMS.

3
RACING ON A SHOESTRING
1930—1936

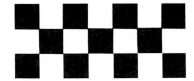

1930 race start. Indianapolis technical rules were completely revised for the 1930 race, encouraging a broader variety of cars and engines that would cost less to build and race. They brought a lot of new blood into the sport. Photo courtesy of IMS.

A NEW KIND OF "BIG-TIME" RACING

The direction of American Championship racing made a complete turnaround in 1930. Overnight we switched from exotic $15,000 specialized race cars with $60 connecting rods to $1,500 backyard buildups using mostly stock passenger-car pieces. Or at best, the cars were hashed-over hardware from the '20s that was cut and fitted to meet the radically changed rules. It was a whole new scene.

Most race fans at the time thought the simplified rules were an answer to tighter economic conditions that came with the Great Depression. Actually AAA officials were talking about the rule changes two years before the 1929 Wall Street crash. Even when the economy was booming in the late '20s, a lot of racing people were concerned about the escalating costs of building and running

the tiny watchlike 91-CID supercharged cars. Only a handful of wealthy sportsmen, or fast-talking owners who could promote piles of sponsorship money, could afford to race the little cars. Grassroots racers who were running their Fronty-Fords on dirt tracks around the country could barely afford a ticket to a Championship race. Just as important, as the cars got more costly the starting fields dwindled. This brought howls from the track promoters.

The AAA Contest Board finally acted in 1929. For the 1930 season they introduced an entirely new set of Championship rules that they hoped would give big-time racing back to the "little guys." It's only coincidence that the new rules came at the beginning of the Depression. Actually, the timing couldn't have been more perfect. After the stock-market crash there wasn't a lot of money left to spend on race cars anyway.

Here's how they worked it out:

- Maximum piston displacement, 6 liters, or 366 cu.in.
- No superchargers on 4-cycle.
- Two valves per cylinder maximum.*
- Two carburetor barrels per engine maximum.*
- Minimum car weight 1,750 lbs., or 7.5 lbs. per cubic-inch.
- Tread between 54—60 in.
- Two-seat bodies with minimum width of 31 in.
- Four-wheel brakes.
- Minimum qualifying speed of 85 mph.

*1931 rules allowed 1 carburetor venturi and 4 valves per cylinder.

It's immediately obvious these rules were designed to encourage modified production-car equipment—not just engines, but chassis and bodies too. By raising the displacement limit to 366 cubic inches, and banning superchargers

Harry Miller built a new series of straight-8 engines for the 1930 rules that were quite successful through the '30s. They were available in a broad range of bores and strokes, with displacements from 180 to 270 cubic inches. Some had vertical intake ports between the camshafts like this. They could develop 1 HP per cu.in. at 5,500 rpm. Nine cam-cover hold-down studs identified these engines. Photo courtesy of IMS.

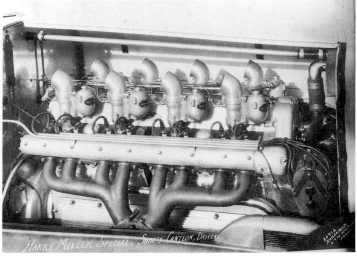

V-16 made from two Miller straight-8's on a common crankcase. Displacement was 301 cubic inches. Shorty Cantlon threw a rod first time out in 1931. Photo courtesy of IMS.

and four valves per cylinder, it was felt that stripped and hopped-up passenger-car roadsters would have a fighting chance at some of the big-time money. Yet there was enough flexibility in the rules to allow use of some leftover engines and cars from the '20s so professional teams with large investments in that equipment wouldn't be left out.

There was a sudden big, big change in Championship cars. It's interesting to compare dimensions of a typical 91-CID Miller of the late '20s to a race car that would comply with the new rules—and then to a typical modified stock car that might run under the new rules as shown below.

See what I mean about a big change in the typical Championship car?

There was a lot of controversy among professional racing people over the new rules. So what's new? Low-budget teams liked them, of course, even though they may not have considered a production-based car. Just the minimum weight of 1,750 lbs. took the pressure off to develop expensive lightweight components. And the 366-CID limit would allow just about anything in the way of an engine, including marine and small aircraft engines! The two-valves-per-cylinder limitation would exclude some special racing engines of the '20s, but there was still a good choice of two-valve engines.

The big-money teams with heavy sponsorship, on the other hand, didn't generally favor the new rules. They were doing fine

on the dirt tracks and board speedways of the '20s. All they could see was a lot more racers, rich and poor, scrambling for dwindling purses brought on by the Depression. They were bound to get a smaller slice of the pie.

But once a racer, always a racer. I never saw a real one quit yet because of anything as minor as money! Everyone just tightened their belts a little.

NEW CARS FROM OLD CARS

Established racing teams that had been in Championship racing through the '30s were faced with quite a dilemma under the new rules. Their cars were single-seaters with body and tread widths too narrow to qualify. The last two-seat cars were used in 1922. Most Miller and Duesenberg 122- and 91-CID engines used in the period from 1923 through '29 had two valves per cylinder which would qualify, but with the new 366-cube limit they would be giving away a lot of pumping capacity to the "stock-block" engines. Today it's customary to put

	Old	New	Stock
Wheelbase (in.)	100	100	114
Tread width (in.)	52	56	58
Body width (in.)	20	31	42
Car weight, dry (lbs.)	1,400	1,750	2,600
Engine displacement (CID)	91	150	336
Horsepower	180	150	170

LEON DURAY MOTOR.

Fine print in the 1930 rules said two-cycle engines could use superchargers. Leon Duray jumped on this and came up with a radical twin-row 16-cylinder two-stroke with articulated connecting rods working a central 8-throw crankshaft. A large Roots blower pumped 10 psi. The car qualified slow and overheated after 6 laps. Photo courtesy of IMS.

different displacement limits on different valve arrangements. An overhead-cam engine gets fewer cubes than a side-valve or pushrod engine on the theory that it would have better volumetric efficiency, and could develop more horsepower per cubic inch. They hadn't started that type of "fine-tuning" of the rules in those days.

So what to do for the established racers with a garageful of ready-to-run Indy cars?

The old-timers had several alternatives. They could resurrect some of the old two-man cars of the early '20s, and update them with more modern brakes, suspension components and drivelines. Quite a few of those cars were still around in 1930. Another possibility was to just get out the torch and tools, and cut and fit a single-seat car of the late '20s to conform to the new rules—widen the frame, body and tread width. No big deal for a clever mechanic with good shop facilities, though definitely expensive. A few chose this route.

Another large group of professional racers took a different approach to the new-car problem: They ordered custom-built cars from a new cadre of specialty builders that grew up practically

overnight to service the revised Championship class. Names like "Cotton" Henning, Herman Rigling, Myron Stevens, Phil Sommers, Clyde Adams, Emil Diedt and "Curly" Wetteroth were suddenly doing the business of Harry Miller and Fred Duesenberg. These specialists quickly developed the shop facilities and recruited the personnel necessary to turn out complete race-car chassis and bodies to custom order. Most of the two-man Indy cars of the early '30s came from these small job shops. A few big-money teams had new cars built by the Miller and Duesenberg shops. But the small specialists could do it for less money and apparently just as well.

Incidentally, these small custom specialists—along with the economic squeeze of the Depression—were what ended the Miller-Duesenberg era of American racing. Within months after the 1930 Indy race, Harry Miller was nearly bankrupt. Fred Duesenberg kept a hand in the Indy scene for a year or two, but he was killed in a highway accident in 1932. That pretty much ended any deep Duesenberg involvement in speedway racing of any kind. The company, then more or less under the direction of

Augie Duesenberg, was still involved with the Model J passenger car for the Cord Corp.

After this the small specialty race-car builders took over the Indy scene. And things really haven't changed that much to the present day. There are no big "semi-production" car builders today who would compare with the fully equipped Miller shops of the 1920's. Race-car building has remained "custom" business since those days.

Engines were another problem in 1930. As mentioned, most of the Miller and Duesenberg 122- and 91-CID engines of the '20s had two valves per cylinder—no there was no big conflict with the new 1930 rules. But the displacements were far below the 366-cube allowance. By boring out the cylinder blocks as much as they dared and machining new crankshafts with the longest strokes that would swing in the tiny crankcases, they could get 20 or 30 more cubic inches than the engines were designed for. Or, by casting new blocks with the cylinder walls moved outward—by re-coring—they could squeeze out maybe another 30 or 40 or 50 cubes. When they got done, some of the old Miller and Duesenberg

Sampson engine of the early '30s consisted of two separate Miller 91's set side-by-side and geared externally to a common driveshaft. This powerplant is confused with the later twin-row 16-cylinder engine from Frank Lockhart's 1928 Daytona Stutz Black Hawk as shown on page 63. It used two Miller 91's set at 15° to each another on a common crankcase geared internally to a single output shaft. Photo courtesy of IMS.

Studebaker factory race cars that ran in 1933 had high-profile streamlined bodies that came up around drivers' shoulders. Running gear was all enclosed in faired sheet metal. Beautiful cars—and definitely the fastest of the semi-stock cars in the early '30s. Photo courtesy of IMS.

Stripped Stutz Bearcat roadster is typical of the semi-stock passenger cars that ran under the new 1930 rules. This was mostly stock except for a light body shell from the firewall back. Overhead-cam straight-8 was rated at 156 HP at 3,900 rpm in stock form, good for 100 mph. The car failed to qualify in '31. Photo courtesy of IMS.

straight-8 engines of the '20s had been expanded to nearly *twice* their original displacements!

There were other possibilities in overhead-cam race-type engines. Miller had built several 4-cylinder, double overhead cam engines for marine racing in the '20s for the 151- and 183-CID classes. Some of these were seen at Indy in the early '30s. Some specially interesting engines were the 16-cylinder Sampson Specials: In the early '30s, two downdraft Miller 91's (2-5/16 X 3 for 202 CID) were set side-by-side, then geared to a common shaft at the rear. The *two*

engines had a common induction system. This setup is confused with Gordon Schroeder's later 1939 16-cylinder Sampson Special driven by Sam Hanks in '46. It used two Miller 91's (2-3/16 X 3 for 180 CID) *on a common crankcase* with one output shaft. Unlike the original 16, this engine had two separate induction systems. Built by Zenas Weisel at the Stutz plant in Indianapolis, this was basically the engine Frank Lockhart had used to attack the world speed record in 1928, but with the superchargers removed. Lockhart crashed fatally on that

attempt, totalling the car. The engine was recovered and ran for many years at Indianapolis.

PASSENGER CAR RACERS

Nearly half of the cars that ran at Indy in the early '30s were modified stock cars. They came in a fascinating variety of shapes and sizes that has not been seen at the speedway since. The new 366-CID limit covered about 95% of America's production cars at that time, so you can imagine the variety of hardware that came out of the woodwork. Many came from low-budget teams that had

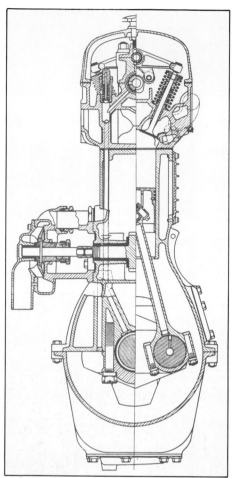

Sections through the main and connecting-rod bearing journals of the Duesenberg Model A passenger-car engine, produced during the '20s. This engine was popular under the 1930 Indy rules, primarily because of the **rugged construction, overhead camshaft and good porting. Though it only displaced 260 cubic inches in stock form, it could be readily hopped up to 140—150 HP for racing.**

Cigar clamped between his molars, Joe Russo adjusts the valves on his Model A Duesenberg Wonder Bread Special in preparation for the 1930 race. Only two carburetors were allowed at that time, restricting power and revs. Photo courtesy of IMS.

been dying to get a crack at Indy for years.

Many concepts were used in building these cars. Some were almost entirely stock roadsters stripped of windshields, fenders, bumpers and running boards, with the stock driveline and various hop-up tricks on the engine. They weighed up to 4,000 lbs. Some used the stock engine and chassis with mods, but replaced the heavy stock body with a light steel or aluminum racing body. Sometimes the owner would keep the stock radiator and hood for identification. Then they went from here to more extensive use of special race-car components. Some used a special body and frame, but with stock engine and driveline and suspension parts. Some would just use the stock engine and driveline, with all other areas special race-only components.

What eventually resulted was a complete special race car with a modified stock engine, and maybe clutch and transmission. There were lots of these. Generally these were old two-man speedway cars that the owner bought for a song without the engine. He couldn't afford a genuine Miller or Duesenberg race engine as these were much in demand for modernized Indy cars. So the next best thing was to take advantage of the light weight of the race cars by building them to the minimum 7.5-lbs. per CID weight limit using modified stock engines. On paper, a combination like this looked pretty competitive considering the tiny Miller and Duesenberg overhead-cam engines displaced only 150—200 cubic inches or so.

Some modified stockers of the early '30s made brutally practical hardware for AAA Championship races in general. The story is told of Russ Snowberger, who built a Studebaker President roadster for $1,500 in 1930. He finished 8th at Indianapolis and 3rd in points on the AAA Championship circuit that year, spending less than $5 for parts! His prize money for the season was many times the original cost of the car. And he had a barrel of fun in "big-time" racing on a shoestring.

Modifying a stock factory engine for more horsepower was a lot different problem in those days. There was practically no bolt-on aftermarket equipment to make the job easier. Today you can build up a "stock-block" engine—and end up without even the stock block. Every piece in the engine can be a special aftermarket part. I

Another Duesenberg A powered race car—this one using stock frame rails, suspension, steering, brakes, etc. Even the stock radiator. The car qualified at 97 mph, but was wrecked. Photo courtesy of IMS.

Chet Miller drove this Hudson factory car in the 1932 race, but dropped out with engine failure. 255-CID straight-8 was only mildly modified, but produced a 111-mph qualifying speed. But the car looked good: low profile, small frontal area and rear-wheel weight bias. More often than not, when a car looks good, it goes good. Compare shoulder-to-tire height with those of other cars of the period. Photo courtesy of IMS.

recall only a few weeks before the 1980 Indy race, USAC officials declared the Donovan aluminum cylinder block legal for the small-block Chevrolet V-8—as there weren't enough special factory aluminum blocks to go around.

In 1930 you made your own hop-up parts. Cylinder heads were milled to increase compression. Intake manifolds were cobbled from factory castings, or fabricated from sheet metal and tubing. Exhaust headers were fabricated from tubing. Camshaft timing and valve lift was altered by regrinding the lobes. Distributors were often replaced by magnetos from aircraft or tractors. Larger valves were scrounged from other cars and trucks, then tediously machined to fit. Lighter pistons were often borrowed from other engines and modified to fit. A lot of extremely clever engineering went into some of these modified stock engines in the '30s. Technology in this area

was pretty crude compared with today, but it wasn't unusual to double the original horsepower of an engine—and that's a reasonable bogie for any backyard hot rodder.

The variety of stock engines that were tried is fascinating. Names like Studebaker, Hudson, Buick, Hupmobile, Stutz, DuPont, Reo, Graham and Chrysler were seen. Even Ford Model T's that were raced on dirt tracks in the '20s were dusted off. And a few more modern Ford A's. One of the most popular production engines for the purpose was the Model A Duesenberg—the 260-CID, overhead-cam straight-8 that powered the

Duesenberg A passenger car in the 1921—'26 period when the company was taken over by the Cord Corporation. Some 1,600 cars were built in this period, and the racers were attracted to the engines partly because of the Duesenberg reputation and partly because of the overhead cam, inclined valves and rugged, race-bred bottom end. With a few mods the engine proved to be a strong, reliable track powerplant.

Fred Duesenberg, in fact, got interested enough to develop a special cylinder head and short-stroke, high-revving crankshaft for Championship racing. The

Phil "Red" Shafer specialized in Buick pushrod straight-8's in the early '30s. He had a magic touch with those unexciting engines. His best finish was 5th place in 1933, with Stubby Stubblefield driving. Photo courtesy of Jerry Gebby.

Shafer's Buick engines were always neat and clean, displaying careful workmanship. Those little aluminum elbows that act as intake manifolds were hand cast. Exhaust headers were fabricated. No over-the-counter speed equipment in those days. Photo courtesy of IMS.

head featured improved porting, and was fitted with a *desmodromic* valve train—cams having special lobes operated dual-finger rocker arms which positively opened *and closed* the valves. The shorter stroke reduced cubic inches from 260 to 240; but it was felt the higher rev range would more than offset the difference. The positive-closing cams were intended to assist the valve springs at these higher speeds. On the track the shorter stroke didn't seem to help. The short-stroker could manage 4,400 rpm—compared with a peak of around 4,000 for a standard engine—but lap speeds were comparable. And on the dyno, both sizes would hit about 140 HP with two carburetors.

BIG-MONEY
STOCK-CAR TEAMS

Up to now I've just talked about private stock-car teams which generally operated on a low budget and did most of their own buildup work. But just as interesting and significant were a number of "big-money" projects which used essentially production equipment.

These were generally sponsored openly by car manufacturers, though it was sometimes funneled through a dealer association or maybe a custom race-car shop. But the money came from the auto industry, not the traditional racing sources. Manufacturers involved in this sort of thing in the early '30s included Studebaker, Hudson, Hupmobile, Stutz, DuPont and Ford. They'd enter from one to six cars in a race.

The whole idea was to sell cars by clothing their products with an image of youth and performance. Not much different than the motives of modern car manufacturers that sponsor race teams and equipment. Some of the companies even keyed selected magazine, radio and newspaper advertising to current racetrack results. I can recall as a child seeing Stutz and Studebaker ads that featured exciting pictures of Indianapolis and the Pikes Peak Hill Climb. We thought that sort of thing was new in the '50s and '60s. It wasn't.

Certainly the most ambitious project of this type was by the Studebaker Corp. in 1932 and '33. Highly developed five-car teams were entered in those two races, and the company hired experienced Indy drivers to see that those cars had a good chance. Furthermore the cars were pretty much Studebakers. The frames and bodies were made by the Indianapolis specialty team of Rigling and Henning. Running gear, engines and drivelines were basically Studebaker President equipment.

Engine modifications included milled cylinder heads giving 7.5-to-1 compression ratio, lightweight Bohnalite pistons, four Stromberg carburetors, reground camshafts, Bosch magnetos, and welded-steel-tubing exhaust headers. Studebaker factory engineers spent many fascinating dynamometer hours fine-tuning these Indy engines. They finally achieved a reported 196 HP at 4,400 rpm from the 336-CID on a 50/50 benzol/leaded-gasoline mixture. That may not sound like much today in terms of horsepower per cubic inch, but it was definitely one of the most success-

Bohn Aluminum Corp. entered a hopped-up Ford V-8 in 1934 to publicize their new aluminum replacement cylinder heads. Engine dynoed 140 HP at 4,400 rpm from 221 CID—good in those days. Driver Chet Miller couldn't get much speed and ended up crashing on the 11th lap. Photo courtesy of IMS.

ful stock-block efforts at Indy in the early '30s. Those old side-valve passenger-car engines didn't have anywhere near the breathing potential of today's efficient over-head-valve designs.

Track performance of these factory Studebakers would also seem to confirm the horsepower figures. Ten-lap qualifying average ran as high as 115.6 mph pulling a 2,600-lb. weight. That would require close to 200 HP with the large frontal area involved. And the cars were durable. By using axle ratios of 3.07-to-1 and 2.92-to-1, and keeping engine speeds down to 4,000 rpm or less, they were able to finish all but two cars in both the '32 and '33 races. Best finish was 3rd in 1932.

Studebaker executives were pleased with the Indy program. In fact they were so enthused about spreading the Studebaker name in the motor-racing world that they considered a plan to sell mildly modified President straight-8 engines. They would be assembled in a special toolroom, for an FOB price of $750—rated 150 HP at 4,000 rpm, and ready to bolt in

One of the 1932 Studebaker factory team cars has been preserved by the Speedway museum. This car finished 3rd that year, with Cliff Bergere driving. He qualified at 111.5 mph. Photo courtesy of IMS.

1932 and '33 Studebaker factory cars used the 336-CID President straight-8 engine, hopped-up by factory engineers to 196 HP at 4,400 rpm. Final-drive ratio held revs to 4,000 in the race. Francis photo courtesy of IMS.

Studebaker factory cars used four Stromberg downdraft carbs on a fabricated manifold, with milled cylinder head and reground camshaft. In those days if it was speed parts you wanted, you made them or modified the existing parts. Note the beautiful hand-fabricated exhaust headers. Francis photo courtesy of IMS.

and race! I don't think the project ever got off the ground. But the fact that it was even considered is strong comment on the good state of stock-block racing in the Depression years.

Another big-money stock-block effort that drew a lot of attention was the team of Ford V-8's fielded by Harry Miller in 1935. This story could make a book in itself. It's not generally known that Ford Motor Co. set up a racing department in 1933 to race semi-stock V-8 roadsters in various road races

around the country—like the Elgin Road Race in Illinois. The company was ripe for the Indianapolis project. It only took Preston Tucker to sell it. Tucker was a race fan, a master professional promoter and the father of the Tucker Torpedo. The Indy idea was his. He went straight to Henry Ford and laid the whole thing on the table. It didn't take much selling—except the old man insisted on two points: Tucker would need to drum up some support among Ford dealers, who he hoped would

promote the Indy program to sell cars. The other stipulation was that Tucker would get Harry Miller to design the cars. The elder Ford had long admired Miller's innovative ideas, consequently he thought his input would be the key to success. If Tucker could promote some dealer support and get Miller's services, Ford promised to build ten cars in his experimental shops in Dearborn, and foot the bill for the program. They say it cost more than $200,000 in Depression dollars.

Well-financed 1935 Ford factory team consisted of ten cars in all— five race cars and five backups. Top personnel were selected for all phases of the program. Cars were built by Ford craftsmen in Dearborn. Photo courtesy of IMS.

Preston Tucker did it all and more. Harry Miller was quickly recruited to design an advanced front-drive speedway car around a mildly modified stock Ford flathead V-8. He was to use as many stock chassis components as possible with a sectioned '35 Ford grille for product identification. Miller was permitted to select his own drivers for a five-car team— which included a youthful Ted Horn from West Coast Dirt tracks. Tucker even got the services of Pete DePaolo, Indy winner in 1925, to manage the team. It was a first-class, big-money effort from the word go.

Needless to say the Miller-designed cars bristled with technical novelty. The front-drive unit was similar to the Miller units of the '20s—transverse change-speed gears on the output side of the ring gear—but this time with only two forward speeds and synchromesh shifting. Unsprung weight was reduced by suspending all four wheels independently on cross links and cantilever leaf springs. Brakes were basically stock Ford. Much attention was paid to streamlining. All suspension parts

Rookie Ted Horn managed to hang on for 145 laps in the 1935 race with his Miller-Ford before the steering "froze" completely. None of the other team cars lasted that long. Photo courtesy of IMS.

were encased in aluminum fairings, including the steering arms. Body panels were perfectly flush, with no protruding parts. Even the gas filler cap was flush. And exhaust-outlet pipes were brought around under the car to a common rectangular duct that ran under the steel floorpan.

Engine modifications were not extensive. Bohnalite aluminum cylinder heads were used with pop-up piston domes to get 9.5-to-1 compression. Intake manifolds were fabricated to mount either two dual-downdraft carbs or four singles. Reground camshafts were included with steel-tubing exhaust headers and special 8-qt. oil pans with fins and tubes built in for oil cooling. Bore and stroke were not touched, so the Fords went forth

All '35 Miller-Ford team cars had different color schemes. This is the No. 43 black-and-white job that Ted Horn drove. Photo courtesy of IMS.

221-CID flathead V-8 used in the Miller-Ford team cars was hopped-up by Ford factory engineers to about 150 HP at 4,200 rpm. They used Bohnalite aluminum cylinder heads, and tried both Winfield and Stromberg carburetors. Finned aluminum heads shown are later aftermarket hot-rod goodies, not the original Bohnalites. Francis photo courtesy of IMS.

to battle with only 221 cubes to fight with. We've heard various reports as to the actual horsepower—generally ranging from 140 to 160 HP, at crank speeds of 4,000 to 4,400 rpm. Similar engines developed by the Bohnalite Company in 1934 dynoed 140 HP at 4,400—so these factory Fords were probably not over 150 HP.

They had pretty decent speed, though. Ted Horn qualified fastest at 113.2 mph, hitting 130 mph on the straights. With the weight and frontal area involved, that should have required at least 150 HP.

The bug that clobbered the whole program was a design defect in the steering gears. In this case, to enclose the steering links inside the body and fairings, Miller located his tiny steering gear right next to the engine block. Pete DePaolo took one look at it and threw up his hands. He immediately informed Miller that the gears were too small, and engine heat would prevent keeping lubricant in the box. DePaolo predicted the gears would lock up after a few laps. Since it was then too late to change anything, he took the best way out and quietly resigned from the team.

And DePaolo was right. One by one the factory Fords dropped out of the '35 Indy race with frozen steering gears. Ted Horn managed to keep going for 145 laps by superhuman effort—but he had to use both hands and brace his feet against the frame to steer the car into the pits!

What could have been a neat piece of image-building for the Ford company turned out to be a scene of frustration and embarrassment. It was Ford's last "official" appearance in racing until the younger Henry was at the helm in the 1950's. The ten cars were eventually sold to private teams, and appeared later in many different forms, with different engines, bodies and chassis parts. Did you know that the famous

Harry Miller designed the '35 factory Ford cars, drawing on features of his earlier cars, including front-wheel drive. Stock Ford V-8 engines were heavily modified with special heads, cams and carburetion, developing about 150 HP. Note streamlined upper and lower suspension-strut halves with radiused leading and tapered trailing edges. Photo courtesy of IMS.

Downfall of the '35 factory Fords was this steering gearbox next to the left exhaust manifold. Heat boiled out the grease, and one by one the cars dropped out with "frozen" steering. A mistake made in the heat of design and construction. Photo courtesy of IMS.

Novi supercharged V-8 was first raced in a modified Miller-Ford chassis from 1935?

MEASURING 'EM UP

It can't honestly be said that the new "low-budget" rules in 1930 made production-based cars truly competitive with the special overhead-cam racing engines. Almost, but not quite. In 1931 these rules were modified slightly to allow four valves per cylinder—in hopes of luring some exotic European sports cars to Indy—and carburetion was increased to one carburetor barrel for each two cylinders—instead of two barrels for the whole engine. This latter change definitely helped horsepower, by freeing up high-speed breathing. Practically all the 8-cylinder engines were immediately fitted with four carburetors, or two dual-downdrafts.

The early '30s also saw the sudden emergence of much higher compression ratios. With superchargers out of the picture, and lead content increased to 6 and 8cc's per gallon in gas/benzol fuels, the door was open for the boys to raise cylinder compression ratios as high as 10 or 12 to 1. Many of them did, especially on overhead-valve engines with compact combustion chambers. Not much was known about things like quench area, flame travel, mixture turbulence, pressure gradients and such. But the racers were anxious to experiment with super-high compression, and see what would work.

These three developments— more carburetion, higher compression, and I should include progress in valve timing—gave considerably higher levels of horsepower per CID in the early '30s than we had seen on the last unblown engines in the early '20s. Some of the short-stroke DOHC race engines could barely exceed one HP per cubic inch at 6,000 rpm. This implies a BMEP of over 132 psi. The bogie for the stock-blocks was a little over 1/2 HP per cubic inch at around 4,200 rpm. Or say 0.6 HP per cubic inch This would require a BMEP of 113 psi. The superior breathing made possible with overhead cams was the difference.

In fact the usable horsepower available from the two types of engines wasn't that much different—for the simple reason that the stock-blocks generally had much larger piston displacements. The average Indy engine in the early '30s, race or stock, developed between 150 and 200 HP. If the pure race cars had an advantage, it was because of lighter weight and less frontal area.

When studying qualifying speeds and race results it becomes obvious the production-based cars were almost competitive. Russ Snowberger, one of the sharpest of the stock-block devotees of the day, put his Studebaker on the pole in 1931, with a four-lap speed of 112.9 mph. Two Millers turned 113 and 116 mph in later runs, but Snowberger was third-fastest in the whole field. In that race Snowberger finished fifth, and 8 of the 15 cars to finish the 500 miles were stock-blocks. The following year Cliff Bergere started in the fourth row with a factory-sponsored Studebaker, and finished third—the best placing for a stock-block during that period.

I guess if it proves anything, it proves that the AAA Contest Board came up with a set of rules that really did give the little guys a chance in big-time racing. It's been attempted, but it hasn't happened since.

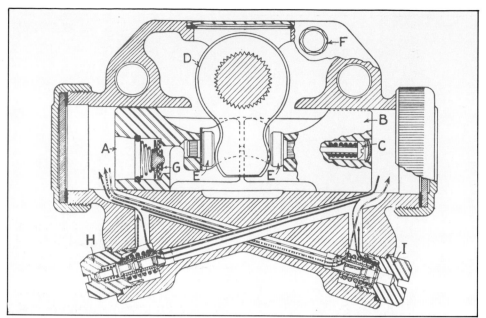

Section through the popular Delco-Lovejoy hydraulic shock absorber. Lever-actuated cam D operates pistons A and B, forcing hydraulic fluid back and forth through orifices and valves at H and I and in the two pistons, damping up-and-down wheel motion. Indy cars switched quickly from friction to hydraulic shocks in the early '30s. Stiffness could be readily changed by removing orifice plugs H and I and juggling springs and jets.

Various types of automotive hydraulic shocks were used on the Indy racers in the early '30s. This is a Houdaille rotary-vane type, as used on early Fords and others. Francis photo courtesy of IMS.

ANOTHER SPEED SECRET

Special mention should be made of one important chassis development in the early '30s that had a substantial effect on lap averages—hydraulic shock absorbers. Race cars had traditionally used lever-type friction shocks, which could be readily adjusted for damping effect by turning a nut. But they were erratic and jerky in action. You usually had either too much shock action or not enough.

Lever-type hydraulic shocks had begun to appear on passenger cars in the late '20s. These used various methods to work the fluid—pistons, rotary valves, rotating vanes, etc. Names like Lovejoy, Gabriel, Hartford, Houdaille and Delco became familiar in this new component market. Some companies originally produced friction shocks, but they quickly realized the benefits of the new hydraulic units. Not only were they much smoother and more predictable in action, but some designs had screw-type orifice adjustments that could change their stiffness as readily as the old friction shocks.

Racers were also quick to see the benefits. The smoother shock action gave better control through the turns. Also, stability on the straights was greatly improved when running over the rough bricks with solid-axle chassis. The switch to hydraulic shocks might have been good for 2 or 3 mph in lap averages at Indy—and even more on the dirt tracks of the AAA Championship circuit.

A RACING ENGINE FOR THE MASSES

One piece of hardware came out of this Depression period that has had perhaps more influence on American speedway racing than any other before or since. That, of course, was the fabled Offy 4-cylinder race engine. Yes, that basic design was laid down in the early '30s. And it hasn't changed much since. It must certainly be one of the most durable mechanical designs in automotive history!

It's interesting the way it came about. It seems that a West Coast dirt-track racer named Bill White was looking for a simple, light, torquey 4-cylinder engine to beat the Fronty-Fords on the dirt. He hit on the idea of the Miller 4-cylinder marine racing engine that had been produced in the late '20s for the 151- and 183-CID hydroplane classes. You could buy one then for $1,100 complete—and parts were still available through the Miller company. White adapted one of the 183s to his sprint car, and started working out the bugs. Fred Offenhauser and Leo Goossen got interested, and designed several new parts that were stronger, better adapted to car use.

The project turned out better than anyone expected. Bill White was soon mopping up on West Coast dirt tracks. The car showed a top speed of 144 mph on Muroc Dry Lake using long "Indy" gearing. The next step was obvious: Enter the car in the 1930 Indy race, under the new "little-guy" rules.

Things continued to go well. White contracted with Shorty Cantlon to drive the car—and he managed to qualify in the front row and finish second. Furthermore they campaigned the car on

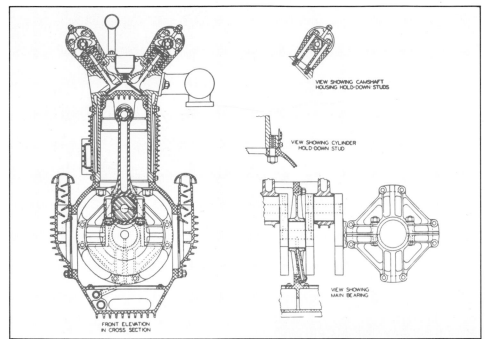

VIEW SHOWING CAMSHAFT HOUSING HOLD-DOWN STUDS

VIEW SHOWING CYLINDER HOLD-DOWN STUD

VIEW SHOWING MAIN BEARING

FRONT ELEVATION IN CROSS SECTION

Miller 4 from Goossen's drawing board in the early'30s was intended to be an inexpensive race engine for the Depression period. Note construction features: separate block and crankcase, integral head/block casting, bolt-on camshaft housings, diaphragm-type main-bearing supports.

the AAA Championship circuit that season, and finished second in points. Needless to say the effort attracted considerable attention. There was suddenly a run on old Miller 4-cylinder marine engines.

But more important, it gave Miller an idea for a brand new kind of simple, inexpensive, off-the-shelf speedway engine. It had to be suitable for either Indy or dirt tracks, and still fit in the tight economic conditions of the Depression years. A 4-cylinder engine, if you will. An engine that could be bought complete for less than $2,000. One that could deliver a reliable 150 to 200 HP at an easy 5,000 rpm or so on gas/benzol fuel, and do it for a whole season of racing with a minimum of maintenance. And yet it must be a small, compact engine of around 400 lbs. that would fit nicely in the smaller single-seat sprint cars of the day.

What came off Goossen's drawing board in 1931 was not a hashed-over Miller marine engine of the '20s. It was an all-new design, specifically aimed at track racing. It incorporated extra beef

Aluminum crankcase castings and forged tubular rods used in the Offy. Parts were very rugged, though weight was held to 385 lbs. on the early models. Crankcase breather vents shown were developed later.

in the right places, and with the latest technology as applied to high-revving, high-output spark-ignition engines. True, it incorporated traditional Miller design concepts—the barrel-type crankcase with bolt-in main-bearing bulkheads, one-piece iron casting for the block and head, right-angle magneto drive off the front, cup-type cam followers, spur-gear

camshaft drive at the front, tubular connecting rods, machined-billet crank, etc.

There were significant differences from the marine design: Four valves per cylinder instead of two; a narrower angle between the valves; larger bearings; a stronger geared magneto drive at the front—on the left instead of right. Also the new track

Cast-iron cylinder-block casting for the Offy included the head and ports to eliminate head-gasket problems. Valves were inserted up through the cylinder bores, and the block was bolted to the crankcase. Note siamesed ports and bolt-on cam towers at left.

An early Offy in Mauri Rose's 1934 car. Winfield racing carburetors were generally used, either updraft or downdraft. A Bosch aircraft magneto was gear-driven off the front. Note he small crankcase breather vents on the early engines. No catch cans here, venting was straight into the engine compartment and onto the track. Venting was radically increased in later years. Note the lead bar bolted to the frame to bring the car up to minimum weight. Photo courtesy of IMS.

engine was scaled up considerably to allow an expansion of the displacement. The original design had a bore and stroke of 4-1/16 x 4-1/4 in. giving 220 CID. Note the near square stroke/bore ratio. This was later expanded to 4-1/4 x 4-1/2 in. for 255 CID—where there wasn't a Sprint Class displacement limitation.

OFFY OR MILLER?

Don't confuse these new Miller or Offenhauser 16-valve engines with the original 8-valve Miller marine engines of the '20s. They were used interchangeably at Indy and on dirt tracks throughout the '30s. They looked quite a lot alike, except the marine versions had squarish cam covers, plain crankcase covers and the magneto drive was on the right instead of left. But some of the marines were bored and stroked to approximately 250 CID. It was easy to confuse them. In fact many thought Bill Cummings' Indy victory in 1934 was with one of the new Offys. It was actually a 4-1/8 x 4-1/8 in., 221-CID Miller marine.

Harry Miller seemed to lose interest in speedway racing after

superchargers were banned in 1930. He neglected the bread-and-butter business in Los Angeles, turning more to exotic custom-built sports cars and aircraft engines. Fred Offenhauser and Leo Goossen pretty much carried on the racing end of the business—and it was during this time the 4-cylinder Miller engine was designed and tooled. But there weren't enough orders initially to keep the high-overhead business afloat, so Miller ended up filing for bankruptcy in early 1933.

The whole thing could have ended right there. But Offenhauser had faith in the future of this racing engine. With a few-hundred dollars he had saved he was able to buy the Offy engine tooling and parts inventory and set up shop in his own garage. There were some lean months before the Offy really caught on for Indy and the dirt tracks. Interest gradually picked up, and orders started coming in. In 1934 Fred formed the Offenhauser Engineering Co. He was able to rehire Leo Goossen to do his designing—plus a couple of former Miller machinists, to turn drawings into steel and aluminum

components.

The team was intact again—and moving. They served American racing for many more years.

Actually those first Offy engines were steady, reliable powerplants for a variety of speedway cars—but they weren't spectacular performers. They were purposely designed with a modest compression ratio of 10.5-to-1 so they would run efficiently on a readily available fuel blend of benzol and premium-grade gasoline with lead which had an octane rating of around 95 by modern standards. On this 50/50 gas/benzol blend with two Winfield updraft carburetors, Offenhauser rated the 220-CID version at 200 HP at 5,500 rpm—and 225 HP at 5,500 for the 255-incher. Quoted weight was 385 lbs. Average price was just over $2,000.

This was representative usage and output for the Offy in those early years in the mid '30s. In 1934 there were 11 of the new 16-valve engines entered at Indy. Kelly Petillo turned the fastest qualifying time of 119.2 mph with his 255-incher. The '34 race was won by an 8-valve marine engine; but the

"Depression" racer was usually a conglomeration of parts. Fred Frame raced this one with great success on dirt tracks around the country. The combination featured a bored and stroked Duesenberg 91, supercharged straight-8 engine displacing 168 CID, Ford transmission and a Bugatti rear axle. It was the last Duesenberg to run at Indy. The year was 1938 when single-seaters became eligible, but it didn't qualify. Drawing by Dave Kimble.

following year Petillo won with the 255. From that point on the venerable Offy was firmly entrenched at the Speedway. And the 8-valve Miller marines gradually faded out.

A NEW PROBLEM: SAFETY

The advent of larger, heavier cars using inexpensive mass-produced components in 1930 brought a new problem to the Speedway—serious crashes. A rash of fatal wrecks in the early '30s culminated in five deaths of drivers and riding mechanics in 1933, during practice and the race

itself. This caused no small amount of concern among AAA Contest Board members. Radical rule changes were inevitable.

They tried two separate approaches in 1933. One was to limit total oil consumption to *6-gallons* per car for the 500 miles. It was hoped this would force the boys to pay more attention to better oil sealing and prevent excessive oiling of the track late in the race. There was even speculation that high-revving race-type engines couldn't run full speed for 500 miles on 6 gallons of oil. The racers did a lot of groaning. But, as

it turned out, only a few cars had any problems—and they were not the front-runners. The stock-blocks had no trouble at all. Some of them finished on only one or two quarts.

The other approach in '33 was to limit fuel-tank capacity to 15 gallons—instead of the usual 40 gals. They felt this would have two effects. It would force two or three pit stops, which in turn would encourage more tire changes and fewer blowouts. Also with the lighter fuel load, there would be less change in car handling between the full and empty tank.

Four Wheel Drive Truck Co. paid Harry Miller a bundle to build this "one-off" 4WD race car in 1933. It had its own exclusive 303-CID V-8 engine, with a drive layout similar to the company's trucks. Nearly 300 HP was available, but the odd drive forces and 2,450-lb. weight made for difficult handling. Mauri Rose drove it to a 4th place in 1936. Photo courtesy of IMS.

Officials felt this had been a factor in previous crashes.

Obviously these new safety rules were ineffective: The 1933 race proved to be the bloodiest in Indianapolis history.

They tried an entirely new tack in 1934—limiting fuel consumption, in hopes of forcing the racers to detune their engines. In previous years it had been common for cars to use 50—60 gals. of gas/benzol fuels for the 500 miles. There was no widespread use of alcohol fuels after superchargers were banned. It was felt that a 45-gal. limit would effectively slow the cars, as it would require an economy of a little over 11 mpg at racing speeds. Also they quoted a 2.5-gal. limit for the 10-lap qualifying runs.

Again the rules were ineffective. Two were killed in 1934, average race speed was up a fraction of a

MPH and qualifying speeds were unchanged. Race winner Bill Cummings averaged an easy 13.9 mpg on his allotted fuel. The mechanics just raised compression, leaned carburetion and geared for slightly slower engine revs—so the cars went just about as fast on 10—15% less fuel.

More of the same in 1935. Three were killed, race speed was up 2 mph, and qualifying speeds increased about 1—2 mph. And all this when the fuel limit was lowered to 42.5 gals. for the 500 miles.

In 1936 AAA and track officials got their heads together and finally found a cure to the terrible string of fatal accidents. The fuel limit was dropped drastically to 37.5 gals.—but that wasn't the key. What did it was a major rebuilding of the four turns on the speedway. Each was widened with a 10-foot

concrete strip around the outside, plus a broad oiled-dirt apron on the inside of the turn, in place of the inner gutter. Then the outer retaining wall was redesigned to slant inward steeply—to deflect spinning cars back toward the track—and a catch space and buffer wall was built around the main outer wall. This latter construction proved very effective in preventing cars from jumping the wall and striking the guard fence. Two cars hit the new wall solidly in turn-4 during practice and neither one left the track. And no serious injuries. This new turn construction proved to be the most effective safety step of all, up to that time.

Incidentally, that 37.5-gal. fuel limit had little effect on speeds. Seven front-running cars ran out of gas before the end. Winner Louie Meyer averaged 14.5 mpg

Typical "Depression" Indy car was often rehashed '20's equipment. Bill Cummings' 1934 winner was a Miller front-drive converted to a two-man body powered by an 8-valve, 4-cylinder marine engine of the '20s. Mechanic "Cotton" Henning got the most from the equipment! Photo courtesy of IMS.

while raising the race record from 100.1 mph to 106.2 mph. There's no easy way to slow a racer down. It's better to make the track safer. We're still learning these lessons today.

THE AMERICAN "DEPRESSION" RACER

At the end of 1936 the typical American Championship car had basically a 31-in.-wide channel frame and two-man body—made by a specialty firm. Miller running-gear components from the '20s, and a 220- or 255-CID Offenhauser engine were used. Very simple. Very durable and reliable. And relatively inexpensive. A perfect type of car to fit the tight economic times of the Depression, yet with enough performance to hold off the big-inch stock-block cars and the lighter Fronty-Fords on the dirt tracks.

These weren't particularly light cars. Remember, minimum weight was still 1,750 lbs., and most of the race-engined Championship cars would go more like 1,800 to 2,000 lbs. Racers thought more of beef and durability for a season's racing than a few extra pounds of weight. Mechanical brakes were in vogue, simply because the old Miller brakes were mechanical. Longitudinal leaf springs were used front and rear, usually, and everyone used hydraulic shocks of one type or another. Special Firestone Speedway tires mounted on 18- or 20-in. wheels. Not a lot of tire development had been done in the last ten years; but experiments were under way on tread grooving and compounds for traction. Pressures were still 30—40 psi.

How fast were these "Depression" racers? Actually almost as fast as the little 91-CID

supercharged cars of the late '20s. Nobody had yet beaten Duray's 1928 lap record of 124 mph, but several 1936 cars could hit lap speeds around 120 mph. Yet their peak straightaway speeds were around 140 mph—compared with 150 mph for the 91s—suggesting that turn speeds increased slightly. This was probably because of improved tires and hydraulic shocks. Let's put average turn speed at 95 mph for a 120-mph lap.

Definite progress was made in these low-budget years of the early '30s. The later cars had power-to-weight ratios similar to the hotter 91's of the late '20s. Because of much additional frontal area with the two-man bodies, they were slower on the straights, but turn speeds were boosted to compensate. It all adds up to lap speed.

They did it for half the cost of those exotic supercharged 91-CID cars of the late '20s . . .

59

4
MORE MONEY, MORE SPEED
1937—1941

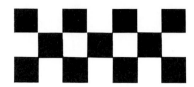

Boyle Maserati that Shaw drove to victory in '39 and '40 was a beautiful maroon that set off the long, sleek lines. European Grand Prix cars gave an entirely new look to Indy racing in the late '30s. Photo courtesy of IMS.

OPENING OF THE RULES

When the reconstruction of the four turns on the Speedway in 1936 proved effective in halting the terrible string of fatal crashes, AAA officials were encouraged to open up the Indy technical rules a little—to allow car designers and builders more flexibility for performance development. Oh, there was still a healthy respect for the dangers of the track. Nobody expected the wider turns to be a cure-all. But Indianapolis had operated under the same general rule structure for seven years. It was time for some new ideas.

It was clever the way the officials opened up the rules and yet kept a tight reign on maximum speeds. At the same time they opened the door to European Grand Prix cars.

They did it in two stages. For 1937 they kept the same general rules that had been in effect since 1930—maximum displacement 366 cubic inches, minimum weight 1,750 lbs., two-man bodies, etc.—but they allowed superchargers on 4-cycle engines and everyone had to run straight gasoline fuel. The reasoning here was that allowing superchargers would stimulate engineering development of the cars and might generate additional fan interest through higher speeds, more noise, etc. Also it would open the door to European Grand Prix cars, which were practically all supercharged at that time. At the same time it was felt that limiting

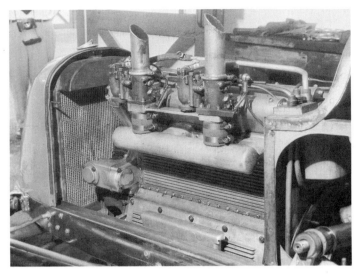

By the late '30s the 4-cylinder "Offy," usually displacing 255 or 270 cu.in., was standard fare in the American oval-track car—in big time dirt racing as well as at Indy. Why not? You could buy one new for $2,500. Photo courtesy of IMS.

the cars to gasoline would prevent them from going a whole lot faster with the extra boost given by the blowers. The two effects would work against each other.

This requires some explanation. It was not the intention of AAA officials to limit the cars to commercial pump gasolines available to all motorists. This would be too hard to police. The idea was just to limit them to gasoline. This could be quickly verified with a hydrometer test—the *specific gravity* of gasoline is much lower than other racing fuels like alcohol, benzol, acetone, etc. Also there were no really high-octane gasolines available then anyway. The better premium pump grades rated about 80 octane by the Motor Test Method and aviation fuels were only in the 80—90-octane range. These ratings were with 1 to 3cc's of lead per gallon. This was not a whole lot different than 1980s unleaded gasolines, which rate about 83 octane by the Motor Method.

So actually you could imagine engine designers in 1937 being limited to fuels similar to today's unleaded regular pump grade. And you know how much performance we can get from 1980s stuff! It's a far cry from the lush days of the late '60s and early '70s when 100+ octane fuels were available at every corner filling station.

The second stage of the Indy rule revolution came in 1938 when American Championship racing changed over completely to International Grand Prix rules. This was a direct turnaround from our go-it-alone rule philosophy of the Depression years. The new international rules stipulated a maximum piston displacement for unsupercharged engines of 4.5 liters (274 cu. in.), 3 liters (183 cu. in.) for supercharged engines, free choice of fuel and single-seat bodies. A complex formula for minimum car weight based on displacement didn't allow much weight break for small-engine cars. It was most practical to run up close to the maximum displacement. Minimum car weights were around 1,850 lbs.—welcome because it was close to the previous minimum of 1,750 lbs.

Many American racing men were surprised when the AAA switched entirely to the international rules. We had followed these rules in the 1920's with some success, but almost everyone accepted the fact that American speedway racing and European road racing had grown far apart in the '30s. It was accepted that cars designed for one type of racing would be entirely unsuitable for the other type—and probably uncompetitive.

Well, everyone believed it except Indianapolis officials Eddie Rickenbacker and Pop Myers.

They were the catalyst that convinced the AAA Contest Board to adopt the international rules. They felt that foreign manufacturers would send cars to Indy if the rules were compatible. Or at least some American racers would buy leftover Grand Prix team cars and run them. Five or six European companies competed on the International G.P. circuit at that time, and there were plenty of interesting cars around. Rickenbacker and Myers thought they could add a lot of zest to the Indy scene and bring it all together with just a simple rule change.

They were 100 percent right.

SPEEDING UP THE TRACK

Indianapolis officials did more than just write new rules in these late Depression years. They spent a lot of money improving their track. The turns reconstruction in 1936 proved so effective in reducing serious crashes that they were encouraged to make other improvements over the next few years, as finances permitted. Keep in mind that the Speedway was an open corporation in those years, with stockholders who liked dividends. So it wasn't possible to plow back all the earnings in track improvements like Tony Hulman did in later years.

In 1937 the four turns and the short chutes at each end were paved over with a rock asphalt.

The following year the approaches to the turns were paved. In 1940 the entire back stretch was paved—leaving only the main front straight with bricks, more or less for sentimental reasons. During these years sections of the dirt aprons on the insides of the turns were paved and the smoothed areas were extended farther into the infield. This gave plenty of room for a spinning car to scrub off speed before hitting the grass. Those inner retaining walls and gutters were murder in the early years.

Lap speeds were helped by the smoother track surface, but perhaps not as much as you'd think. That early rock asphalt was much coarser than the paving on the track in 1981. In fact the first result of paving the turns was to trigger 70 tire changes in the 1937 race—three times more than the previous year on the brick surface. Firestone engineers had to hustle to come up with new tread designs and compounds to resist the increased abrasive wear. Of course the mechanics had to recalibrate springs and shock absorbers to take full advantage of the smoother surfaces in the turns. Later, when the back straight was paved, gear ratios were lowered slightly to permit higher top speeds back there. This was the period when cars would hit 5—10 mph higher peak speeds on the back stretch than on the rougher front straight.

All in all, the paving changes had a very beneficial effect on both speed and safety. There were scattered fatal accidents in the years just before and after World War II; but nothing like the bloody record of the early '30s.

NEW BLUEPRINTS FROM GOOSSEN

The reallowance of superchargers in Championship racing in 1937 accomplished exactly what race officials hoped: It stimulated a surge of performance development on all types of engines. Just as important, it triggered the design and construction of three brand new full-race engines. These were to have a deep influence on Indy racing for years to come.

Not surprisingly, Leo Goossen laid out all three of them, working in cooperation with the Offenhauser Engineering shop in Los Angeles. Fred Offenhauser was also deeply involved in the engines all the way. Working from Goossen's drawings, and with only sketchy instructions from customers who ordered the engines, Offenhauser procured patterns and castings and did the basic machining. At this point the engines were released to the buyers who did the final minor machining, trimming and tuning. The basic patterns, castings and machined pieces came out of one of the few shops in the country that was capable of doing that kind of work in the '30s. You don't pick complete racing engines off trees. Not everyone can design one. Not everyone can build one. If you wanted a competitive racing engine in the '30s, and had the money to finance it, your course was clear: Go to Leo Goossen, give him a basic idea of what you wanted, and let him design it on the drawing board in a way that would work. Then give the drawings to Fred Offenhauser and tell him to make two or three sets of basic pieces. A good mechanic could take it from there—and maybe have a pretty competitive engine.

Yes, it did cost a bundle of money. Only a handful of die-hard enthusiasts had the determination and resources to tackle a project and see it through. What usually happened was an innovative race mechanic or car builder would come up with an idea for a new engine design, perhaps with just a few sketches to illustrate it. With the Goossen and Offenhauser names to pull the whole thing together, he would search out a prospective sponsor with plenty of money to get the project financed.

Skilled labor rates were still reasonable enough to make this sequence of events possible. Whether it could still happen in the '80s—even given a designer/builder team like Goossen and Offenhauser—is debatable. Pattern making, gear cutting, foundry casting, and machining costs are totally out of sight today. Only big companies have the resources to scratch-build engines today.

Even so, it could and did happen several times after the 1937 rule changes freed up engine design somewhat. Here's a run-down on those three important new engines I mentioned . . .

SPARKS-THORNE SIX

Art Sparks, a young race designer and clever innovator of special chassis and engine parts, was the catalyst for this unusual 6-cylinder engine. After sketching out the general design, he sold Joel Thorne—wealthy owner of Thorne Engineering—on financing a team of cars and engines. Thorne had plenty of money and it was a first-class effort all the way. Adams was commissioned to design and build the chassis and Sparks took his sketches to Goossen for finishing and polishing.

The choice of six cylinders in-line was to be a compromise between the light weight and torque of a 4-cylinder and the high-revving ability of an 8. The 6 would also have inherent dynamic balance, like an 8, and should have less friction. Sparks felt it might be an ideal combination for the fast Indy track.

But this engine wasn't in any way just a 6-cylinder version of Goossen's original Offy. Sparks outlined several design features that deviated radically from classic Goossen philosophy. One, the connecting rods were forged-steel H-section, rather than tubular. Sparks had a slight hump in the center of the web to provide for a drilled hole to feed oil up to the piston pin. He felt the H-section

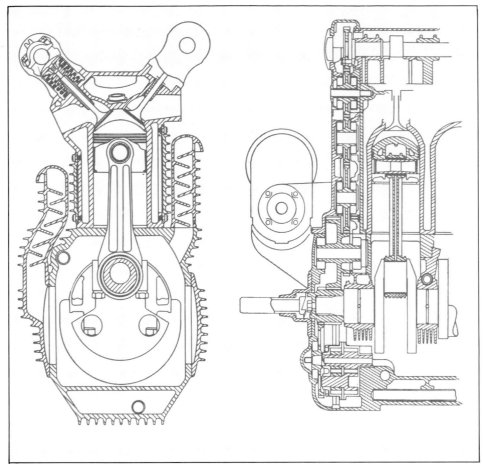

Gordon Schroeder working on the 1946 version of the '39 Sampson, formerly the Stutz Black Hawk engine. Riley Brett built the chassis using ideas from Mercedes: de Dion rear suspension with torsion bars. Photo courtesy of Gordon Schroeder.

Art Sparks' 6-cylinder engine for Joel Thorne had many "non-Goossen" features, even though Leo made the drawings. Main-bearing diaphragms were bolted into the block, not the crankcase—and H-section connecting rods, not tubular, with drilled holes for pin oiling. Very rugged engine.

rods would be lighter, which they were, and he felt pin oiling was important at Indy. Sparks also deviated from the classic diaphragm-type main-bearing bulkheads. He still used a barrel crankcase; but the bulkheads bolted up into the block with long through-bolts, rather than around the periphery of the crankcase. This was to give additional rigidity to the block/crankcase assembly.

Sparks also plowed new ground in his supercharger-drive system. Right-angle-gear drives were brought off the front of the block on each side. The magneto was on the right. The left gear drove a long torsion shaft down the outside of the crankcase to the supercharger unit on the left rear of the engine. The small-diameter shaft twisted enough to isolate shock loads from the supercharger gears.

Another benefit of having the supercharger at the left rear was that it could feed directly into a finned manifold for some inter-cooling effect.

This engine was designed in late 1936 when the 366-CID limit was still in effect at Indy. Sparks selected a brutal bore/stroke combination of 3-7/8 x 4-3/4 in.—giving a total of 337 CID, and tremendous power and torque potential even on pump gas. With a modest 10-psi supercharger boost, they claimed over 450 HP at 5,000 rpm; in excess of 550 lbs.ft. of torque coming off the turns at 3,500—4,000 rpm. Those must have been real ponies because driver Jimmy Snyder had no trouble beating Duray's nine-year-old lap record at 130.49 mph prior to the 1937 race. He accelerated close to 160 mph on the back stretch!

Sparks-Thorne Six, introduced in 1937, had 337 CID and developed over 450 HP at 5,000 rpm on a modest 10-psi supercharger boost. It was the most powerful engine to run on the bricks up to that time. Photo courtesy of IMS.

Thorne's crew chief, "Chickie" Harishima, inspects the huge supercharger for the '37 Sparks engine. Early versions such as this one drove the blower through gears off the back of the crankshaft; later they used a cushioning torsion shaft along the left side of the crankcase. Photo courtesy of IMS.

3-liter Sparks-Thorne Six supercharger-drive torsion shaft along the left side of the crankcase. Francis photo courtesy of IMS.

When the international rules were adopted in 1938 the displacement of the engine had to be pulled down under 183 cu.in. But this didn't reduce power proportionally because the shorter stroke allowed higher revs and less friction. Higher revs meant more boost from the supercharger because boost increases roughly as the square of speed with a centrifugal blower. Sparks reported an flash dyno reading of 412 HP at 7,200 rpm and 22-psi boost on an ethyl-alcohol fuel in the later 3-liter configuration. The engine was never turned above 6,500 rpm on the track. Even then Jimmy Snyder was able to beat his own lap record at 130.76 mph in 1939 with the smaller engine—and the same car won the first postwar Indy race in 1946 with George Robson driving.

The Sparks-Thorne Six was definitely one of the stronger independent efforts at Indy in the late '30s.

MEYER-BOWES STRAIGHT-8

This was a relative low-budget project compared with the massive Thorne expenditure on the Sparks 6. And yet the screaming Bowes Seal-Fast straight-8 had a more loyal fan following than probably any previous Indy racer. It ran the bricks for more than 10 years, first with Lou Meyer driving, then Rex Mays. Louie Meyer, two-time Indy winner and first-class racing businessman, was the idea man. The Bowes Seal Fast Co., was the manufacturer which provided the money.

It didn't have to be a whole lot, thanks to Meyer's unique idea for a hybrid 8-cylinder "Offy" made from two 4-cylinder Offys. The engine was conceived right after the international formula was announced for the 1938 season. Ed Winfield put this engine package together by placing two Offy blocks back-to-back on a common crankcase, with one cam-gear tower facing the back and the

other the front. The back gear train drove the two long camshafts. They were drilled through for a long, thin torsion bar that ran all the way to the front for driving the supercharger gear train. Here again the torsional twist of the shaft cushioned blower-gear shock loads. To make sure the torsion bar wouldn't break, it was machined from SAE 6150 steel. It never broke.

You can see the beautiful simplicity of this whole engine. Only a few special new components had to be made: crankcase, crankshaft, camshafts, front gear train, etc. They used existing blocks, rods, pistons, main-bearing diaphragms, valves, etc. Lou Meyer can be credited with a great idea in go-fast economics: When you can't afford a new and bigger engine, graft two successful small ones together!

This new hybrid did go. Meyer insisted on running gasoline fuel for tank mileage, however this

With 450 HP on tap, Jimmy Snyder had no trouble breaking Duray's nine-year old lap record at 130 mph with the big Sparks-Thorne Six. He accelerated to nearly 160 mph on the back stretch. Wildest ride to date at Indy. Photo courtesy of IMS.

When rules restricted displacement of supercharged engines to 183 cubic inches in 1938, the Sparks-Thorne engine output dropped below 400 HP. Jimmy Snyder still turned the same lap averages—though his straightaway speeds were down a little. Photo courtesy of IMS.

Louie Meyer, with the aid of Ed and Bud Winfield, conjured up a successful straight-8 by putting two Offy cylinder blocks back-to-back on a common crankcase. Leo Goossen filled in the blanks and Myron Stevens built the chassis. Photo courtesy of IMS.

Meyer's Bowes Seal Fast Special, first seen in 1938, was one of the fastest cars on the track. It usually qualified in the front row. Best finish was 2nd in '40 and '41, with Rex Mays driving. Meyer liked to run gasoline, so output was probably not over 350 HP. Photo courtesy of IMS.

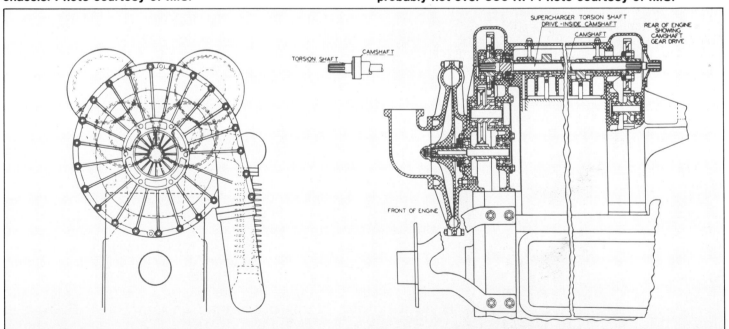

Goossen used a new idea to drive the supercharger on the Meyer-Bowes straight-8. Long torsion shafts ran inside the hollow camshafts, from the rear to the front, driving the blower step-up gear train. Splined into the cam drive gear at the back, the bar could twist its full length to isolate the gears from shock loads. This drive was troublefree.

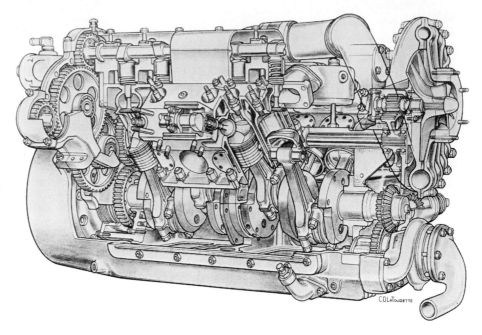

Fabled Novi V-8 had a long and brilliant career that started before World War II. Goossen designed this one to Ed Winfield's specifications. It had a lot of Offy design features—integral head/block castings, diaphragm main-bearing bulkheads, etc.—but it was always a free-revving engine that developed gobs of power. H-section connecting rods were adopted after the war. Original Novi weighed a hefty 575 lbs! Drawing by C.O. La Tourette.

limited the output to 350 HP at 6,500 rpm on 12—15-psi boost. The Stevens chassis was light and Meyer was usually a front-row qualifier. In fact, his 1939 qualifying speed was only 0.6 mph slower than Jimmy Snyder's lap record in the Sparks-Thorne car. The two cars were very evenly matched for several years. Unfortunately, the famous Bowes Seal-Fast straight-8 never had quite the combination to win. Their best finishes were 2nd in 1940 and '41 with Rex Mays driving. The car won plenty of money—both at Indy and on the Championship circuit—but never the checkered flag at Indy.

WINFIELD-WELCH V-8 . . . NOVI

This is the famous "Novi" supercharged engine that made so much rich Indianapolis history. Did you know it first went on the drawing board way back in August, 1940—some 25 years before its final appearances at Indy? It was one of those lucky designs that had a lot of reserve that could be tapped a little at a time over a period of years. Only a few racing engines, like the Offy,

have had that rare spark.

Credit Ed and Bud Winfield, of the Winfield racing carburetor family, with this one. Leo Goossen should get some of the credit too. Ed just wanted a strong, supercharged V-8 engine to power his modified Miller-Ford front-drive chassis. He liked front-wheel drive, and he was satisfied with his updating of the '35-Miller design. But he wanted a whole lot more horsepower than he was getting with his little Offy. Because the car was originally designed for a V-8 type engine, this was the logical layout to build on. Also Winfield was able to get sponsorship from Lou Welch, who did a booming business in rebuilt Ford V-8 engines in Novi, Mich. Welch was also interested in promoting the V-8 type engine, and he wanted to name the car after his home town. The "Novi" name stuck down through the years.

Actually Ed Winfield gave Goossen a pretty free hand in designing the engine, as long as it was a V-8. Thus, as expected, the engine had a lot of traditional Offy design features. Like the aluminum barrel-type crankcase,

three bolt-in diaphragm-type main-bearing bulkheads, and with the usual iron head/block castings bolted to the case—but this time in a 90° V arrangement. Valve gear was also conventional: Two valves per cylinder, angled about 70°, with one spark plug slightly offset in a hemispherical combustion chamber. Cup-type cam followers and dual valve springs were used, allowing very high revs with the lightweight valves. Connecting rods were originally tubular, but were later changed to drilled H-section forgings, like those in the Sparks engine.

The crankshaft was a special problem. Offenhauser machinists had most of their experience with single-plane cranks, but a single-plane crank in a 90° V-8 engine gives a wicked secondary unbalance that can rattle your teeth at high revs—though it has a back-and-forth firing order that can help intake and exhaust tuning. It was decided to go with the tried-and-true, unbalance and all. And it worked. They revved those engines as high as 8,200 rpm in later years.

Goossen again came up with a

Novi V-8 first powered Ed and Bud Winfield's old '35 Miller-Ford front-drive chassis. It was a handful to drive—but Ralph Hepburn managed to qualify it in the 4th row for the 1941 race and finished 4th. Photo courtesy of IMS.

When Indy adopted the International racing rules in 1938, a number of European Grand Prix cars were brought over to compete. Rex Mays qualified this Italian Alfa-Romeo in the front row that year, but dropped out early with supercharger trouble. Straight-8, Roots-blown engine was reported to develop 310 HP at 6,000 rpm. Photo courtesy of IMS.

Wilbur Shaw blew off everyone with the beautiful "Cotton" Henning prepared Boyle Maserati in 1939 and '40. The car was not competitive in Europe against the German Mercedes and Auto-Unions; but it sure was right at Indy. Photo courtesy of IMS.

clever torsion-bar supercharger drive. This time he used a gear step-up off the back of the crankshaft and ran the torsion shaft through the top of the crankcase to the front super-charger—where the camshaft would normally be located in a pushrod V-type engine. Again, it worked fine. The key to these successful torsion blower drives was merely the perpetuation of the idea from the '20s that you just had to include some cushioning in the crankshaft-to-impeller drive. It didn't matter what—torsion shaft,

coil spring, rubber pads, clutch plates. The torsion shaft proved to be the simplest for most gear drives.

There is no question that this Novi V-8 had more potential than any of Goossen's previous efforts. It practically screamed at you from the blueprint. But that potential didn't come easy, make no mistake. For one thing, Winfield's Miller-Ford chassis didn't handle as well as expected with the additional power and 175 lbs. extra engine weight. Furthermore, there is reason to believe the original

supercharger impeller and outlet scroll weren't too efficient. Impeller tip speeds exceeded 1,700 ft./sec., way above Mach 1, and it's possible less than 15-psi boost was available—plus a lot of heating of the air and subsequent power loss. Ralph Hepburn did well to qualify the combination in the 4th row at 120.6 mph, and finish 4th in the race. He attracted a lot of attention just from the noise of the alternate-firing V-8.

But the greatest years of the Novi were to come after the war. It was developed over a period of 25

Maserati chassis featured excellent brakes, independent front suspension, low CG and unusual rigidity. Crew chief "Cotton" Henning found it easy to "tune" for bite in the turns. Photo courtesy of IMS.

more years, and eventually became one of the most powerful engines ever to run at Indy.

ANOTHER EUROPEAN INVASION

I've mentioned that Indy's adoption of International Grand Prix rules in 1938 was done partly to lure well-known European cars and drivers. This was very successful in the World War I period and European Grand Prix racing was even more competitive and well publicized in the late '30s, after government-backed German teams came in. Indy officials even hoped to draw some of these biggies.

The "European plan" was only half successful. No Germans showed. No European factory teams came at all. Several well-financed American owners did buy some leftover G.P. cars from the Maserati and Alfa-Romeo stables in Italy—and ran them with considerable success in the immediate prewar years. The most successful effort was Mike Boyle's Model 8CTF Maserati which Wilbur Shaw drove to victory in 1939 and 1940.

Actually it took a lot of ingenuity and faith to tackle a project of running a foreign car at Indy

without any direct factory support. Boyle bought a ton of spare parts, but he could only buy one complete car. He didn't have spares for everything by any means. More than once he had to go to Fred Offenhauser and Goossen to have spare parts made to fit. Many capable Indy mechanics and builders were eventually involved in Boyle's crusade. It was a fascinating project costing a bundle of money. But they won.

The question is, how? Wasn't it an accepted fact that European road-race cars could never be competitive on an American oval speedway? They weren't designed for this type of racing.

Let's take a closer look at the 8CTF Maserati, and see if we can figure out why it was able to beat our best speedway cars twice at Indy . . .

First, its chassis was more sophisticated than most American cars. The rigid frame consisted of welded box-section side rails and crossmembers with the rear half tied together by a massive magnesium casting that doubled as the oil tank. CG was kept low by using torque-tube drive to a spur gear step-up on the nose of the rear axle. Front suspension was independent with lateral links and tor-

sion-bar springs. At the rear a solid axle was supported by quarter-elliptic leaf springs. This chassis had low unsprung weight, good wheel control and a minimum of frame flexing—so it stuck good in the turns.

Brakes were also a factor. Most American cars had rudimentary mechanical brakes that were never touched in the race. The Maserati had huge 16-in. magnesium drum brakes, hydraulically operated, with special high-temperature friction shoes on iron liners. There was no "fade" under hard braking. Wilbur Shaw often drove deep into the corners in traffic, using the brakes to slow down—and he would often gain three or four car lengths on competitors who had to coast into the corners.

The Maserati engine wasn't weak either. A straight-8 with double overhead cams, it had two big gear-driven Roots-type blowers on the front that pumped 15-psi boost. The factory rated the engine 350 HP at 6,500 rpm on 80% methanol. That was not earth-shaking at the time. The key was the positive-displacement Roots blowers provided nearly full boost coming off the corners—where the American centrifugal super-chargers would drop 1/3 — 1/2 of

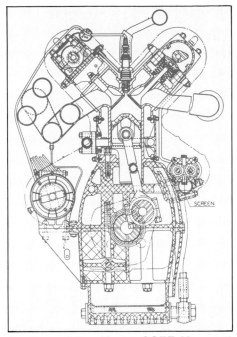

Section of the Model 8CTF Maserati engine like that used in the Boyle car shows the Offy-like integral head/block construction, tubular rods, bolt-on cam housings, etc. Unlike the Offy, crankcase/main-bearing-web assembly was split in half, with long through-bolts to give maximum rigidity. Engine's weakest point was its long 4.9-in. stroke.

Twin gear-driven Roots-type superchargers on the front of the Maserati pumped 15-psi boost, giving 360 HP at 6,500 rpm on alcohol. Roots blowers gave more mid-range torque than our centrifugal type, helping acceleration off the corners. Good engine for Indy. Note the independent front suspension with torsion-bar springing. Bar runs forward along the top of the frame rail, into the upper-control-arm inner pivot. Big brakes were well ducted. A lot of details to study. Photo courtesy of IMS.

Maserati intake manifolding from the twin Roots blowers was carefully designed for even air/fuel-mixture distribution between cylinders. Throttle response off the turns was sharp and crisp. Francis photo courtesy of IMS.

Huge 14-in. Maserati front brakes used magnesium drums with iron liners secured by shrinking and riveting. Designed for more demanding road racing conditions, the extra braking capacity helped Shaw maneuver in traffic and go deeper into the corners. Francis photo courtesy of IMS.

European G.P. cars seemed better designed for seating and driving comfort. The Boyle Maserati controls were within easy reach and worked smoothly. Francis photo courtesy of IMS.

their boost in the turns. This gave the Maserati more torque. You could see this as the cars came off the turns together. Shaw could out-pull most of the other cars, although his maximum straightaway speeds were no greater—he just got there quicker.

If the 8CTF Maserati had one weakness it was the long 4.9-in. stroke, making for a delicate bottom end when observing the 6,500-rpm factory red line. Some Maserati engines threw rods. Boyle's mechanic, "Cotton" Henning, took care of it by gearing Shaw's car for a maximum of 6,000 rpm. No problems after that.

Admittedly no other team using the Italian G.P. cars at Indy had anywhere near the success of the Boyle team. They weren't outclassed, but not quite competitive. Boyle had the combination—top mechanic, top driver, good car—and lots of money!

FASTER AMERICAN HARDWARE

At the end of 1941, the Offy 4-cylinder engine in a conventional solid-axle chassis with longitudinal or cross-leaf springs was still the combination to beat. This was the combination our mechanics and drivers knew. They knew how to

set up these suspensions for higher cornering speeds. Chassis "tuning" had come a long way in these ten years. Drivers knew how to handle the cars in the turns, how to get through quickly and reasonably safely. They knew how to drive them fast without brakes. Years of schooling on short dirt tracks around the country had left American drivers and mechanics uncomfortable with anything very sophisticated in the way of chassis design. Nothing had come along yet to shake everyone up. The Maserati wins in '39 and '40 caused little more than a ripple in Indianapolis technical evolution.

Even so, there was definite progress in the late '30s. When the international rules were adopted, for instance, and unblown engines displacing up to 274 cubic inches were allowed, Fred Offenhauser introduced a larger 270-CID version of the popular 4-cylinder, with 4-5/16 x 4-5/8-in. bore and stroke. He also increased the height of the cylinder block and cam-gear tower at this time, and lengthened the rods to allow further expansion to over 300 CID for unrestricted dirt-track racing. Weight increased about 60 lbs.

He adopted a new engine-dress policy, in keeping with the free fuel allowance of the international rules. His standard 270 setup used 13.2 to 1 domed pistons and was rated 300 HP at 5,000 rpm on straight methanol fuel with two Winfield carburetors. Actually relatively few racers used high-alcohol fuels at Indy in the late '30s because of the desire to get good tank mileage and limit pit stops. So the average Offy in those days didn't develop anywhere near 300 HP, at least in the race. An increasing number were using more alcohol for qualifying—and this is where the highest lap speeds with Offys were occurring. The effects of the smoother track surface must also be considered, of course.

On the other hand the 183-CID supercharged cars, usually with some alcohol in the fuel, could develop probably 100 HP more than the average Offy. This showed up in 3—5 mph higher lap speeds. Sometimes the first two rows were all supercharged cars in prewar races. But they didn't always win. Higher fuel consumption, more tire wear, more pit stops, less reliability—these have always worked against cars with gear-driven superchargers at Indy. It's only been the modern turbosupercharger that has changed this pattern.

It should also be mentioned that many old straight-8 Millers from the '20s were still running suc-

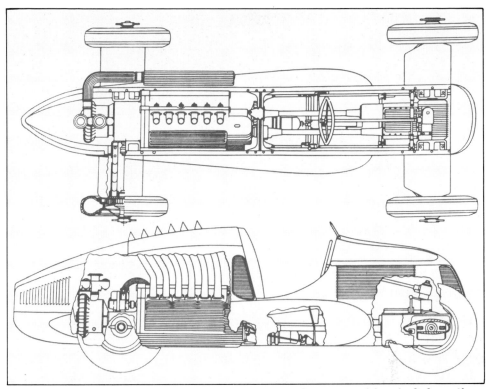

Harry Miller's controversial 4WD cars of the late '30s had a driveshaft from the midship-mounted engine to the front wheels—then a long one from the front to the back wheels. With side fuel tanks, weight distribution was near "ideal"—45% front, 55% rear.

cessfully in Championship racing in the late prewar years—even some Miller front- and rear-drive chassis modified to meet the late rules. They say good race cars never die—and it certainly proved out at Indy up to this point. It was not unusual for a particular basic car to compete for 15 or 20 years with only minor changes. This may not speak well for the pace of technical progress, but it certainly made it possible for a lot of low-budget racers to get into big-time racing.

As an example, the Miller front-drive that Mel Hansen qualified in the 2nd row in 1940 was basically a re-bodied version of the two-seater that Fred Frame drove to victory in 1932. Harry Hartz owned and campaigned it successfully through the '30s and into the '40s. This was the last complete race car built in Harry Miller's Los Angeles shop.

Certainly the most unusual cars raced at Indy in this period were the four-wheel-drive Miller

Specials—designed by Harry Miller himself, and financed to a merry tune by the Gulf Oil Co. The cars were ultra-radical and never did anything of note. This was because they were destroyed before the many sorting problems could be corrected—one in the Gasoline Alley garage fire in the early '40s and the others on the track.

Those cars incorporated just about every feature that race-car designers dreamed about for years. Like four-wheel disc brakes. They were designed like a plate clutch, with one friction disc pressed against the other hydraulically. The four wheels were suspended independently on cross-leaf springs. The engine was located behind the driver, driving forward through a shaft to the gearbox at the front—and then back to the rear wheels through a parallel shaft. The clutch was on the forward end of the engine.

Just as novel as the chassis, the engine was a 180-CID DOHC 6-

Al Miller qualified this Miller 4WD in the 5th row for the 1941 race, but dropped out early with transmission failure. The cars used a lot of advanced ideas, but were never developed. The original sponsor, Gulf Oil, soon lost interest. Photo courtesy of IMS.

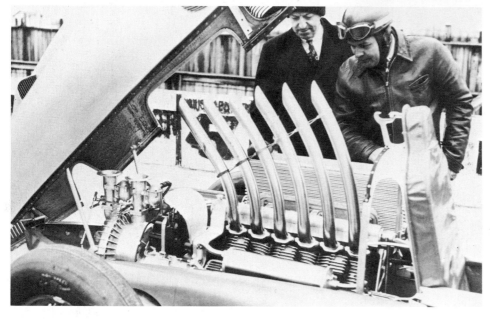

Harry Miller and driver George Barringer inspect the supercharged 6-cylinder engine in the 4WD Miller. It featured an integral aluminum block/crankcase casting, dual-entry supercharger, and developed 300 HP at 7,000 rpm on 80-octane gasoline. Photo courtesy of Jerry Gebby.

cylinder laid over 45° to get proper driveshaft alignment. Block, head and crankcase were combined in a single aluminum casting, with dry iron sleeves and steel valve-seat inserts. The supercharger was unique in using a double-entry impeller—vanes on both sides of the disc, with air inlets on each side—and a spring-cushioned planetary gear step-up designed into the casting. Miller claimed 20-psi boost and an output of 300 HP at 7,000 rpm on Gulf 80-octane premium pump fuel. This fuel handicapped their performance.

The cars looked good on paper, but erratic handling in the turns didn't suggest any advantage for four-wheel-drive. The relatively high 2,100-lb. weight hurt acceleration on the straights. Qualifying speeds were modest. Engine and driveline bugs kept the cars from ever finishing a race.

In concluding our look at the prewar years at Indy, a word about lap performances. The fastest supercharged cars were hitting top lap averages in the 128—130-mph range. Turn speeds were up from 95 mph in the early '30s to 105—110 mph by 1940, due largely to chassis tuning and the smoother paved track surfaces. Tire development was not yet a big factor in turn speeds. Firestone engineers were busy with the problem of tread wear on the more abrasive asphalt surface. This was the big reason for the trend to 19- and 20-in. wheels—to get more tread circumference to absorb more wear. Additional unsprung weight from the larger tires actually hindered cornering speeds. At turn speeds of 110 mph tread wear was very rapid. The cars rarely went fast in the race as opposed to when they were qualifying.

Straightaway speeds? The stronger supercharged cars, with around 2,000-lb. dry weight and 350 HP or so, could accelerate to 150—155 mph on the straights. The Offys, with 75—100 HP less, could hit about 145 mph.

Lou Moore owned and wrenched the 1941 winning car, co-driven by Floyd Davis and Mauri Rose. It was a classic example of the open sprint-type car that was still the dominant force in American racing at this time. A handful to drive, but easy to build and service. Photo courtesy of IMS.

5
POSTWAR POTPOURRI
1946—1952

Thorne Engineering Special that George Robson drove to victory when racing resumed in 1946. A good example of a prewar car dug out of mothballs and polished up to race again. It was one of the Thorne cars such as Jimmy Snyder drove in the late '30s. Photo courtesy of IMS.

DUSTING OFF THE PREWAR CARS

When racing resumed at Indianapolis after World War II it's not surprising there wasn't much in the way of new machinery. The racing fraternity had been deeply involved in the war effort—as engineers, tool designers, machinists, fabricators—and fighting men of course. The Offenhauser shop was a beehive of war work, and several race-car designers later received patents on advanced-weapon designs. There wasn't much time for race cars. Any racing was done over a bench.

Most of the cars that ran in that first postwar Indy race in 1946 had been on the bricks many times before. In fact, 20th place that year was our old friend, the Miller-Hartz front-drive Fred Frame won with in 1932—this time with a young Tony Bettenhausen. It didn't go any faster than it did before the war!

With one exception American Championship racing stuck with the prewar international rules in the immediate postwar years: The minimum weight limits were dropped. This was done to open up

the field to a wider variety of prewar cars, to fill out the dirt-track fields after four years of practically zero activity. In other words, prewar international rules called for minimum car weights around 1,850 lbs. with maximum-displacement engines. But many Sprint-class cars weighed 1,600—2,700-lbs.—they made interesting competition on Championship tracks with the 270 Offys.

Besides, immediately after the war the International Grand Prix rules were switched to reduce supercharged engines from 3 to 1.5 liters, or 91 CID. Unblown engines were kept at 274 CID. This meant our supercharged cars wouldn't be eligible under international postwar rules, and European supercharged 91-CID cars probably wouldn't be competitive at Indy with such a big displacement handicap. It was a rough choice. But both Indy and AAA officials decided it would be best to stick with the prewar rules, drop the weight limits and make as many existing American cars eligible as possible.

It proved a good choice, because

American Championship racing made a swift and strong comeback in the first few years after the war.

Another significant event in 1946 was that Louie Meyer and Dale Drake bought out Fred Offenhauser's engine business. They also hired back Leo Goossen full time for the design work. This assured a supply of new and improved Offy engines for Championship—and Sprint-car racing. It would sustain an expanding sport for years to come. Fred had made good money during the war and was anxious to retire after some 34 years in the sport. Meyer and Drake, with adequate financial backing and years of racetrack experience, felt the greatest days of the venerable Offy engine were still ahead. Getting Goossen's services gave them a handle on just about any design problem that might come up. It was a team that served U. S. auto racing well for another 20 years. They made astonishing improvements to a basic engine design that started out 15 years before as a compromise engine to sell in a Depression economy.

THE FIRST POSTWAR BOMB

Certainly the most impressive new car to appear in 1946 was an updated version of the famous Novi V-8 that first appeared just before the war. This time it was combined with a brand-new front-drive chassis and sleek body designed specifically to handle the tremendous power and torque of the supercharged Novi. You recall the engine was originally installed in a Miller-Ford chassis dating from 1935. It proved entirely inadequate in its first outing in 1941, even though the car did finish 4th in the race. Driver Ralph Hepburn had a handful.

The new front-drive transmission was designed by Leo Goossen, and the rest of the car was done by a budding Los Angeles builder named Frank Kurtis. The 3-speed gearbox was unique in having the input shaft located low so engine height and CG could be kept as low as possible. There was a diagonal gear step-up at the front for the differential pinion gear. Change-speed gears were parallel with the input shaft, below the axle line. This layout permitted the engine to be positioned just about as low as desired.

Front suspension was independent, on parallel links with longitudinal torsion bars for springing. A conventional steel-channel frame had tubular crossmembers and the rear axle was a solid tube on leaf springs. Nothing radically new, just one evolutionary step from the classic full solid-axle, leaf-spring chassis. The car weighed a hefty 1,920 lbs. with full-length aluminum body and huge 85-gallon fuel tank. Because the Novi engine was said to produce over 500 HP at 7,500 rpm in the postwar setup, no one was too worried about a little extra weight.

The track performance didn't disappoint anyone. Driver Ralph Hepburn had no trouble beating the prewar lap record at 134.45 mph, accelerating to a reported

6-cylinder Sparks engine in the '46 Thorne car dynoed 412 HP at 7,200 rpm. But it was never revved above 6,500 on the track and rarely exceeded 15-psi boost pressure. Being conservative was Sparks formula for success! Francis photo courtesy of IMS.

Many race fans don't know that the Granatelli brothers—Andy, Vince and Joe—were involved at Indy as far back as the late '40s. They bought one of the 1935 Miller-Fords and raced it as the Grancor Special in 1946, with Danny Kladis driving. It was disqualified because of illegal pit work. Photo courtesy of IMS.

Prewar Meyer-Bowes straight-8 appeared in several post-war races, running alcohol fuel to develop near 400 HP. Rex Mays could still get plenty of speed out of it; but reliability suffered at the higher power levels.

RALPH HEPBURN IN NOVI GOVERNOR SPL.
FASTEST LAP EVER MADE - 134.449 MPH
Indianapolis Motor Speedway, 1946

Leo Goossen and Frank Kurtis designed a brand new front-drive chassis for the powerful Novi V-8 engine in 1946. It was instantly the fastest car ever to run on the Speedway. Driver Ralph Hepburn set a new lap record of 134.45 mph, hitting nearly 170 mph on the straights. The noise alone was worth the price! Photo courtesy IMS.

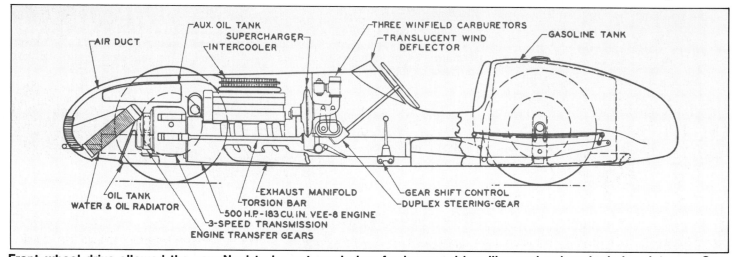

AUX. OIL TANK
SUPERCHARGER
INTERCOOLER
AIR DUCT
THREE WINFIELD CARBURETORS
TRANSLUCENT WIND DEFLECTOR
GASOLINE TANK
OIL TANK
WATER & OIL RADIATOR
EXHAUST MANIFOLD
TORSION BAR
500 H.P. - 183 CU. IN. VEE-8 ENGINE
3-SPEED TRANSMISSION
ENGINE TRANSFER GEARS
GEAR SHIFT CONTROL
DUPLEX STEERING-GEAR

Front-wheel drive allowed the new Novi to be extremely low for improved handling and reduced wind resistance. One problem was the change in handling with the change in fuel load. If the car was set up for neutral-steer with a full fuel load, it progressively understeered as the huge rear-mounted fuel tank quickly emptied—the engine burned a gallon of alcohol per lap. The other alternative was a dangerous oversteer setup with a full tank—handling would change toward neutral-steer before progressing to understeer as the fuel load lightened.

1949 version of the famous Novi had a beautiful silver paint job with bright red magnesium 20-in. wheels. The noisy, flashy cars were real crowd pleasers. Photo courtesy of IMS.

Mechanic "Radio" Gardner checks engine adjustments on an early postwar Novi. They used an intercooler above the engine, fed by large duct from the front grille opening. Photo courtesy of IMS.

Intercooler radiator above engine, used on the early postwar Novis, was probably not very efficient, due to small surface area. It was soon discarded to save weight. Francis photo courtesy of IMS.

Argentine sportsman Raul Riganti campaigned this prewar Type 8CL Maserati Grand Prix car for several years. It was an update of the Type 8CTF Shaw used—but with four valves per cylinder, shorter stroke, improved superchargers. It was said to develop 60 HP more than the Shaw car, but never went as fast. However a similar 8CL Maserati with factory backing finished 7th in 1946. Photo courtesy of IMS.

Louie Durant qualified this prewar Alfa-Romeo G.P. car in the 2nd row in 1946 and finished 6th. It was said to be an easy, comfortable car to drive. Prewar European G.P. cars could be bought for reasonable prices in the early postwar years; but spare parts were always a headache. Photo courtesy of IMS.

170 mph on the straights. Hepburn reported responsive handling in the turns—if a little heavy on the steering. He waxed positively lyrical when describing the acceleration for the first thousand feet out of turns 2 and 4! No reaching "terminal" speed here. The Novi would yank your head back at any speed. One of them exceeded 220 mph in tests at Muroc Dry Lake.

Very soon the real problems surfaced: Tire wear and fuel consumption. Although the Novis were clearly 2—3 mph faster around the track than other cars in the immediate postwar years, they went through fuel and tires too fast for a 500-mile race. They had to run high-alcohol fuel blends to keep from burning pistons and valves. This meant huge fuel loads which caused increased tire wear. If they ran at competitive lap speeds the tires wouldn't last as long as the fuel. Eventually they increased tank capacity to 115 gallons, and tried to strike a happy medium on lap speed. But it still didn't work. The Novis had to make at least one more pit stop than most of the other teams. The best they ever finished was 3rd in 1948.

Don't ever forget that those big Novi V-8's were perhaps the most fabled and exciting cars ever to run on the bricks. You haven't heard a racing engine unless you heard one scream down the front straight at 8,000 revs! That's when everyone appreciated the back-and-forth firing order of that single-plane crankshaft!

Certainly the fastest and noisiest of all European G.P. cars was this 3-liter V-12 Mercedes-Benz. Owner Don Lee entered it in several postwar races, but it never finished one. Photo courtesy IMS.

MORE HARDWARE FROM EUROPE

When I mentioned dusting off prewar cars to fill out early postwar Indy fields, that included a bunch of prewar European G.P. cars, too. At the end of the war there were probably at least 10 or 12 ready-to-go Maseratis and Alfa-Romeos stored in this country. They were still very competitive. Four or five more G.P. cars were brought in for early postwar races. So in the late '40s we had a situation where perhaps one out of five cars in the race was foreign. The fans always liked them, possibly because of their very noisy Roots-blown engines.

I discussed the Model 8CTF Maserati in detail in the last chapter. This is the type Shaw won with in '39 and '40. It also finished 3rd in '46 and '47, and 4th in '48 with Ted Horn driving. It was one of more consistent money-winners in Indianapolis history.

It's interesting that an improved Maserati G.P. car introduced in 1940, the Model 8CL, had no such good record at Indy. The updated engine had four valves per cylinder, square stroke/bore ratio, and was factory-rated at 420 HP at 6,800 rpm—70 HP more than the 8CTF. There were also improvements in the rear suspension and brakes. Those three or four 8CL's never did anything at Indy. The best they could muster was 7th in 1946, with Italian Luigi Villoresi starting from the back of the field with a modest 121.2 mph qualifying speed.

Incidentally, this was a genuine Italian factory team effort. They called themselves the "Corvorado Filippini" and they brought three cars. The other two were postwar G.P. Maseratis built to the new 91-CID formula. In effect they just chopped the 8CL engine in half and made a "4CL" out of it. This cut the power in half—to around 200 HP—but the prewar chassis was lightened by 200—300 lbs. to compensate. The 4CL was almost as fast at Indy as the 8CL. The Maserati team finally hired Duke Nalon to drive a 4CL. He qualified it at 119.7 mph. In the race a U-joint failed on the 48th lap.

Undoubtedly the most interesting European racer to run at Indy was the prewar 3-liter Mercedes-Benz that millionaire Don Lee brought over in 1947. The car was spirited out of Germany after the war, and Lee bought it in England for a reported $25,000. It was by far the most exotic and advanced race car ever to be seen in this country. The engine was a four-cam V-12 with an aluminum crankcase and separate bolt-on cylinder block/head units, somewhat in the Miller tradition. The blocks were unique as the cylinder jugs were formed from steel forgings, then the ports and outer water jackets were formed from welded sheet metal! Extremely complex construction, but very light and durable. The engine also featured two-stage Roots supercharging, giving 24-psi boost and strong mid-range torque with a minimum of top-end power loss. The engine was said to produce 480 HP at 7,600 rpm on a basic alcohol fuel.

The chassis was just as exotic: Frame side rails were fabricated steel tubing having an oval cross-section. Torsion-bar springing all around. De Dion rear suspension.

Don Lee's two-stage Roots supercharged V-12 Mercedes-Benz was rated 485 HP at 7,600 rpm, giving the car a flat-out speed of nearly 200 mph. Photo courtesy of Wayne Ewing.

Independent front suspension, with large finned aluminum brakes all around. The 4-speed gearbox laid across the rear end to save space and get the CG down. The driveshaft ran under and to one side of the driver's seat. Nothing was left to chance in getting durability and miminum weight. Even at that, there was too much there to get really lightweight. The car was as heavy as the Novi—over 1,900 lbs.

The race program was a long shot from the start. Without factory mechanics and a ready supply of fresh parts, it's hard to race such a complex piece of machinery. Don Lee did right by hiring Duke Nalon to do the driving. They often got Duke to drive these oddball cars because he had the reputation of being a fearless, gutsy driver who would get the ultimate speed out of anything he jumped into. In fact his qualifying speed of 128.1 mph with the Mercedes in 1947 was 2nd fastest in the field. However, the car was never designed for long distances at sustained high revs. They burned a piston on the 119th lap.

Don Lee brought the car back in '48, with Chet Miller driving. They again qualified well, but dropped out with an oil leak. The car was eventually sold to Joel Thorne, who pulled the 12-cylinder engine and dropped in one of his own Sparks Sixes. It never qualified again.

To sum up on the postwar foreign car invasion at Indy: They were noisy and colorful. While they attracted a lot of crowd interest, they didn't take home a whole lot of our prize money.

SOME ODDBALL CARS OF OUR OWN

American car designers had their share of wild ideas for world-beating speedway cars in the early postwar years . . .

Like the Fageol Twin Coach Special. In 1946, Lou Fageol, one of our big bus manufacturers at the time, wanted a car with a more perfect balance of weight and tractive effort—with no big change of this balance as fuel was consumed. He started with two Offy midget engines, destroked them to 90 CID and installed Roots superchargers. He installed one engine at each end of his car, driving the wheels at that end. The driver sat in the middle, alongside of the fuel tank. The engines drove their respective wheels through '35 Miller-Ford front-drive units but were otherwise unconnected other than by throttle controls.

It was a "different" handling car. Driver Paul Russo qualified it in the front row, depending on straightaway acceleration with the 320 HP available from the two engines. Things got a little spooky in traffic during the race. Russo rammed the turn-3 wall on the 16th lap, totalling the car.

Lou Fageol came back again in 1948 with one of his 6-cylinder bus engines designed by Ed Winfield in a more conventional rear-drive car. They did the full stock-block hop-up treatment, claiming 260 horses at 5,000 rpm on a gas/benzol fuel blend with three Stromberg carburetors. Driver Bill Cantrell managed to qualify it in the 3rd row—but had to drop out of the race with steering failure.

That same year we saw the radi-

Fageol Twin Coach Special in 1946 had a supercharged 90-CID Offy midget engines mounted at each end of the car, driving the wheels at that end. Only connection between the two engines or drivelines was their throttle linkages—handling was different. The car was totalled with Paul Russo driving.

A Fageol bus engine was tried at Indy in the late '40s. It featured an overhead cam and three valves per cylinder—one intake and two exhausts—and was hopped-up to 260 HP at 5,000 rpm.

One of the most unusual cars to run at Indy was the 6-wheel Pat Clancy Special in 1948. Tandem rear axles were used to get more rubber on the track for better traction. Increased weight offset any improvement in traction. Photo courtesy of IMS.

Rounds Rocket Special of 1949 was inspired by the rear-engine German prewar Auto-Unions. Workmanship was beautiful and the chassis had many advanced ideas—too advanced considering the lack of understanding of basic suspension theory. Rear-suspension control arms and non-pivoting radius rods worked against the de Dion tube, binding up the rear suspension in vertical travel and roll. It was too heavy to handle well. Photo courtesy of IMS.

cal Pat Clancy 6-wheel car. Another attempt to get more rubber against the track for better bite in the corners. It was more or less a conventional sprint chassis with two tandem rear axles connected by a short U-jointed driveshaft. The idea was to spread the driving forces over four wheels instead of two. The bug was weight—about 250 lbs. more than normal for that type of car. Driver Billy DeVore qualified fairly well. However he couldn't keep up race speeds, and was black-flagged after 100 laps.

In 1949 came the Rounds Rocket Special. This attempt to get better weight distribution located the engine *behind* the driver. The car featured a deDion rear suspension and independent suspension on torsion bars and the rear *transaxle* unit was a take-off on the Goossen-designed front-drive unit in the Novi and Moore Blue Crown cars. This rugged transmission/final-drive unit seemed equally at home at either end of a car.

Though displaying exquisite

design and workmanship, the radical Rounds car could never get up to qualifying speeds. It just weighed too much.

LOU MOORE HAS A BETTER IDEA

No car owner ever dominated the Indianapolis race quite as completely as did Lou Moore from 1947 through '49. With Mauri Rose and Bill Holland driving, Moore's ''Blue Crown'' Specials finished 1st and 2nd in '47 and '48, 1st in '49—and Holland might

This illustrates the very low profile of the Blue Crown front-drive racers of the late '40s. Without a driveshaft going to the rear, the driver could sit partially on the underpan. Photo courtesy of IMS.

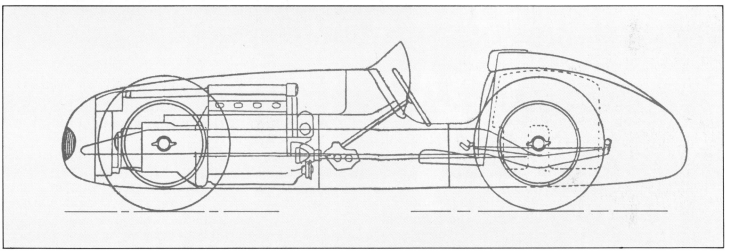

Lou Moore's famous Blue Crown front-drive cars of the late '40s were basically very simple. They were light, good handling, good riding, and easy on tires. Front-wheel drive was still a very viable option at that time.

have won the 1950 race if Moore's strategy wasn't fouled up by a sudden rainstorm that shortened the race to 345 miles. Holland was in 2nd place and moving, according to the race plan. Then the rains came.

Lou Moore's basic plan to win the bulk of the Indy prize money in the early postwar years was really quite simple. His idea was to build a team around two identical and extremely light cars, utilizing front-wheel drive in a configuration that could get around the Indy track at competitive speeds on minimum horsepower. He wanted to power these cars with very simple, basic 270-CID Offy engines running on straight gasoline.

Gasoline fuel was the key to the whole thing. Moore was counting on new grades of super-high-octane aviation gas that had been developed for military aircraft during World War II. Some of these had become commercially available shortly after the war. The best of them was a 115/145 Performance Number grade—with an octane rating of about 110 at the air/fuel ratios Moore was running. This was about equivalent to iso-octane plus 1.5cc of lead per gallon. He could run the standard Offy compression ratio of 13.2-to-1 on this fuel without any detonation or pre-ignition problems. With this high compression ratio, in conjunction with the high BTU content of the fuel, Moore was delighted to find 260—270 horses from the Offy at an easy 5,000 rpm. Fuel economy was 10—12 mpg at competitive lap speeds.

Moore set up the Blue Crown engines more for fuel economy than power to allow one pit stop only. They used a high compression ratio, mild cams, gasoline fuel—and he even tried aircraft carburetors (shown here) to get the leanest possible air/fuel ratio. Cars got 12 mpg at race speeds. Photo courtesy of IMS.

Blue Crown cars were the toast of the Speedway in the late '40s when steady, consistent running with one pit stop could win the race. Drivers Mauri Rose (shown here) and Bill Holland were easy on equipment and got the most out of the cars. Photo courtesy of IMS.

The rest was easy. Firestone's Indy tires would easily go 300 miles at race speeds on a fairly light car. On a one-stop strategy with the superb fuel economy, only 30 or 40 gallons of fuel had to be carried. This helped keep weight and tire wear down. Less weight also meant better acceleration with the modest power available. Any racing man knows that taking off weight is every bit as good as adding horsepower.

Everything fell into place: Run the race at competitive lap speeds on one pit-stop—instead of the two or three stops everyone else was making. The time saved could very easily win the race.

Which it did.

Did you know this was no overnight dream? Lou Moore was planning the Blue Crown racers in detail all through the war. Leo Goossen designed the front-drive-transmission unit in 1943 and this basic design had already been used on the Novis. As mentioned above, the real key to the plan was the availability of high-octane aviation gas. Moore followed this

development avidly during the long wartime nights of tinkering and bench-racing. He knew these postwar fuels were a far cry from anything ever dreamed of in the '30s. Lou Moore richly deserved his Indy victories for looking ahead and planning.

The Blue Crown front-drives weren't complicated cars. The front-drive unit, like the Novis, had the gear step-up at the front. This setup let the input shaft pass under the differential so the engine could be set lower in the chassis. Suspension was similar to the Novi: Cross links and torsion-bar springs at the front and leaf springs at the rear, off the conventional channel steel frame. The most significant difference from the Novi was the Blue Crowns had their front drum brakes inboard, next to the front-drive gearbox. This was done to reduce front-suspension unsprung weight, and possibly reduce tire wear. Tire wear had proven a weakness of the Novis in 1946. Moore chose Rzeppa constant-velocity U-joints for the front end. He felt they would

be more durable than the Bendix Hooke-type U-joints used on the Novis.

And then there was the weight—only 1,650 lbs. dry! It was a real engineering triumph to combine these advanced features under a sleek, streamlined body in a package weighing no more than a simple sprint car of the period. If those cars had needed to lug 200 or 300 more lbs., the "Moore plan" might never have worked.

But it did. The other Indy teams couldn't cope with the new one-stop strategy. At first they didn't believe you really lost that much time on one pit stop. They thought they could beat Moore with 1 or 2 mph more lap speed. Some tried bigger fuel tanks—but the extra weight just wore tires faster. So did the higher lap speeds. Some tried to copy the Moore formula, but with little success. He had the whole Indy fraternity talking to themselves in the late '40s.

As quickly as the one-stop formula blossomed, it faded. Reason: Tire wear increases very rapidly as lap speeds go up. Just a 3 or 4 mph

INDIANAPOLIS MOTOR SPEEDWAY 1949
JIMMY JACKSON

Needless to say, there were several copies of the Blue Crown layout in the late '40s. Jimmy Jackson drove this Howard Keck Special to 6th place in 1949, making two pit stops. Emil Deidt built the chassis using the Blue Crown's plans. Photo courtesy of IMS.

Frank Kurtis caught the attention of the Indy-car builders in the late '40s. This typical Kurtis Kraft chassis used a tubular space frame, solid axles, and longitudinal torsion-bar springs. He also built many cars with an independent front suspension like this one. Photo courtesy of IMS.

increase can readily double tire wear. You've heard of cars wearing out a set of tires on four qualifying laps. It works that way. So what happened was that lap speeds increased so much in the early '50s that the tires would only go 200 miles instead of 300. That shot the one-stop strategy right there.

And Lou Moore's "better idea" flickered out overnight.

CHASSIS DESIGN ADVANCES

It wouldn't take much studying to see that chassis design hadn't progressed very far at Indianapolis in the 20 years before World War II. The first postwar cars used solid axles and leaf springs in configurations not a lot different than the Millers and Duesenbergs of the '20s. Hydraulic shocks and hydraulic brakes were the biggest changes.

Racing mechanics justified the situation by pointing to all the dirt tracks on the AAA Championship schedule. Anyone knows sophisticated suspensions don't work on dirt. Solid axles and "broadslide" cornering is the only way to go. Which could be true. One thing for sure, they sure weren't trying to prove otherwise. They're still arguing about this 35 years later!

Whatever, chassis design finally started to progress at Indy in the early postwar years. Perhaps it was new blood. The old-guard car builders of the '30s—Adams, Wetteroth, Rigling, Henning, Stevens—were slowing down or retiring. In their place was emerging a new generation of builder-engineers with a host of new ideas.

Names like Emil Deidt, Luigi Lesovsky, Ed Kuzma, Gordon Schroeder—and the most prolific of them all, Frank Kurtis. These men completely changed Indy-car design in the first five or six years following World War II.

Never forget the contributions of component suppliers. The two Conze brothers, for instance, developed the quick-change rear axle and disc brakes. Ted Halibrand introduced the magnesium disc wheel during this period. Stuart Hilborn developed a brand new type of fuel injection.

Monroe Auto Equipment Co. engineered tubular-type shocks for Indy cars. Cleveland Graphite Bronze helped put insert bearings in the Offy engine. These companies and individuals all made a lot of money as a result of these Indy developments. I'm sure they would have been in there helping if there hadn't been a dime in it. They were "racers" too.

Taking a broad look at chassis design in the late '40s, you can see the major aims were to increase the torsional stiffness of the frame and to reduce front unsprung weight. The stiffer frame was to aid individual wheel "loading" to get better bite in the turns. Any reduction in unsprung weight at either end can only improve tire bite on an uneven surface.

Frames progressed quickly from channel-steel rails to large-diameter tubes to "space" frames made of welded chrome-moly steel tubing. A space frame is designed somewhat like a truss bridge so the torsional loads are distributed over a network of diagonal, horizontal and vertical tubes. You can get about any stiffness you want by merely increasing the depth of the structure. This gradually went from about 5 in. to 12—14 in. during the '46 to '48 era. Frame stiffness was no longer a factor in car handling. And the space frames were even lighter.

Front unsprung weight was reduced by merely suspending the front wheels independently on A-arms, usually with a longitudinal torsion bar for the spring. Torsion bars were favored as springs because you can vary the preload on the wheel by merely turning the anchor screw. Leaf springs required "wedging." Torsion bars also began to be used for solid rear axles for this same reason, but this required additional locating linkages, so there was no weight saving.

Frank Kurtis experimented with a de Dion rear suspension in 1948 in an attempt to reduce rear unsprung weight. He was obvious-

Halibrand magnesium pin-drive wheels on the Kuzma built 1953 Dean Van Lines upright car. Lightweight webbed wheel went on the left rear only. Clint Brawner prepared the car and Jimmy Bryan drove it to a 2nd place finish in '54 against the new roadsters. Car has been restored by Jack Layton. Photos by Tom Monroe.

ly influenced by the exotic German Mercedes that ran the previous year. Tommy Hinnershitz drove the new car, qualified well and finished 9th. Because there seemed no clear advantage with the setup—the car was said to have unusual handling characteristics— no more was done with the idea.

Credit car owner Eugene Cassaroll for the first use of direct-acting telescoping shock absorbers. He approached the Monroe people in 1950 for a cure to his wheelhop problems on the Auto Shippers Special. They engineered a special set of tubular direct-action shocks that transformed the handling. The direct action gave more precise wheel control than the old lever-type shocks that had always been used. Word got around, and within two years everyone wanted tubular shocks. Monroe executives saw an opportunity for valuable publicity, so they launched a program to develop special adjustable shocks exclusively for Championship cars. They supplied technicians at the Speedway to help select and valve them. Shock sets were supplied at a fraction of cost. Sure it cost a bundle. But Monroe can say their shocks have been on the win-

ning Indianapolis car almost every year since 1953. That's good advertising.

Disc brakes had an equally interesting evolution. These began to catch on in the late '40s, when the racers discovered the Goodyear-Hawley "spot" brakes on the Crosley miniature passenger car. Remember it? These were small brakes; but they proved adequate for speedway cars. They were much lighter and less expensive than current drum brakes. The Conzes went further. They adapted their aircraft brakes for use on Indy cars in 1951. Ted Halibrand, then manufacturing race-car axles and wheels, picked up on the disc-brake idea and began producing them specifically for racing purposes. Their use on Frank Kurtis' first roadster-type car in 1952—the Howard Keck Special—started the snowball rolling.

Speaking of Halibrand, his unique cast-magnesium disc wheels contributed much to chassis progress in this immediate postwar period. Ted felt there had to be a better answer than the expensive, hard-to-manufacture Rudge-type wire wheels that had been used on most of the world's

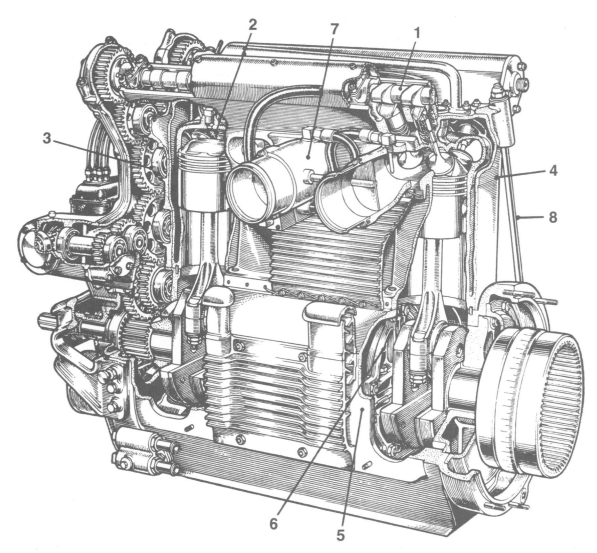

After Louis Meyer and Dale Drake took over the Offy engine business in 1946, they proceeded to make a number of important engine improvements over the next five years or so: (1) improved camshaft profiles; (2) first experiments with forged pistons; (3) more durable cam drive gears and bearings; (4) revised water jacketing; (5) undercut crankshaft-journal fillets; (6) insert-type main and rod bearings; (7) Hilborn fuel injection; (8) block bracing bars. Drawing by C.O. La Tourette.

race cars for over 30 years. He began experimenting with cast-magnesium disc wheels in 1947, gradually developing their strength and stiffness to levels beyond wire wheels—with half the weight of a wire wheel. The magnesium disc wheel took over the Indy scene completely in only three or four years. The light weight and rigidity did a lot for car handling.

One thing that made Rudge-type wire wheels so expensive was the slip-on hub machined with 88 fine serrations or splines, to transmit the torque. Halibrand located his magnesium wheels with four or six simple dowel pins

with pilot guides for quick wheel centering, plus a pressure plate behind a conventional 3-lug wing nut. Not everyone embraced the new pin-drive concept. Even though they liked the lighter wheel, Halibrand had to make both hub types for years.

UPDATING THE OFFY

When Lou Meyer and Dale Drake took over the Offenhauser engine business in 1946 there had been very few changes in the Offy design since its inception 15 years earlier. This pattern was to change under the new ownership. Even though there was no real competition for the basic Offy engine in

big-time American track racing, Meyer and Drake vowed to try to improve the design in years to come—not just grind out identical engines to fill orders.

Several important improvements were made in the late '40s. Believe it or not, Offy engines were still using poured-babbitt main and rod bearings in the post-war years. This was long after passenger cars had switched to the superior insert-type bearings. The break came when a salesman for a Cleveland bearing manufacturer got involved with an Offy midget race car in 1948. They machined the engine to accept commercial steel-backed copper-lead insert

Riley side-draft, single-throat carbure-tors were used on nearly all Offy race engines in the late '40s—prior to Hilborn fuel injection. They were a takeoff of the Winfield vertical carbs of the '30s, but with the more convenient, horizontal layout. Francis photo courtesy of IMS.

Hilborn constant-flow fuel-injection system used large air-intake barrels with butterfly throttle valves. Nozzles behind the valves sprayed in the fuel. Throttle shaft was linked to the fuel-control metering valve. A modified Pesco positive-displacement aircraft fuel pump was driven by the engine and the fuel metering valve was opened with the butterflies, so fuel flow increased with engine speed and throttle position.

bearings. To everyone's amaze-ment the engine ran the whole season with the same bearings. This contrasted to poured bearings which had to be renewed every four or five races. Word got around quickly, and within a few months Lou Meyer contacted the "Clevite" bearing people to sup-ply heavy-duty copper-lead inserts for experimental use in the big Indianapolis Offys. They raced first in 1949. Within a year prac-tically everyone was using them.

Other improvements during this period included strengthened bronze castings for the main-bear-ing bulkheads, undercut crankshaft-journal fillets—a new refinement at that time—and the first experiments with forged pistons. High-rev durability was becoming more critical in those years because Indy rules required racing with the same gear ratio as that used for qualifying. To turn

adequate qualifying speeds, some teams had to rev their Offys beyond safe limits in the race. Everyone was glad to see this rule dropped in 1952.

Certainly the most important performance breakthrough in the late '40s was fuel injection. Meyer & Drake had nothing to do with this. A young California hot rod-der, Stuart Hilborn, began getting orders for bolt-on systems for Offy midgets—which were at a peak of popularity on the West Coast at that time. He set up shop, and the next logical move was a system for the big 270 Offy.

The whole thing was so simple no one thought it would work: A rotary fuel pump driven off the camshaft supplied fuel pressure that increased more or less in pro-portion to engine speed, up to a maximum of around 35 psi. A throttle body on each port con-tained a fuel-spray nozzle and

throttle butterfly. A fuel-metering valve placed between the pump and nozzles was calibrated to open and close with the throttles. This ensured increased fuel flow as engine speed increased, while the metering valve cut off flow under part-throttle and idle conditions. Fuel/air-ratio control was obviously somewhat cruder than a conventional suction carburetor. But for speedway racing, where the engine operates in a fairly nar-row range of RPM and load, the mixture could be quite closely tuned. It helped that alcohol fuels aren't very sensitive to air/fuel ratios.

Of course the big advantage of the system was that it eliminated most of the breathing restriction of carburetors—the tight venturi throat, the nozzle bar, the thick throttle blade. In the late '40s the Riley sidedraft carburetor pretty much replaced the old Winfield

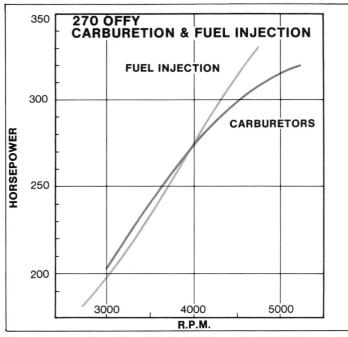

Dyno curves show the effect of Hilborn fuel injection on the performance of a standard 270-CID Offy engine on methanol fuel. Carburetors gave a little more power at the low end because of more accurate air/fuel mixture control. But airflow with the injectors helped the top end—where it counted.

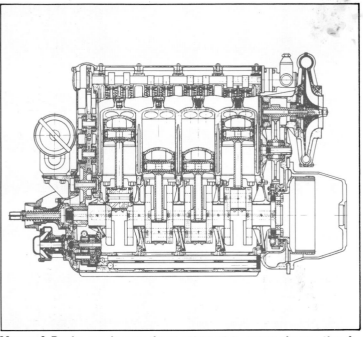

Meyer & Drake made a serious attempt to supercharge the 4-cylinder Offy in the early '50s, using a destroked 220 sprint-car engine (177 CID) with a Goossen-designed centrifugal blower on the back. Main drive gear on crankshaft had a spring-cushioned hub for shock-load isolation. The engines were always hampered by poor mid-range torque.

updrafts and downdrafts. This helped performance somewhat. But Hilborn fuel injection added an instant 10% or so on top of this. That was about 30 HP and 1 or 2 mph in lap speed *right now!* Accompanying graphs show comparative power curves for a standard 270 Offy with twin Riley carbs and with fuel injection. With the improved cams available in the late '40s, a good 270 kicked out more than 350 HP at 5,400 rpm on methanol.

Hilborn fuel injection was first tried on the Howard Keck Special at the Speedway as early as 1949. Its adoption was delayed several years by the need for low fuel consumption, when race strategy called for only one or two pit stops. Consumption rates were always a little higher with injectors. At first many of the teams would qualify their cars on injectors, running a straight methanol fuel. Then they'd switch to carburetors and usually a 40/40/20 blend of methanol, gasoline and benzol for the race. This fuel gave a good compromise between performance

and fuel economy, and the carburetors assured more precise tuning of air/fuel ratios. Actually the benzol served only as a blending agent, because gasoline and alcohol won't stay in a stable mixture in these proportions. Gasoline was for economy—alcohol for power.

This was the situation in the very early '50s. It wasn't long before increasing lap speeds boosted tire wear to the point where three or four pit stops were necessary. Under these conditions fuel consumption was eliminated as a factor. Pit stops were determined by tire wear. Practically overnight the guys went to injectors and straight alky for both qualifying *and* the race. By 1953 the switch was complete.

Meyer & Drake introduced an interesting variation of the Offy theme in 1950—an under-3-liter supercharged version. Starting with the 220-CID sprint engine, they reduced the bore and stroke to give 177 cubes, cut the piston domes for 8-to-1 compression and designed a beautiful gear-driven

centrifugal supercharger on the back of the crankcase, pumping through a finned cast-aluminum intercooler to a special log manifold. Leo Goossen tried to design all the latest wartime technology into the supercharger with 5.35-to-1 gear step-up. They got nearly 30-psi boost at 6,500 rpm and 460 HP at this speed on methanol fuel using a large aircraft carburetor.

Results on the track were less than impressive. Four cars with these engines qualified for the 1950 race, and Fred Agabashian put one of them in the front row at over 132 mph. All were slowed by various engine ailments in the race. When the race was stopped for rain at 345 miles the three were still running, but they were far behind. In 1951 Meyer & Drake got another 20 HP by adapting Hilborn fuel injection at the ports. Throttle response off the turns improved, but by then these engines had a reputation for poor torque on acceleration. No top teams used them after that. It's ironic too, because Tony Bet-

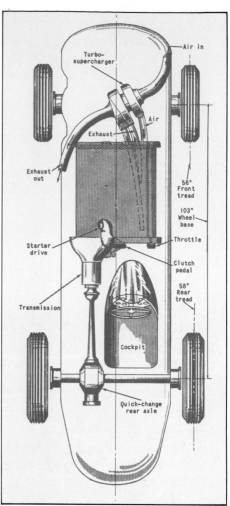

Turbocharged Cummins Diesel, driven by Freddie Agabashian, was the most sensational car on the track in 1952. He qualified on the pole, setting a new 139-mph lap record in the process. The allowance of 402 CID for diesel-type engines got the Cummins people interested. Photo courtesy of IMS.

Layout of the Cummins Diesel roadster that ran in the 1952 race. Driveline was offset to the left to shift weight to the "inside," and the engine laid over to the right to lower CG and reduce frontal area. The turbocharger—first to be used at Indy—was positioned ahead of the engine.

tenhausen was very competitive on the AAA dirt tracks in 1950 with one of these blown engines in the lightweight Belanger Special. He won several races. They just never seemed to be able to do anything at Indianapolis.

EVEN DIESEL ENGINES

In 1950 AAA officials tried to encourage some new blood at the Speedway by allowing diesel-type engines a large displacement advantage. Diesel-displacement limit was set at 402 CID, supercharged or not. This immediately attracted executives at the Cummins Engine Co. in Indianapolis, as they had sponsored several diesel cars for publicity purposes in the early '30s. These weren't competitive on

speed; but they could run the 500 miles without a pit stop and get 15 or 20 mpg—which proved well worth the effort in free publicity.

This new displacement advantage was too much of a temptation to resist. Cummins had a 6-cylinder truck diesel that could be raised to 401 CID with a 1/8-in. overbore, so it could be used with the original rods and crankshaft. They stuck a big gear-driven Roots-type blower on the front, and started experimenting on the dyno. It wasn't long before they were reading 340 horses at 4,000 rpm on 15-psi boost pressure! So why not? Frank Kurtis was contacted in Los Angeles to build a new rear-drive car to accept the big diesel. Cummins was off to the races.

That first attempt in 1950 was not too successful. Driver Jimmy Jackson did manage to qualify the car in the last row at 129.2 mph—slowest in the field—but dropped out on the 52nd lap with supercharger-drive failure. Probably without impressing anybody.

But Cummins didn't give up. They planned an even stronger program for the 1952 race, with a brand new state-of-the-art car from Kurtis, and with the engine upgraded with one of the funny new "turbochargers" that were just beginning to be seen on trucks and tractors. This marked the first use of a turbocharger at Indy. Not much was known about the science of matching a turbocharger to a specific engine at that time. Waste gates were not generally used, and you selected the turbine/compressor combination to give some peak boost pressure at peak engine RPM, with that pressure just more or less trailing off at lower speeds. Thus the Cummins engineers used a relatively large turbo unit to give 20-psi boost at 4,000 rpm engine speed, giving them a very nice peak output of nearly 400 horses. Acceleration off the turns was sluggish. Boost was only 11 psi when the throttle was punched in the turn, and it took 3—5 secs, for the turbine to speed up enough to give 15—20 psi down the straightaway. A simple waste gate and a smaller turbine would have made that engine much more responsive for track racing. Lessons that came 15 years later.

But even with this crude turbocharging system, the car/engine combination permitted driver Freddie Agabashian to break the Indy lap record at 139.10 mph and sit on the pole for the 1952 race. In fact the car was almost as radical as the engine. To reduce frontal area and lower the CG as much as possible with the large, heavy engine, they laid the engine flat on its right side, with the crankshaft to the left, and ran the driveshaft down the left side of the chassis to an offset rear axle. The driver sat down low to the right of the driveshaft. It was a beautiful car and probably the lowest at the Speedway at that time. If the car had a serious weakness it was weight. Just too much engine and turbocharger plumbing. It weighed 2,480 lbs. dry. Needless to say it was hard on tires. Agabashian wore a set down to the cords on his four qualifying laps.

Tire wear, then, was a major concern in race strategy. Which was a double pity because the diesel engine had the potential to go the whole race at competitive speed on 50 gallons of fuel. It was

Turbocharger on the Cummins Diesel was positioned ahead of the engine to reduce body height and frontal area. The mistake was locating the turbocharger inlet so it could suck dirt and rubber particles off the track. A clogged turbocharger inlet put the car out after 175 miles. Francis photo courtesy of IMS.

'52 Cummins Diesel was the first "roadster" type car built by Frank Kurtis. Driveshaft to the left of the driver allowed a very low seating position. Francis photo courtesy of IMS.

finally decided to set up the chassis for minimum tire wear—even with some sacrifice in handling—then run at somewhat slower lap speeds, hang back in 5th or 6th place, and hope to run without the pit stop. They thought this might be possible because tire wear was much less at lap speeds only 5 or 6 mph slower than maximum.

Unfortunately the strategy was not needed. The turbocharger did them in. Due to its position in the laydown engine installation, the air inlet was only a few inches from the track. As you can imagine, it acted like a huge vacuum cleaner, sucking dirt and rubber dust off the track at a merry rate. It took about 175 miles to clog up the

Classic sprint-type cars reached a peak of performance in the early '50s. Lee Wallard's Belanger Special, 1951 winner, was a perfect example. Cheap to build, easy to set up—but hard cars to drive compared to later roadsters. Note the Halibrand cast-magnesium wheels—no more "lacing them in or out." Photo courtesy of IMS.

inlet. That was the end of the Cummins diesel effort at Indy.

THE PEAK OF THE UPRIGHT CARS

The time period covered in this chapter, through 1952, saw the last wide use of the classic upright or "sprint-car" configuration at Indianapolis. This layout has the centrally located engine upright in front, with center driveshaft and conventional rear axle. The driver sits above the driveline and the fuel tank is in the tail behind him. A solid front axle is generally used—though a number of successful sprint-type cars were using independent front suspensions by the early '50s. Torsion-bar springing was widely used for both independent and solid-axle suspensions.

Anyway, the peak of the performance potential of sprint-type cars

at the Speedway occurred in the early '50s. The highest official lap speed for this type of car was Walt Faulkner's 138.12-mph record in the Agajanian Special in 1951. On that run the car was geared to turn up to 6,200 rpm on the straights, and mechanic Clay Smith had the chassis tuned razor-sharp. Walt was getting through the turns at 120 mph. The 270-CID Offy also had the benefit of fuel injection and methanol fuel, plus Clay Smith's personally designed camshafts. I assume Faulkner had 360—370 HP available down the straights, pulling a car that weighed under 1,700 lbs. dry. There certainly wasn't much more to be had from a basic sprint-type car in that day.

There were already plenty of indications in 1952 that the classic sprint configuration had lived out its usefulness at Indy. The first

By the early '50s even the classic upright "sprint" cars were using tubular frames for improved rigidity. Cross-loading of the suspension worked much better with a very stiff frame. This car used a beam front axle and cross-leaf spring, a la Ford.

Contrast this shot of the Belanger sprint car with the Cummins roadster on page 89. Driveshaft down the center of the chassis required the driver to sit above it, raising the car's CG and increasing frontal area. Francis photo courtesy of IMS.

new "roadster"-type cars from Frank Kurtis were the Cummins Diesel Special and the Howard Keck car for Bill Vukovich. They were getting through the turns anywhere from 5 to 15 mph faster than the older designs. They were able to turn higher lap averages without the tremendous horsepower required for high peak straightaway speeds.

It's interesting to compare turn speeds, peak straightaway speeds and lap averages for several different types of cars competing in 1952:

	Turn	Straight	Average
Typical sprint type	120	150	135
Novi supercharged	115	170	139
Cummins Diesel	128	150	138
Kurtis roadster (Keck)	130	150	138

This tells the whole story. The sprint-type car, with its high center of gravity and high polar moment—with the heavy fuel load behind the driver—was obviously no longer the best way on a high-traction banked track like Indy. Maybe on the flat dirt tracks. But not at Indy anymore.

So we entered the age of the roadster . . .

6
AGE OF THE ROADSTER 1953—1962

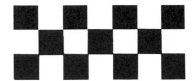

Right side view of the Vukovich Kurtis roadster shows driver's seat positioned far to the right, with the deep body cutout on that side only. High body side resulted in the term "roadster." Photo courtesy of IMS.

FRANK KURTIS CHANGES THE PICTURE

Not all Indianapolis historians make a point of it, but the little Kurtis "roadster" Bill Vukovich drove in 1952 made more of an impression on Speedway designers and mechanics than perhaps any car in the previous 20 years. You didn't need any insight to see it was inherently the fastest car on the track. This came without any long process of chassis tuning and de-bugging. Mechanics Jim Travers and Frank Coons twisted a few wrenches, then "Vuky" just jumped into the cockpit and went fast!

His 1952 qualifying average of 138.2 mph was 3rd fastest in the field and the highest of any unsupercharged car. His turn speeds of 130 mph were the highest to date. His high lap speeds seemed effortless. And he was just as impressive in the race. He gradually moved to the front, made three planned pit stops, and was leading and going away when a steering arm broke and put him into the wall only 22 miles from the finish.

No wonder the Speedway fraternity was a little shaken by this radical new type of car.

It's hard to pinpoint credit for the unique layout of the car. It wasn't all Frank Kurtis' idea. Mechanics Travers and Coons huddled with Kurtis on design and construction ideas. Jim Travers also happened to be a partner with Stuart Hilborn in the new fuel-injection business. He was a wizard with Offy engines, so the new car had the double benefit of a strong, durable engine as well as a good chassis. Don't forget car owner Howard Keck. An oil millionaire, he never scrimped on equipment and facilities that might strengthen his racing team. It was said he spent $25,000 on the car alone—a lot of money in those days. It was strictly a team effort that launched the roadster-type car on the Indianapolis scene in 1952.

What was so special about it? And what was a "roadster" anyway?

The trick that distinguished this new Kurtis-Kraft 500A chassis was simply offsetting the driveline approximately 9 in. left of center,

and positioning the driver's seat to the right and about on the drive-shaft level. Plus the engine was tilted 36° to the right, to lower its center of gravity. Then, because of the low seating of the driver, the car body was more or less up around him. Only the driver's head and shoulders projected out—in contrast to the classic sprint-type car, where the driver sat high and pretty much out in the open.

So the car ended up several inches lower than a sprint car, with a lower center of gravity and less frontal area. Consequently, it had a cleaner body, with considerably less aerodynamic drag at high speeds. Perhaps the most important benefit was its left-side static-weight bias. With the major mass of the driveline moved 9 in. left of center, and allowing for the tilt of the engine to the right, there was about 150 lbs. more weight on the left tires than on the right with the driver and a partial fuel load.

What was so great about this? Think about it. When turning left, as at the Speedway, natural centrifugal force acting at the

WINNER
Bill Vukovich
Indianapolis Motor Speedway
=1953=

Bill Vukovich drove the first Kurtis roadster in the 1952 race and almost won. He did win the 500 in 1953 with the same car. The Kurtis' weight offset and low CG helped handling and tire wear tremendously. Photo courtesy of IMS.

Team of Bill Vukovich, Frank Coons (right), Jim Travers and the first Kurtis roadster was hard to beat in the '52—'55 period. Good car, good driving, good preparation, good pit work—a combination that always works. Photo courtesy of IMS.

Offy engine was laid over 36° to the right in the early Kurtis roadsters to reduce body height and frontal area. Driveline was offset to the left.

center of gravity, generates a moment arm that unloads the left tires, transferring it to the right-side rubber. This additional load on the outside tires causes them to lose traction and break away sooner than the inside tires. So by transferring more weight to the inside tires in a static condition, all four tires are more evenly loaded in the turns. More ultimate traction and higher cornering speeds resulted with more even tire wear as a bonus.

I'll put a few numbers on it. Assume a car weighs 2,000 lbs. with driver and partial fuel load. Normally this means 1,000 lbs. on each side. But the 150-lb. weight bias actually puts 1,075 lbs. on the left side and 925 lbs. on the right. In a 130-mph corner on the Indianapolis track, allowing for the banking angle, groove radius and an approximate CG height/track relationship, roughly 20% of the total car weight transfers from the inside to the outside wheels due to

centrifugal force. That's a 400-lb. weight transfer.

So now what do we have in tire loads? Without any built-in weight bias, of course, there is simply 800 lbs. on the inside wheels and 1,200 lbs. on the outside. But our 150-lb. weight bias narrows this down to 875 lbs. on the inside and 1,125 lbs. on the outside. It was still not *even* weight distribution in the fast turns, but it was much better than the upright high-CG sprint cars. At slower lap speeds in the race,

Quick-lift air jacks for fast pit work appeared in the '50s. There was usually one at the front and two at the rear, giving a "tripod" stance. An air hose plugged in the side during a pit stop raised the car immediately.

1952 Vukovich Kurtis roadster was one of the first to use Monroe tubular shock absorbers at Indy. They gave much smoother wheel control than the usual lever-type shocks. Monroe Auto Equipment has supplied special Indy shocks ever since. While you're looking, note the left-side cross-torsion-bar anchor immediately behind the shock. This and the combination right-side torsion-bar lever/ upper front-suspension radius rod outboard of the shock made for a light and easy-to-tune suspension. Photo courtesy of Chrysler.

the tire loads were almost even all around. This improved traction and reduced tire wear.

Everyone started calling the new cars *roadsters* because the shoulder-high bodywork resembled a passenger car. Mechanics who had to try to tune their sprint-type cars to compete against the new layout knew all too well that the difference was more than mere bodywork!

It should also be mentioned that Frank Kurtis used solid axles front and rear on the new 500A chassis. It was mentioned earlier that independent front suspensions were used quite extensively in the late '40s, as designers groped for new suspension arrangements to improve front-tire wear. Not much was known in those days about suspension geometry, roll centers, roll rates, scrub radius, etc. As we look back at some of those early independent-front-suspension systems, it's obvious that there was a lot of camber change and tire scrub due to too quick suspension-geometry/wheel-travel change. This had a detrimental effect on handling when the chassis would roll in a turn.

By the early '50s chassis designers were beginning to have second thoughts about i.f.s. When Kurtis made this major switch to offset drivelines with the milestone 500A chassis, it's significant that he also went back to a tubular front axle. In fact the front-suspension linkage was rather unusual on this car. Transverse torsion bars were behind the front axle, with the wheels pivoting up and down on two "leading" arms. At the rear the torsion bars ran along the frame rails, with transverse control arms for the wheels.

Kurtis didn't stick with this arrangement very long. On his 500B chassis for the 1953 season he located the torsion bars ahead of the front axle, with the wheels pivoting on trailing arms. Then at the back he put the torsion bars behind the axle, with leading arms—like he used at the front in '52. The idea here was to get a longer "spring base." That is, the pitching and bouncing motion of the car when going over dips and bumps would be centered about these front and rear torsion-bar pivot axes. The farther they were

Ted Halibrand introduced the first specialized Indy disc brakes in the early '50s. They were very light and efficient. Driver Jack McGrath points out the caliper. The year is 1955. Photo courtesy of Halibrand.

spread, the better the suspension control became. With the 500B suspension setup, the effective front-to-rear spring base was actually about 20 in. longer than the wheelbase. On the 500A it was 10 in. shorter. The longer base helped tire adhesion as well as providing a smoother ride for the driver.

Chrysler engineers built a special stock-block 331-CID Hemi in 1952 that developed over 400 HP on alcohol. On a demonstration run—pit stops and all—it averaged over 134 mph for 500 miles in a Kurtis chassis. It shook the Establishment. Photo courtesy of Chrysler.

To make a long story short, Frank Kurtis' new roadster-type cars revolutionized Indy track performance in only two or three years. Billy Vukovich went on to win the 1953 and '54 races with the Keck 500A car. By 1955 Kurtis-Kraft roadsters made up more than half of the starting field at Indy. The new chassis layout was a breakthrough in every sense of the term. The upright sprint car continued to hold forth on the dirt tracks; but on a smooth banked speedway like Indianapolis the new trend was toward weight bias, more precise wheel control, lower CG's and better streamlining. Very importantly, driver comfort was beginning to get some attention. These new roadsters rode like luxury cars compared with the old sprint cars. When you added the wind protection of the body sides, the 500-mile race was getting to be a Sunday cruise.

MORE STOCK-BLOCK ATTEMPTS

Interest in stock-block engines at Indianapolis has always seemed to go in cycles. There was another upsurge in the early '50s. Probably what triggered it was a widespread rumor throughout the sport in 1952 that the AAA Contest Board was considering a program to encourage lower-cost stock-block engines in Championship racing by allowing unsupercharged versions an extra liter of displacement over the all-out race engines—or 335 CID. At that time this limit would have covered all the new overhead-valve V-8's from the various car companies.

At this point Chrysler Corporation officials made a move which later proved a serious mistake. They gave their engineers the green light to develop a race version of their 331-CID Firepower hemi-head V-8. They contracted with the Roger Wolcott race team to furnish a competitive Kurtis race car to test the engine on the Indy track in the fall of 1952. The Chrysler brass not only wanted to be ready for any new opportunities to demonstrate the performance potential of their engine, but wanted to show AAA officials that well-engineered stock-block engines could add to the excitement of Championship racing.

This they did. The engineers were able to get over 400 HP on alcohol fuel at a loafing 5,200 rpm from the 331 cubes, with 100-hour reliability on the dyno. Installed in the Kurtis car, driver Joe Sostillio lapped the Speedway easily at 137 mph—actually averaging 134.35 mph for 500 miles with pit stops for tires and fuel. That performance would have been more than enough to win the race in 1952.

Where Chrysler made their mistake was in doing the development and testing for the world to see. Their cooperative, benevolent attitude toward Championship racing backfired badly. As had happened so often in the past, the old-guard car owners stiffened and froze out any new-blood competition that might threaten their investments in 4-cylinder engines. After a lot of behind-the-scenes bickering, the announcement came down from the AAA in February, 1953 that stock-block engines would not be given any displacement advantage over the Offys.

Chrysler officials were crushed. They had the choice of pulling out quietly or try the impossible—make a rocker-arm engine compete cube-for-cube against dual-overhead camshafts. They decided

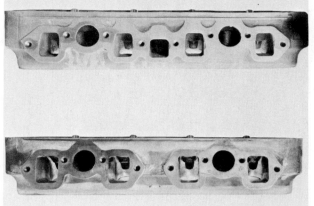

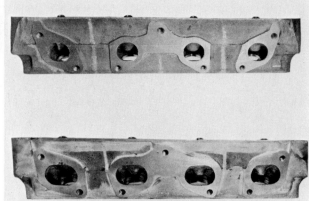

Chrysler made special cylinder-head castings for the Indy engine, with much larger intake-port cross-section. Compare the intake ports in the special head (bottom) to those in the stock head (top). Photo courtesy of Chrysler.

Just as the intake ports of the special Chrysler Indy head were enlarged, so were the exhaust ports—stock head is at top. Photo courtesy of Chrysler.

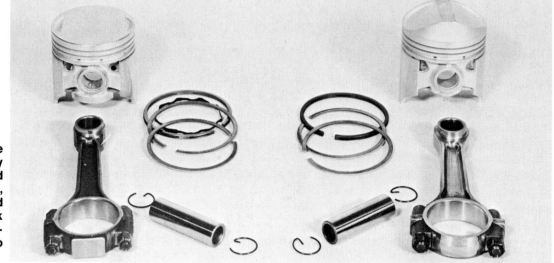

1953 Chrysler Indy engine piston-and-rod assembly (right) shows the domed high-compression piston, light pin and polished rod compared to the stock parts. This was factory hopping-up 30 years ago. Photo courtesy of Chrysler.

to try the impossible. And they used every known trick: special cylinder-head castings, Hilborn fuel injection with tuned ram stacks, roller cam, machined lightweight valves, forged-steel rocker arms, billet connecting rods, forged pistons, dry-sump lubrication, etc. They managed to pull more than 350 HP on alky at 5,800 rpm, with a safe range to 6,500. Reliability looked fairly good on the dyno, and fuel consumption wasn't increased enough to cause problems with pit stops. There was reason to hope when Chrysler sent ten engines to the Speedway for the Wolcott and Belanger teams in May of 1953.

But no way. They said it was poor torque coming off the turns. The Chryslers couldn't accelerate with the Offys—even when geared tighter to peak at 7,000 rpm on the long straights. Lap speeds were down to 133—134 mph, compared with Sostillio's 137 mph with the big engine. None of the Chryslers could even qualify. That was the end of it—Chrysler never showed any interest in Championship racing again, though they became very active in other forms of racing.

Studebaker was another interesting stock-block project. Willie Utzman used the small 232-CID V-8 block expanded to 269 cubes. He had Leo Goossen design special cylinder heads with gear-driven dual overhead camshafts. The improved porting layout gave much better breathing, plus the reduction in valve-gear reciprocat-

ing mass extended the safe rev range to 7,400 rpm. They actually achieved a dyno output of 372 HP at 7,200 rpm on methanol fuel. Mid-range torque was not good; but it was hoped that tight gearing would compensate.

They never really got a chance to assess performance. With Clay Smith doing the wrenching, the engine was mounted in an Agajanian sprint car. Through a foolish mistake, the welded-on nose of the crankshaft was not strong enough to transmit the 1,800 lbs.ft. torque of the starter motor. It snapped the third time they engaged it. There wasn't time then to machine another part, so the car was parked. No big-money attempts were made to run the engine at Indy in later years.

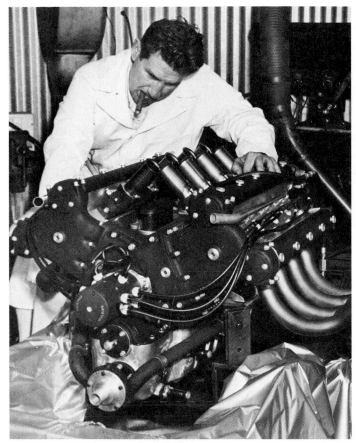

Willie Utzman dyno testing his brain child, the overhead-cam fuel-injected 1953 Studebaker stock block. It was said to develop 372 HP and good torque on alky. A broken crank eliminated the car its first time out. Photo courtesy of Wayne Ewing.

First major breakthrough in tire design in years came in 1953, when tread width was increased 1.5 in. (right). Nylon cord was adopted the following year.

Some cars still used huge 20-in. wheels in the '50s, with the idea of getting better tire mileage due to the longer footprint with the large tread circumference. The heavy Novi-powered cars used 20-in. wheels for years.

Score zero for stock-block efforts in the early '50s.

NEW TIRE TECHNOLOGY

Firestone hadn't done any extensive development of their Indianapolis tires since compounds and carcass designs were modified to adapt to the new paved track surface in the late 1930's. More synthetic-rubber compounds were used after World War II development; but the shape and construction of the tires had not changed radically through the early '50s.

The '53—'54 period saw a substantial tire-design revolution. Tire sections and treads were widened 1 to 1.5 inches, wheel rims were widened a like amount, inflation pressures were increased from 40 to 50 psi. Nylon cord was used for the first time—though it had been used for some years in passenger-car tires. Slightly softer rubber compounds were also adopted and the tread layer was made thicker to give the same tread wear with the softer rubber.

The whole idea was to improve tire traction on all parts of the track—on straights as well as in the turns—without any disastrous increase in tire wear. Wider treads and wheel rims, coupled with the softer rubber compounds, took care of the traction. The higher inflation, cooler-running nylon cord and the slightly thicker tread layer combined to give equal tire life at slightly higher lap speeds than the narrow pre '53 tires.

Racers were generally enthusiastic about the new Firestones. Turn speeds increased an average of 2 mph, so a number of cars were hitting 130—132 mph in the turn-1 time trap. Traction was so much better on the rough bricks down the front straight that some drivers reported tachometer readings of 300 rpm less with the same gearing but at slightly higher speeds. The difference was reduced wheelspin over the bumps. Johnny Moore, head Firestone engineer at the Speedway, said slip rates of 10—15% were common on the bricks at 150 mph!

It took a few years for the boys to learn how to use "pop"—nitromethane. A good many Offy engines were junked in the process.

Offy crankcase had to be heated when fitting the diaphragm main-bearing supports. Tight-fitting main-bearing diaphragms held up better when using high nitro fuel loads for qualifying.

Overall we can probably credit the new tires with 2 to 3 mph lap speed increases during this '53—'54 period. And there was no significant increase in tire wear. In fact wear was further improved to the point that only 12 tire changes were made during the '57 race—for the whole field!

POPPING WITH "POP"

It wouldn't be fair to credit improved tires with 2 or 3 mph in lap speeds without giving a couple of miles per hour to the use of an exciting new fuel additive they called *pop* in the early '50s. Actually nitromethane. A compound of nitrogen, oxygen and hydrogen that forms an explosive mixture at relatively low temperatures and pressures—yet is fairly stable to handle and mixes readily with alcohol. The stuff generates too high pressures and temperatures in the cylinders to be used as a straight fuel for long-distance racing. Also fuel-consumption rates became very high, as the optimum air/fuel ratio is only about 1.7-to-1. When mixed in a proportion of 10 to 20% in methanol, using the cooling effect of the alcohol, another 30 to 50 HP could be gained from a tired old Offy.

This is the way some of the guys were qualifying with more than 400 effective horses from their 270-CID Offys in the early '50s. You might get 350 HP at 5,200 rpm on straight methanol, but 390 or 400 HP with 15% nitro in the mix. Easy speed, if you didn't overdo it. Tricks were involved in using the stuff right, and many teams blew up many engines learning the ropes. For instance nitromethane has a slow burning rate, so you have to increase spark advance to control internal temperatures. A rich mixture of both the nitro and alky is required to avoid detonation. Hilborn fuel injection was ideal for this situation because air/fuel ratios could be changed in a minute by just changing the by-pass jet, or "pill," in the fuel-return metering valve.

Was it practical to run some nitro in the race? Not really. Maximum lap speeds were not required and you just risked engine damage. Fuel consumption was higher, especially when you richened the alky to keep things cool. Very little nitro was ever used in the 500-mile race. It was mostly a quick-fix "boost" for qualifying.

Can we pin the credit for nitro? First recorded use of the chemical for racing was by California hot rodders on the dry lakes and drag strips in the late '40s. They pioneered the tuning tips necessary to use the stuff sanely. It was a quick and natural step to bring it to Indy. It's still there today—though you don't see so much of it in recent years with turbochargers, as it's terribly touchy to use with high manifold pressures.

STREAMLINING HAS ITS DAY

Since the earliest days of oval-track racing, car designers wondered if lap performance could be improved with full-enveloping bodies that could theoretically slash wind resistance in half at any given speed. The Germans ran extensive wind-tunnel tests on their Grand Prix cars in the '30s and found the open wheels accounted for about 90% of the total air drag. The car body itself contributed only 10%—and their experiments showed total drag could be cut as much as 60 or 70% by enclosing everything in a streamlined shell.

These concepts intrigued two Indianapolis teams enough in the '55—'56 period to encourage them to spend thousands of dollars on beautiful fully streamlined bodies for their more or less conventional Kurtis roadsters. Chapman Root installed a full shell on his Sumar Special. Sandy Belond, well-

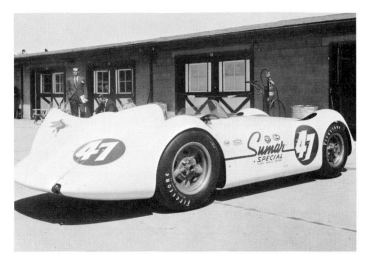

There was a flurry of interest in fully streamlined cars in the mid '50s. The Sumar Special had probably the best-looking body, but the body panels were gradually stripped off to make the car more stable at high speeds and lighter for cornering. Drivers never liked the streamliners.

Belond streamliner had fairings between the wheels and a fully enclosed cockpit. The cockpit canopy was the first to go!

known California muffler manufacturer, used a more conservative faired shell on the Miracle Power Special for Jim Rathmann. Belond's car had the wheels open with broad fairings filling the turbulent areas behind the wheels and at the back of the body. On the Sumar car the body shell covered the wheels, with side cutouts for tire cooling. Neither car was tested in a wind tunnel; but the Sumar would have had a considerably lower drag coefficient.

Either way it didn't work. The increase in car weight from the extra bodywork—about 200 lbs.— just about offset any slight gain in top-end acceleration on the straightaways from the reduced air drag. It was a standoff. More weight offset less drag. If the cars could have been built with exotic materials to get the same weight, there might have been a very slight gain.

Meanwhile drivers Jimmy Daywalt and Rathmann, didn't particularly like the cars. Not only did they have to contend with unusual aerodynamic lift and side-force effects, they had a problem with something that may have been psychological. Driving through the turns was difficult when they didn't have a clear view

Like Jack McGrath and crew, practically all the teams were using Kurtis roadsters by the mid '50s. The "inside" weight bias helped tire wear a lot, and the low CG helped cornering and streamlining. A great setup for Indy at the time. Photo courtesy of IMS.

of the front wheels. It ended up that Daywalt pulled all the side panels off the Sumar car, qualifying it in "nudist" form—with less weight and more speed. Rathmann stuck with the original side panels on the Belond, but removed the driver's head canopy. He qualified also, though well back in the field. Both cars were running at the finish.

And that's the last we saw of fully enveloping bodies at Indianapolis.

VARIATIONS ON THE KURTIS THEME

From the first time Bill Vukovich went out on the track in 1952 with the first Kurtis roadster, it was obvious to the sharper Indy car builders that there was much potential in left-side weight bias and lower CG's. When those premises were accepted it was inevitable that the boys would try to go farther with the concept and attempt to squeeze out the full potential. An age-old racing adage

270 Offy intake and exhaust could be switched from side to side by merely redrilling camshaft oil passages in the block and turning the block around on the crankcase. This was handy with the radical engine installations during the roadster era. Francis photo courtesy of IMS.

As the roadster era progressed cockpit seating and padding were improved to give more driver comfort. These cars were much easier and more comfortable to drive than the old upright sprint cars. Francis photo courtesy of IMS.

Most roadsters had steering arms with several holes drilled for the drag link. Steering ratio could be changed in two minutes to suit the driver.

Stripped chassis of a typical late-'50s Watson roadster being cleaned with solvent spray after qualifying. Axle center section is located considerably to the left to accommodate the left-side driveline. Dry car weight was eventually brought down to about 1,550 lbs., using much fiberglass, aluminum and magnesium.

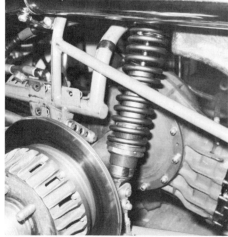

Monroe introduced the first *coil-overs*—coil spring/shock units—in 1961. Suspension could be "jacked" or ride height changed by merely threading the spring seat up or down on the shock body.

First "laydown" roadster was made by Quinn Epperly for the Belond team in 1957. Engine was laid over 72° to the right, giving a cowl height of only 20 inches. Sam Hanks won with the car the first time out. Photo courtesy of IMS.

Offy engine had to be modified somewhat for laydown operation—revised sump, oil-drainback lines and breather caps. Long, curved stacks made fuel-injectors more accessible.

seemed to take over: If a little is good, a lot should be better—and too much could be best of all.

Three car builders were majorly involved in these experiments in the late 1950's—A. J. Watson, Quinn Epperly and Ed Kuzma. Consider their individual design:

Watson—A. J. Watson burst upon the Indy scene quite suddenly when his first car won for Pat Flaherty in 1956. The layout here was not a lot different than the then-current Kurtis roadsters, except A. J. went a few steps further. He set the Offy engine upright, rather than tilting it 36° to the right, and he moved the entire engine and driveline farther to the left of center—about 12 in., rather than 9 in. In later years he also narrowed the track widths 3 to 5 in., which had the effect of shifting a still greater percentage of the car's static weight to the inside tires. Finally, he actually positioned the frame and body 1.5 in. to the left of the center of the track, so you could notice the offset positioning from the front or back.

The result was a maximum left-side weight bias of about 260 lbs.,

a hefty 16% of the total car weight, because Watson was always shaving weight by liberal use of magnesium and fiberglass. His cars generally ran between 1,550 and 1,650 lbs. dry weight. So the large weight bias was especially effective in equalizing tire loads in the turns without any serious effect on straightaway stability.

Other chassis features included solid axles front and rear, transverse torsion-bar springs, trailing-link suspension front and rear, and highly developed tubular-steel space frames. Watson even tried coil springs. The Monroe people had recently introduced commercial overload springs for cars and trucks. These had a conventional tube shock absorber inside a coil spring, all in one unit that could be bolted on. They made up special "coil-over-shock" units for Championship cars in 1960—and Watson was one of the first to grab them. He felt he could save over 50 lbs. in linkage, plus the units made it easy to adjust individual wheel loading by merely threading the spring seat up and down on the shock body. These Monroe "coil-overs"

appeared on a number of Indy cars in the early '60s. After the rear-engine cars took over in the mid '60s, the coil-over shock became the almost exclusive form of suspension springing and damping.

Epperly—Quinn Epperly collaborated with owner George Salih to introduce the "laydown" engine installation for the winning cars in 1957 and '58. This layout was much like Kurtis' original 500A chassis, except the driveline was 2 or 3 in. farther left, and the engine laid over 72° to the right instead of 36°. The engine appeared to be laying almost flat when viewed from the side. The idea of the new arrangement was to get about the same left-side weight bias of 150 lbs. as the early Kurtis roadsters—but to get a still lower CG and less frontal area by laying the engine down flatter. These laydown cars were only about 20-in. high at the cowl. It was hoped this combination would have near optimum lateral weight distribution for fast cornering and minimum tire wear, and that the reduced frontal area and improved streamlining would boost straightaway speeds.

Leading and trailing-arm suspensions were popular on the roadsters, with torsion bars running diagonally across the chassis. Solid axles were used in most cases. Light and compact, and everyone understood them.

Laydown engine installation in the Epperly-Salih roadster that won the '57 and '58 races. Left-side weight bias was not as much as the Watson roadsters. Francis photo courtesy of IMS.

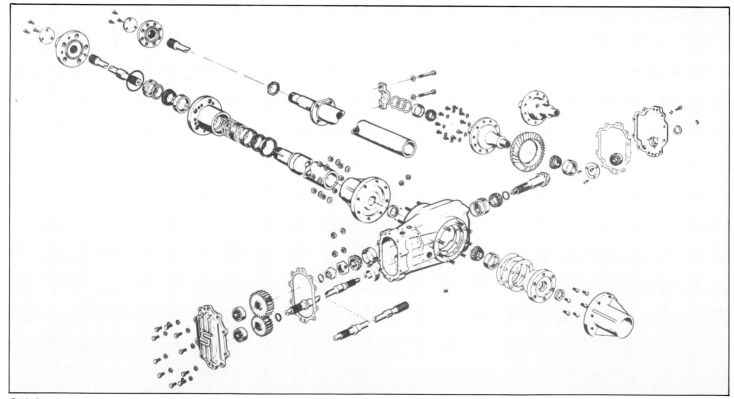

Quick-change rear axles appeared in the '40s and were used by everyone in the '50s. The Conzes introduced the first. This Schiefer design of the '60s is basically like the Halibrand. Final-drive ratio could be changed in minutes by simply changing the two spur gears at the back of the housing.

Car builder Ed Kuzma tried to beat everyone on left-side weight bias by laying the engine nearly all the way over and out the side of the car—9 in. outside the cowl line! He got more than 300 lbs. additional weight on the left wheels.

Whether it was the improved chassis or the good wrenching of George Salih that won for Sam Hanks and Jimmy Bryan in '57 and '58, I don't know. The combination seemed to have Indy by the tail in those days. Epperly received orders for a number of laydown cars in the late '50s. They all seemed to handle well. His suspension systems were similar to Watson's, with transverse torsion bars front and rear, trailing arms front, leading arms rear, with a Watts-link arrangement for lateral axle control. This layout was convenient from the space standpoint, light in weight, gave the desired long spring base for ride, and the torsion-bar springs were easy to adjust for wheel loading.

It should also be mentioned that the Meyer & Drake engine people had to make minor modifications on the Offy to allow it to be laid almost flat in the car. These included a new oil-sump casting rotated 72°, larger bottom cam cover to handle larger volumes of oil in the top of the engine and new oil drain-back lines. Also, the fuel-injection throttle-body castings were curved to keep the fuel-metering components horizontal.

I might also mention that the original Offy engine design lent itself very nicely to these extreme installation positions. When Leo Goossen laid out the design in 1931 he made the block so it could be turned on the crankcase after redrilling the camshaft oil passages. This meant the exhaust and intake could be switched to opposite sides by doing some minor machine work and reassembling the engine with the block turned in the opposite direction. In a Watson roadster, where the engine was upright and far to the left, they would take the exhaust directly out on the left, for minimum heat buildup inside the body. On these laydown cars they would put the intake on the left for accessiblility to the fuel-injection components and run the exhaust out on the right, underneath the car.

Many Indy fans never noticed this very convenient design feature of the Offy.

Kusma—Ed Kuzma is the guy who might have said, "Too much could be the best of all." He went all the way with his left-side weight bias: Driveline far to the left, with engine laid over 72° to the left—actually projecting 9 in. outside the body line. This required a special cowl housing around the top of the engine and the cars looked a little different. Kuzma got slightly over

300 lbs. of weight bias on the left wheels. Allowing for the low CG with the laydown engine mounting, wheel loadings must have been very nearly equalized at normal turn speeds in the race.

It's unfortunate that some unrecorded bug in the lateral-control components of the suspension of these cars fouled up their handling from the start, so we never got a clear picture of the effect of his high left-side weight bias. Kuzma built three or four in the late '50s, but none of them ever went very fast. Quinn Epperly also built some cars with this layout later on and they seemed to handle better. Bobby Marshman qualified one in the front row in 1962.

If we eliminate handling considerations and just try to judge these three general layouts on a basis of tire wear, the nod would probably go to the Watson layout. Those cars seemed consistently to show less tire wear than the laydown cars—frequently to the extent of one less pit stop in 500 miles. It's risky to be dogmatic about these things because minute suspension adjustments can have a big effect on tire wear. The Watson cars definitely had 100 lbs. more weight bias than the Epperly laydown cars, so you might predict

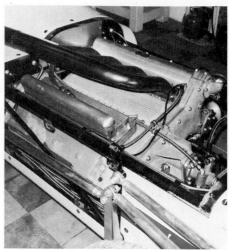

Builder Luigi Lesovsky surprised everyone by laying his engine over to the left and running the driveline down the right side of the car. Driver was seated on the left. Less weight bias, but he still *got the low CG.*

Like most sprint cars of today, very simple "Jacobs Ladder" arrangements were often used to laterally locate solid axles. Light, simple and efficient.

One of the last Kurtis roadsters. It used an independent front suspension with massive fabricated trailing arms. A beam-axle type tie rod was used, making the wheels steer in vertical travel—spooky to drive.

Agajanian crew chief, Frank McGurk, an old-time hot rodder, experimented with "tuned" exhaust stacks in the mid '50s. Separate pipes of equal length were used for each of the four exhaust ports. The idea didn't work. Separated stacks have to be much shorter than one common outlet.

they would show slightly better tire wear.

The Kuzma left-side laydown, with 50 lbs. more bias than Watson, should have shown the best of all. Those cars didn't handle well and we shouldn't judge them too sharply. The best showing of an Epperly left-side laydown was Bobby Marshman's 5th place in 1962. Look at the record: He made four tire stops in 500 miles, compared with three for Rodger Ward's winning Watson car.

You be the judge.

ANOTHER LAYOUT . . .

All the above cars featured left-side weight bias in varying degrees. There was also a flurry of interest around 1960 in roadster-type cars with tilted engines, but with practically no static weight bias. These cars had their drive-lines on the right, drivers seated on the left and engines tilted in varying degrees to the left. Standing still without load they might have 100 to 150 lbs. more on the right wheels. But with driver, and fuel tankage biased toward the

left, wheel loads were about equal when running straight on the track. They still had the benefits of a low CG and small frontal area.

Builder Luigi Lesovsky was first with this layout in 1959, with a beautiful roadster for the Racing Associates team, Johnny Thomson driving. The combination was a success from the start. Thomson put the car on the pole and finished 3rd in '59. He then qualified second-fastest in '60 and finished 5th. Importantly, tire wear was comparable with the

Some cars used elaborate scoops to supply air to the fuel injectors in the '50s, hoping the "ram" effect would increase power at high speeds. Results were inconclusive.

faster Watsons at the time. This was also true of similar chassis by Epperly and Floyd Trevis that appeared later. They handled well and tire wear was moderate.

Where does all this leave our conclusions about the effectiveness of left-side weight bias? You could argue that it had no real benefit at all—that the major advantage of offset roadster construction was merely lowering the height of the car. Here's all these different layouts with fast cars using each one, with no big differences in tire wear that can be positively pinpointed. Perhaps I should just cop out by blaming it all on suspension designs, and how the individual mechanics adjusted the chassis. Race cars have never lent themselves to simple slide-rule analysis.

DOWNSIZING THE OFFY

After nearly 50 years of administering all big-time auto racing in the United States, officials of the American Automobile Association decided to confine their attentions to pleasure driving in 1955. This decision was largely due to the terrible Pierre Levegh accident at LeMans in the same year which claimed the lives of Levegh and over 80 spectators. AAA could see themselves with a similar situa-

tion. Disbanding of the AAA Contest Board suddenly left a big gap in the Indy scene. A new United States Auto Club (USAC) emerged a few months later that was probably stronger and better equipped to serve the growing sport. Indy Speedway owner Tony Hulman initiated the meeting that brought USAC into existence in September, 1955. Former driver Duane Carter was elected the first Director of Competition. A strong Competition Committee backed him.

One of the first major rule changes under USAC was to cut piston-displacement limits in the Championship class by 300cc for unsupercharged engines and 200cc for superchargers. That would give about 256 and 171 CID respectively, or 4.2 and 2.8 liters. The idea was to slow the cars down a little and make for safer racing. Lap speeds at Indy at the time were approaching the 150-mph mark, and there had been a rash of tire failures and spectacular crashes in the mid '50s. Reducing engine displacement had always been the simplest way to slow cars down. By going down only a few cubic inches, there wasn't the problem of obsoleting a lot of expensive engines. Just a short-stroke crankshaft and set of pistons with the correct compression heights would

cover these moderate cuts first used in 1957.

Actually, Offy owners had several ways to meet the smaller displacement limit. For one thing, there was to be an ingrained belief among Offy devotees that the engine's long stroke was the prime factor in its impressive torque advantage coming off the corners. They felt this initial torque off the turns was more important to lap speed than peak horsepower down the straights. It was no surprise, that most Offy owners responded to the smaller cubic-inch limit by merely reducing bore diameter and keeping their long 4-1/2 and 4-5/8-in. strokes. Some sleeved the cylinder block, others bought new smaller-bore blocks. Those long strokes were sacred.

There was only one dissenting voice that first year in 1957—A. J. Watson. He had a whole different philosophy. A. J. figured a shorter stroke might be the way to go, if it was combined with shorter, lighter connecting rods to reduce bottom-end inertia. The plan was to get a more favorable ratio of stroke length to rod length. The 270 rod was a big brute of a thing, with an 8-in. center-to-center length. Watson realized that the shorter lengths might sacrifice some mid-range torque; but they should give more top-end potential by reduc-

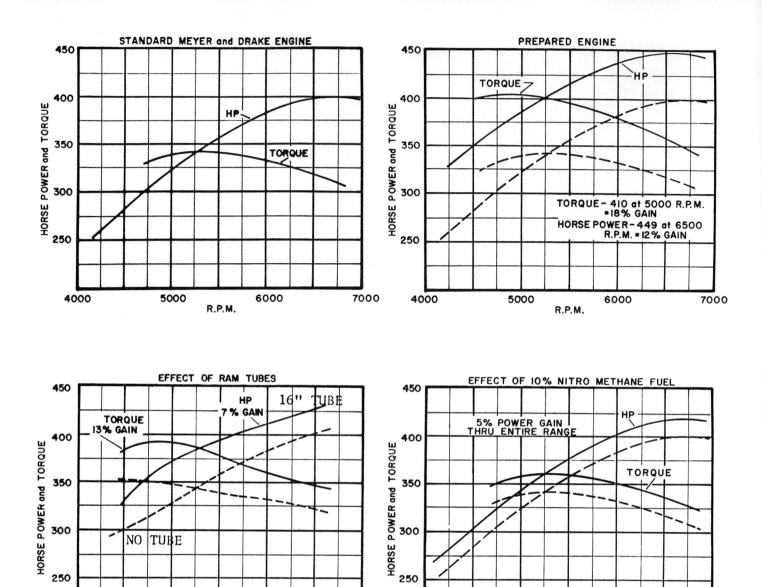

Meyer & Drake "factory" curves generated around 1960 illustrate the performance of the standard 252-CID Offy using various hop-up tricks—nitro fuel, ram stacks, and a "prepared" engine with all the tricks. 450 HP from only 252 CID naturally aspirated took some sharp tuning.

ing friction and bearing loads.

It's clever the way he scrambled standard Offy engine parts to arrive at these new stroke/rod relationships. He chose a 4-3/8-in. stroke and matched this with the 7-1/2-in. rods from the smaller 220-CID Offy sprint engine. This required a special crankshaft machined to the smaller 220 crankpin diameters. The cylinder bores in the 270 block were too high for the shorter stroke and rods. So he milled 5/8 in. off the bottom of the block, to equal the

220 block height. He then bolted the 220 gear tower on the front to drive the overhead cams! In effect he had a hybrid engine with the big valves and ports of the 270, but with the short stroke and rods of the 220. A bore of 4-9/32 in. gave a displacement of 252 cubic inches.

A. J.'s performance projections proved to be right on target, too. By using the shorter stroke and rods, only about 10 HP was lost on the top end after dropping 18 cubic inches. Here are typical dynamometer figures for these three bore/stroke/rod combinations, using standard No. 4 Offy cams and straight methanol fuel:

	Max HP @ rpm	Max Torque lbs.ft. @ rpm	Max RPM
270 CID, long stroke, long rod	370 @ 5,600	380 @ 4,500	5,800
255 CID, long stroke, long rod	350 @ 5,800	340 @ 4,800	6,200
252 CID, short stroke, short rod	360 @ 6,200	320 @ 5,200	6,600

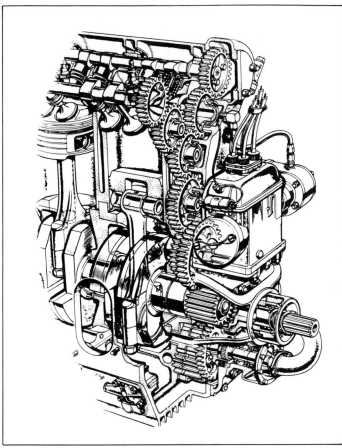

Smokey Yunick was a controversial crew chief at Indy for years. Always plenty of new ideas, never a follower. They didn't all work, but he kept things interesting.

When the Offy was downsized below 256 CID for 1957, a conglomeration of 270 and 220 parts were used. A 270 block had 5/8 in. removed from its bottom surface to match the stroke reduction—and shorter 220 rods and cam gear tower provided the right match-up. The shorter stroke worked better. Berris drawing courtesy of AUTOCAR.

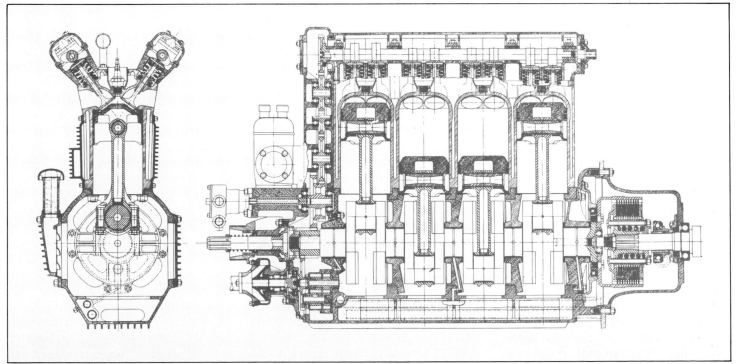

New 255 and 252-CID Offys of the late '50s. The engine was noticeably shorter in overall height. It can be identified by the two rows of cam-cover studs.

Extended ram stacks with bellmouth inlets were fitted to the Offy in the '50s. They gave a good boost in power and torque by utilizing the ram effect of bouncing pressure waves generated by valve closure. A 16-in. stack-to-valve length was popular.

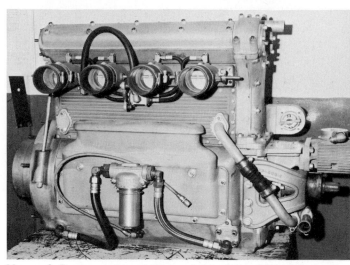

Meyer & Drake reduced the weight of the 252 Offy in the early '60s by using an aluminum block, aluminum main-bearing diaphragms, lightened crank, magnesium gear covers, etc. Weight got as low as 355 lbs. complete.

These dyno figures pretty much tell the story. The short stroke and rods in the Watson setup did sacrifice some mid-range torque. By taking advantage of the higher usable rev range and gearing to hit 6,600 rpm at the shut-off point on the straightaways, Watson's cars were able to come off the turns at 5,500 rpm—so the engines were at or near their peak power on all sections of the track. Engine speed never got down to the max-torque range at race speeds.

Of course there was no way the new 4.2-liter cars could be as fast as the 270's at their peak in 1956. Lap speeds dropped 2—3 mph for the first couple of years with the smaller engines. This is what USAC intended. But gradually speeds began to inch up again and the Indy lap record was clipped several times by a fraction of a second in the late '50s. By the early '60s the small engines had far surpassed the power of the 270. This could be attributed to camshaft development. The stronger ones were developing 405—410 HP at 6,400 rpm without nitro, and could be turned to 6,800 rpm on the straights with some degree of reliability. By that time everyone was using Watson's short-stroke 220 hybrid setup. In 1962 Parnelli Jones broke the 150-

mph barrier with one of these engines.

No one really thought much about long strokes after that!

NEW LIFE FOR THE NOVI

After the glory days of the late '40s, the fabled Novi supercharged V-8's fell on hard times at Indy. They always had plenty of power, but there were a lot of other problems. The front-wheel drive and high weight wore tires too fast. High fuel consumption required huge tanks and heavy fuel loads. This meant a big change in car handling as fuel was consumed. To top it, the cars were never easy to drive through the corners. Real handfuls in traffic. Several times in the early '50s the cars couldn't even qualify.

In l956 owner Lou Welch commissioned Frank Kurtis to build him two brand-new rear-drive cars that they hoped would take better advantage of the engines' tremendous power, and be considerably lighter than the front-drives.

Kurtis did a good job. He used the latest chassis technology of the period—space frames, tube axles, cross torsion bars, engines and drivelines offset 4 in. left, driver seated low on right. Total fuel capacity was 82 gals. in two tanks. The dry weight of 1,875 lbs. was

about 150 lbs. less than the earlier front-drive Kurtis cars built right after World War II. Welch seemed satisfied with the weight, considering the 575-lb. weight of the engine and the large fuel tankage.

The new rear-drive Novis seemed considerably faster right off due largely to the wizardry of chief mechanic Jean Marcenac, a name which became synonymous with Novi. Driver Paul Russo lapped at 146 mph in practice, qualified 2nd in the 3rd row, but then fell victim to one of the rash of tire failures in the '56 race. What was encouraging was that his turn speed was a healthy 125 mph—a good 10 mph faster than the front-drive chassis. In 1957 Russo finished 4th in the race. In '58 he dropped out with radiator trouble. Teammate Bill Cheesbourg finished 10th. In 1959 neither car could qualify. The same old story. Chassis technology was passing them by again.

Finally in 1960 Welch gave up on the Novis. He sold his cars, all spare parts, patterns and drawings to Andy Granatelli for $10,000! Granatelli was then manufacturer of Paxton bolt-on superchargers and an up-and-coming promoter whose name was to become legend at Indianapolis. Andy was no stranger to the brickyard. In the

Granatelli updated the Novi in 1963 with a new Kurtis roadster chassis and body. These cars fell victim to the rise of the rear-engine car about that time, and were not successful. Today they are museum pieces. Photo courtesy of IMS.

The Granatelli's rejuvenated the 20-year old Novi V-8 engine in the early '60s. They claimed another 300—400 HP at 7,600 rpm after updating the ignition, supercharger and inlet ducting. Francis photo courtesy of IMS.

New rear-drive Kurtis roadster chassis, built to accept the Novi V-8 engines in 1956, had large tailfins for aerodynamic stability at speed. There is no conclusive evidence the fins helped, but they certainly looked impressive.

Andy Granatelli bought the Novi cars in the early '60s and began immediately to update the engines. Here's Andy testing one of the Novis on his Paxton dynamometer in Santa Monica. Photo courtesy STP.

late '40s, when a young speed-shop owner in Chicago, he bought one of the old '35 era front-drive Miller-Fords and raced it at Indy several times. No success, but he got the bug. In act this was a team effort. Andy's brother Vince was in on the early Indy efforts. He stayed on with Andy in the supercharger business and finally crewed at Indy. They were both ex-hot-rodders and sharp promoters.

The first thing they found when they started playing with the Novi hardware was the supercharger wasn't very efficient. When Andy tested one on his dyno in California, it was claimed it developed less than 500 HP at 7,000 rpm on 25-psi boost. The hooker was fuel consumption—a merry 142 gals. per hour! This calculates out to enough fuel to generate 700 or 800 HP with an efficient supercharged engine.

Using experience gained with the Paxton passenger-car unit—originally designed by McCulloch Engine Co. engineers—and drawing from technical papers on aircraft designs of World War II, the Granatellis immediately enlisted the help of Jean Marcenac to redesign the supercharger internals. Impeller diameter was reduced from 10 in. to 8 in., to reduce tip velocities. Inducer and diffuser vanes were blended into the impeller and housing. Result: 640 HP at 7,600 rpm on 35 psi boost—and with a fuel rate reduced 15% to 120 gals./hr. Andy tested the new supercharger for a power consumption of 75 HP at 7,600 rpm engine speed, almost 40,000-rpm impeller speed. Also significant: Straightaway speed up from 167 to 180 mph.

It was a classic exercise in engine performance sleuthing. Unfortunately, by 1961 the mid-'50s Kurtis chassis needed more than horsepower to keep up with the hot Offy-powered roadsters. The Granatellis couldn't get either car qualified the first two years.

Buick passenger-car brakes were popular on low-budget Indy cars in the '50s. Large finned aluminum drums gave good fade resistance and were reasonably lightweight.

1960 start. Completely repaved with a widened pit apron separated from the main track, the Speedway was much safer and faster. Photo courtesy of IMS.

Suspension problems, engine breakage, lack of top drivers—they had all the classic headaches. They got both cars in the field in '63, with Jim Hurtubise and Bobby Unser driving; but Unser crashed and an oil leak put Hurtubise in the pits.

Andy turned his attentions to the 4-wheel-drive Ferguson . . .

THE ROADSTER PEAKS

You recall the first Kurtis 500A roadster in 1952, with Bill Vukovich driving. It turned a lap speed of 138 mph by combining 130 mph turn speeds with peak straightaway speeds of about 150 mph. This was with a 270 Offy developing about 350 HP.

Ten years later, at the peak of roadster development, Parnelli Jones set a new Indy lap record of 150.73 mph in a Watson roadster powered by a 408-hp, 252-CID Offy. Jones' clocked speed through the number-1 turn on this run was 142 mph, with a peak of about 160 mph down the straights.

These figures tell the whole story of performance development during the roadster era. Admittedly it is a story mostly of engine and chassis development. There wasn't a whole lot of tire development during this period, other than the widening of treads and rims and the switch to nylon cord in the '53—'54 period. You must also consider track improvements: The track was *completely* repaved in 1956, except for a 3-foot strip of bricks left at the start/finish line for sentimental reasons. This smoother surface all around added probably 2—3 mph to turn speeds and straightaway peaks. Otherwise, lap-speed increases were pretty much a result of more power and torque, stiffer gearing and far superior chassis due to improved weight distribution and precise suspension tuning. Indy-car chassis construction was becoming a design science as well as a tuning art.

Everything was looking pretty good for the roadster-type car in the early '60s. Except for a couple of disturbing developments in one corner of the Indy garage area . . .

SEEDS OF A NEW TREND

It really started back in early 1960. Jim Kimberly, wealthy American sports-car enthusiast, almost jokingly suggested to England's John Cooper that he take a crack at Indianapolis with his current world-champion Formula I Grand Prix car. Cooper, you may recall, is the one who started the trend to lightweight rear-engine race cars in the late '50s. At that time his top driver, Jack Brabham, was busy winning the world G.P. championship with a 4-cylinder Climax engine in a tiny car weighing only 1,050 lbs. dry. The European G.P. displacement limit was 2.5 liters at that time, so the engine only developed about 240 HP. Hardly promising fodder for the fast Indy track.

Cooper was intrigued enough to send his winning car and driver over to Indianapolis in October, 1960 to run some track tests. To everyone's astonishment, Brabham lapped easily at 144.8 mph! The little engine could only get him up to 150 mph on the straights; but the light weight, sticky tires and sophisticated suspension got him through the turns at a surprising 141 mph. That was faster than any American car had been clocked at that time. Brabham could actually drive

Jack Brabham turned Indy upside down with the tiny rear-engine Cooper Grand Prix car in 1961. He could run competitive speeds with 150 HP less than the big roadsters. He had to use Dunlop tires, though, and these caused some concern.

almost flat out all the way around the track with the tiny Cooper.

Needless to say, John Cooper was suddenly very excited about the big prize money at Indy. The front-row qualifiers for the 1960 race had been in the 146 mph bracket. He figured he could match that by boring and stroking the tiny Climax engine to its limit of 2.8 liters, which should provide another 15 or 20 HP and some extra mid-range torque. Some left-side weight bias could be achieved by tilting the engine a few degrees to the left and adding extra fuel tankage to the left. A little beefing here and there on the chassis, and Cooper figured he could have a good shot in the 1961 race with minimum hassle.

Well, the Cooper-Brabham team did not win the 1961 race. They qualified in the 5th row at 145.1 mph and finished 9th. What clobbered them, unexpectedly, was tire wear. They were tied to the British Dunlop Tire Co. by contract and Dunlop engineers had no Indy experience. The special 16-in. tires they sent over proved to wear two or three times as fast as equivalent Firestones.

1961 Indy Cooper was essentially a standard Grand Prix model with the weight biased slightly to the left, larger fuel tanks, and the 4-cylinder Climax engine output increased 15—20 HP. Its approximate weight was 1,200 lbs. Drawing courtesy of AUTOCAR.

Mickey Thompson got the Harvey Aluminum Co. to finance a team of radical rear-engine cars in the early '60s, using the small GM aluminum V-8 and minimum weight construction throughout. They were surprisingly competitive.

Extensive testing indicated Brabham would require five tire changes at lap speeds of 145 mph, but only three if he would hold it down to 140 mph. Cooper decided the latter course would be better, especially as their crew was not experienced in quick pit work. They were taking twice as long as the Americans to change tires. They did well to finish 9th under the circumstances.

Don't think this little Cooper project didn't make a profound impression on a number of our top racing people. It started some head-scratching that completely changed the face of the sport in only four or five years.

In fact there was a major American rear-engine attempt just a year later—still in our time frame of the roadster era. Mickey Thompson, an aggressive California hot rodder, master mechanic and prolific promoter, succeeded in getting sponsorship from the Harvey Aluminum Co. to build a

pair of super-light rear-engine cars using little Buick aluminum V-8s that had just been introduced in some GM passenger cars. This engine could be readily bored and stroked to 255 CID, and weighed only 280 lbs. in racing trim. With all the bolt-on aftermarket goodies—fuel injection, roller cam, billet rods, ported heads, forged pistons, etc.—they were able to get a reliable 330 HP at 6,500 rpm. By extensive use of aluminum and light construction throughout, dry weight was held to 1,150 lbs. The chassis was actually constructed by John Crosthswaite, who had been with the Lotus G.P. team in England, so he had experience with rear-engine chassis techniques.

The cars went surprisingly well for coming right off the drawing board. Dan Gurney and Chuck Daigh were hired as drivers because of their G.P. experience. Both lapped consistently in the 146—148 mph range in practice,

with good turn speeds around 138 mph. Engine problems kept Daigh from qualifying, but Gurney qualified one car in the 3rd row at 147.9 mph. Unfortunately he dropped out of the race early with gear failure in the hybrid Halibrand transaxle unit.

Thompson came back in '63 with all-aluminum small-block Chevrolet V-8's supplied by the factory. Both cars made the field, with Al Miller finishing 9th. The cars were faster and more reliable with the Chevy engines, but nagging suspension problems caused undue tire wear. It's always been true in racing: It takes more than speed to win.

Here again these super-light Thompson rear-engine cars turned heads at Indy. After Brabham's showing in '61, more and more Indy car owners, designers and mechanics were wondering if the roadster really was the way to go, or if the roadster "had to go."

The revolution was upon us . . .

First serious attempt to run a gas turbine car at Indy was the John Zink "Trackburner" in 1961. It used a 375-HP Boeing gas-turbine engine. This initial test was on a Tulsa airport. The car made only a few laps at Indy. Photo courtesy of Boeing.

Thompson-Harvey rear-engine cars used front and rear independent suspensions, tube space frames, Buick and Chevy stock-block engines, and at one time tried special 12-in. Firestone tires. Always plagued by poor handling and reliability. The major contribution of this car was the trend it started toward wider, low-profile tires.

Roger Ward in the pits on his way to winning the 1962 500. Car on air jacks, four new tires, a drink for Roger and fuel from A. J. Watson. The car was rolling 5 seconds later. Photo courtesy of Goodyear.

7
COMPLETE REVOLUTION
1963—1968

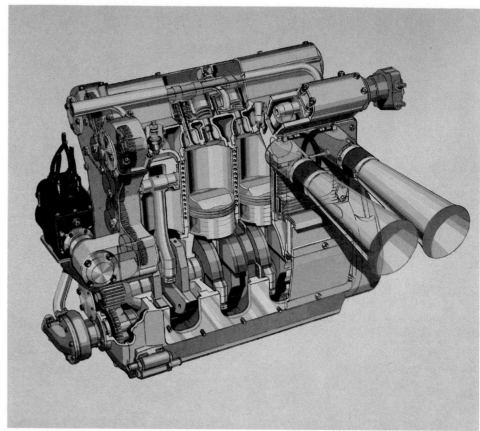

Last-design Offy; 255 CID with dry-sleeved aluminum block. Note drilled water passages between siamesed cylinder bores. Drawing by Dave Kimble.

ENGINES TO THE REAR

At no time in Indianapolis history did such rapid design changes or performance improvements occur as in the mid 1960's. Everything seemed to happen at once. Rear-engine technology from the European Formula-1 scene came across the Atlantic like a tidal wave. Ford Motor Co. spent millions developing a new overhead-cam V-8 racing engine. Goodyear challenged Firestone for top spot in the speedway-tire picture, after sitting on the sidelines for 40 years. Andy Granatelli squeezed millions in sponsorship money out of the Studebaker-STP combine, and used it to develop four-wheel-drive and gas-turbine race cars. Turbocharging was first used seriously and developed extensively during this period. And the world saw the first hints that the science of aerodynamics might be used for something other than drag reduction.

Indianapolis and Championship auto racing in general have never been the same since the wild days of the mid '60s.

I don't think there's any doubt that Jack Brabham's impressive showing with the Formula-1 Cooper in 1961 started the revolution. That project proved conclusively that a race car could get around corners faster if the engine was placed toward the rear of the car. By moving this major mass toward the rear, and positioning the driver toward the front gave three benefits: (1) higher percentage of the total car weight on the rear wheels helped handling coming off the corners; (2) grouping the high-mass components toward the center of the car reduced the polar moment of inertia so responsiveness to steering inputs improved and a car was less apt to spin; and (3) shifting the weight distribution toward the rear reduced the understeer tendency which makes

front-engine cars tend to "push" in the corners.

It must be admitted that American race-car builders were nowhere near as knowledgeable in suspension design technology as the European Formula-1 people at that time. I don't know why, but they never were. Even back in the '30s and '40s, concepts like roll centers, roll rates, camber change, bump steer, scrub radius, etc. were lost on the typical American race-car builder. We just built cars like they'd always been built—with a few minor twists here and there like weight bias, independent suspension, lower CG's, etc. If it worked, race it. Major changes were resisted. In fact, designers backed with solid theory, were met with suspicion—even contempt in many instances. Meanwhile the European designers were digging into textbooks. This is why they beat us to the rear-engine configuration. It was

Last gasp of the roadsters. A.J. Foyt won the 1964 race in a Watson roadster against formidable rear-engine opposition—the last victory for a front-engine car. Photo courtesy of IMS.

Dan Gurney was one of a handful of American drivers who made it big in Grand Prix racing. He was a key factor in bringing Ford and Colin Chapman together to create the Lotus-Ford race cars in the '60s. Gurney has been very active at Indy as both driver and builder since then.

Jimmy Clark pondering while the crew works. Original Lotus-Fords in 1963 were painted the traditional British racing green, with pit crewmen dressed in green coveralls. The operation was "low-key" in many respects—compared to many private American programs with a fraction of the money. Photo by Rowell.

"right" on paper as well as on the racetrack.

It was inevitable that the Brabham-Cooper success in '61 would soon attract other overseas Formula-1 teams to the huge Indy purse money. It looked so easy. Even a 3rd or 4th place at Indy would pay more than a whole season of successful racing in Europe. The way things happened was almost a perfect sequence of events to establish the rear-engine car firmly on the Indy scene in just three years.

So the story goes, Dan Gurney, one of a handful of American drivers who ever made it big in European road racing, was the catalyst who brought Colin Chapman's Lotus race cars in contact with a factory-developed Ford engine with the potential to win the Indy race. Gurney was tremendously impressed with Chapman's new monocoque Formula-1 Lotus he saw at the Dutch Grand Prix in May, 1962. He offered to foot the bill to bring Chapman to Indianapolis where Gurney was scheduled to drive one of the new Mickey Thompson rear-engine cars later in the month. One thing led to another. Before Chapman went home, Gurney had arranged a meeting with Ford officials—and a contract was signed for Chapman to build three Formula-1 type cars to meet Indy rules for the 1963

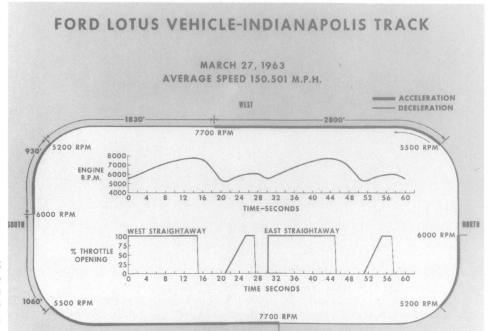

FORD LOTUS VEHICLE-INDIANAPOLIS TRACK

MARCH 27, 1963
AVERAGE SPEED 150.501 M.P.H.

Ford engineers instrumented a prototype '63 Lotus-Ford to check throttle angles and rpm limits on a fast 150-mph lap on the Indy track. This type of analysis was used to set up a dynamometer test program to prove durability on prototype engines. Drawing courtesy of Ford.

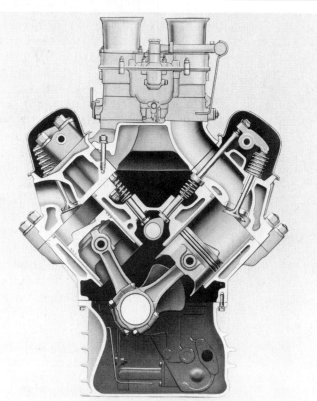

'63 Ford Indy engine developed 376 HP at 7,200 rpm with four 58mm Weber dual-downdraft carbs on 103-octane gas. Mid-range torque was good. A 5-hour dyno cycle up to 7,700 rpm proved reliability! Photo courtesy of Ford.

Ford's 1963 Indy engine was basically a Fairlane passenger car V-8 with a dry-sleeved aluminum block, special aluminum cylinder-head castings, and a beefed-up crank and rods for 7,000-rpm-plus speeds. Lubrication was completely revised. Drawing courtesy of Ford.

'63 Ford Indy block was a beefed-up aluminum casting from the production small-block Ford 260-CID patterns. It used cast-iron cylinder sleeves and O-rings around the bores to avoid gasket problems. Studs and nuts were used rather than the conventional bolts. Also, bosses were added directly below each cylinder to accommodate four additional cylinder-head studs for improved cylinder-head retention. Photo courtesy of Ford.

'63 Indy Ford had an extremely light cast-magnesium oil pan that increased bottom-end rigidity considerably. It was carefully shaped and baffled to maintain good oil control. Photo courtesy of Ford.

race. They would be built to accept special Ford V-8 engines. Chapman was to set up the cars, select the drivers and manage the team. Ford would supply the engines and pay the bills.

You have to appreciate Ford's special position at this time. They were just launching a multi-million-dollar racing program to enhance their image in a mushrooming youth/performance market. They were wide-open to an ambitious plan like this. In fact the project eventually expanded to a reported $10 million a year and encompassed a worldwide program including LeMans, Indianapolis, NASCAR, drag racing, Formula 1—even Bonneville speed records. Colin Chapman was in the right place at the right time!

Ford Motor Co. jumped into this project with both feet—no expense or engineering brainpower was spared to get the job done. For instance they brought a standard Lotus Formula-1 car to Indy in October, 1962 and tested it thoroughly with the small Climax engine. With these figures Ford engineers set up computer equations to determine what horsepower and weight would be required for a potentially winning performance in the '63 race. The computer spit out roughly 350 HP and 350 lbs. maximum engine

weight. With these figures as a guide, it was decided to maintain as much passenger-car image as possible by using an aluminum version of the 260-CID Fairlane pushrod V-8, reduced to 255 CID, and using gasoline and carburetors instead of the usual fuel injection and alcohol. They felt they could achieve the power and weight objectives with this combination.

They did it—but with a lot of intense engineering and tedious test work in the following six months. The resulting engine ended up with very few stock Fairlane components. The aluminum block and heads were cast with stock patterns, but the cores were trimmed to change wall thicknesses, cylinder-head intake- and exhaust-port contours, block-deck thickness, etc. Bosses were cast in the block to accept four additional cylinder-head *studs*—not bolts—per side. Forged crankshafts and pistons were used. Other major changes included shaft-mounted rocker arms, gear camshaft drive, cast-magnesium oil pan, dry-sump lubrication, electronic ignition, aluminum water pump, vacuum-melt-steel valve springs. The combination was as rugged and reliable as it was strong.

And it was strong! Ford engineers very quickly exceeded the 350-HP bogie by experiment-

ing with radical camshaft grinds, high compression ratios and huge 58mm Weber downdraft carburetors. By May, 1963 they were pulling 376 HP at 7,200 rpm on 103-octane gasoline and getting 500-mile reliability. This was confirmed through testing by cycling the race engines under load for five hours between 5,500 and 7,700 rpm on a dynamometer, simulating acceleration and deceleration sequences on the Indy track. It was also possible to project fuel-consumption rates from these tests. The engines were as ready as automotive science could make them. They met the weight bogie, too: 344 lbs. complete with stub exhaust pipes.

Meanwhile Colin Chapman was busy building three new Model-28 Lotus cars in England. They were very similar to his current Formula-1 cars—monocoque structure, four-wheel independent suspension on coil springs, Girling disc brakes, Colotti transaxles. They were modified to arrive at a 5-in. longer wheelbase (to 96 in.), 46-gal. fuel tankage and with the body offset 3 in. to the left on the suspension for a weight-bias effect. The cars weighed a bit less than 1,300 lbs. dry with the aluminum Ford engines. Again, within the original weight objective of Ford engineers. Chapman even gave the project a little extra push by bringing his top Grand Prix driver, Jimmy Clark, to head up the team. Dan Gurney was recruited to drive the second car. A third car and eight spare engines provided in-depth backup.

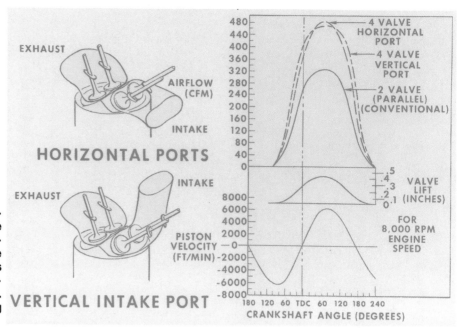

Ford engineers "flowed" several combustion-chamber and port layouts while developing the 4-cam '64 Indy engine. As illustrated by the upper graph, the 4-valve head with vertical and horizontal intake ports flowed considerably more air than the conventional 2-valve setup of the '63 engine. Ford went with the vertical layout. Drawing courtesy of Ford.

It was certainly the most highly financed team project ever to run at Indy up to that time.

It will always be argued whether they could, or should, have won the race. They had it all planned out: One pit stop, lap speeds of 145—148 mph, moderate qualifying speeds to get them started well up in the field. It should have been enough. Things did go according to plan, except that leader Parnelli Jones started leaking oil toward the end of the race, just when Jim Clark started to make his move from 2nd place. The leak got worse, and two cars spun out in the gap between Jones and Clark. There was a heated rhubarb at the starting line between Chapman, J.C. Agajanian—Jones' car owner—and race officials whether Jones should be black-flagged. They never did. Clark decided it was the better part of valor to hang back and settle for 2nd rather than to chance putting it into the wall on the oil-slick track.

We'll never know whether the Lotus-Ford would have whipped Jones' Watson-Offy in a showdown battle on a clean track.

FORD'S BETTER IDEA

Fortunately it didn't make a lot of difference in the broad sweep of Indianapolis history. The really important benefit of Clark's good showing in the 1963 race was to fire up the enthusiasm of Ford company officials to develop an engine with the potential to dominate the Indy scene for several years to come—for sale to all takers, with a big Ford nameplate on it. Even knowing full well that it might cost more than $5 million to develop and tool such an engine, the idea snowballed. Within a month after the '63 race project engineers had been appointed, budgets approved, and the thing was rolling. The timetable called for testing a completed engine on Ford's Kingman, Arizona test track not later than February, 1964—and to win the Indy race the following May!

The new design objectives were very simple: Increase output by 50 HP over the '63 engine, to 425 HP, with a weight increase of not more than 50 lbs., or 400 lbs. total engine weight. The 500-mile reliability had to be proved by the unique dynamometer cycling that had proved so successful with the '63 engines.

It was accepted from the start that the new engine would have to turn in excess of 8,000 rpm and would thus require some form of twin-overhead-camshaft/cylinder-head setup to control valve-train stresses and give an optimum porting and combustion-chamber layout. Ford engineers designed and flow-tested a number of configurations, including full hemispherical combustion chambers, horizontal and vertical ports, twin spark plugs, and two valves as opposed to four valves per cylinder.

What finally evolved was four valves in a pentroof-shaped combustion chamber, single plug at the center, with the intake port routed between the two camshafts. The exhaust port went inward and exited on the inside of the cylinder banks. This layout had two important advantages. Flow tests showed the vertical intake port gave slightly better volumetric efficiency than a conventional horizontal port. It also had the benefit of accessibility of carburetion between the camshafts with the V-8 cylinder arrangement. Bringing the exhaust ports out in the center of the V also gave more flexibility for designing tuned exhaust-pipe systems. This had been a real headache with the conventional side ports of the '63 pushrod engines. With the convenient inside ports on the four-cammer, Ford engineers experimented with six or eight exotic pipe layouts, all giving significant

First prototype 4-cam Ford engine used conventional inboard intake ports and outboard exhausts. This layout gave less power than the vertical intakes and center exhausts. No expense was spared to make sure which arrangement worked best. Photo courtesy of Ford.

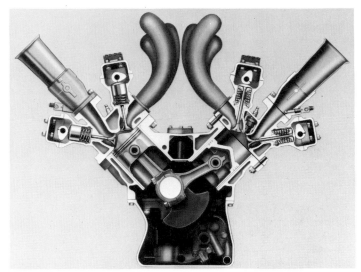

Front section of the final '64 Ford Indy design shows intake- and exhaust-port layout, valve angles, and very rugged block construction. A great deal of flow-bench work was done to assure optimum port sizes and contours for operation up to 9,000 rpm. Drawing courtesy of Ford.

power boosts over conventional straight stacks.

A few components were carried over from the '63 engine. The original aluminum cylinder block proved adequate for heavier duty and the cast-magnesium oil sump and dry-sump lubrication system with dual internal scavenge pumps were carried over with minor improvements. The '63 pushrod engine had already been fitted with gear drives for the camshaft, water pump, oil-pump and alternator in the magnesium front housing. For the new engine it was merely necessary to run an upper gear train off the center cam gear to drive the overhead cams. An aluminum tube was cast in place of the original cam for oil drain-back and block strengthening for 1965. The water pump, oil pumps and alternator—were retained.

For 8,000+ rpm operation, it was decided to beef-up the connecting rods and pistons considerably. Very little weight was added, but the metal was more carefully distributed to reduce stress concentrations. Both rods and crankshafts were forged from chrome-moly steel, then hardened and shot-peened. Tri-metal bearings capable of sustaining 10,000-psi loads were used.

It was determined early in the

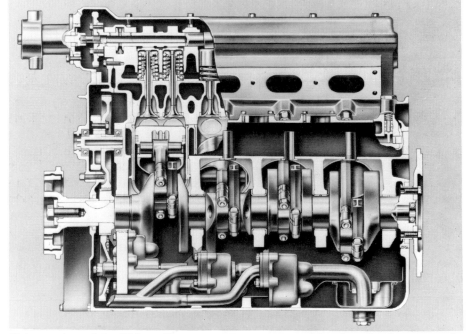

Side section of the '64 engine shows the cam gear drive, bearing layout, and dual scavenge pumps in the oil sump. Extensive dyno testing revealed a number of weak spots. Drawing courtesy of Ford.

Connecting rods were strengthened for the '64 Ford 4-cam engine. The '64 rod had a lot more "meat" in it: larger bolts, larger piston pin, and was twice as strong as the '63 rod. Photo courtesy of Ford.

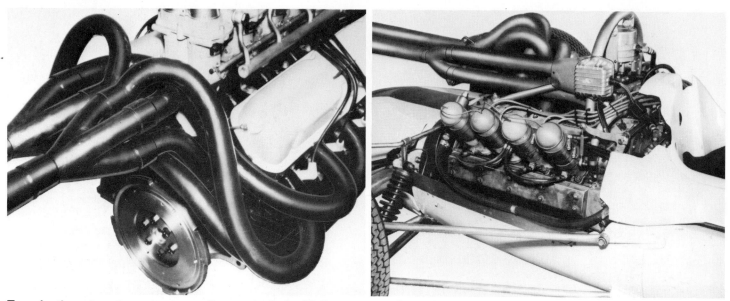

Tuned exhaust systems were greatly compacted with the center exhaust ports of the Ford 4-cam engine. Outboard ports of the pushrod engine required considerably more room to bring the primary pipes up behind the engine—this made installing the engine in a chassis more difficult. This is one big reason Ford used the center ports. Outboard exhaust ports would've been worse with the 4-cammer. Photo courtesy of Ford.

program that the 58mm Weber downdraft carburetors used in '63 would not be adequate for the increased air-flow demands of the four-cam engines. Because these were the largest Webers available and no other automotive carburetor would fit, there was little choice but to turn to Hilborn constant-flow fuel injection. Ford engineers were not anxious to do this, as it was well known that the Hilborn method of fuel metering was very imprecise over a broad speed and load range. This wasn't too much of a handicap with alcohol fuels because engines would tolerate broad deviations from the optimum air/fuel ratio without much loss of power. Gasoline was more fussy, but Ford was determined to run with gasoline for at least the first race with the four-cam engine.

Ford technicians literally re-engineered the Hilborn metering system for more precise air/fuel curves. Spring-loaded economizer valves and secondary by-pass jets shifted the curves to more nearly match the engine's fuel demand when accelerating off the corners—and on up through the speed range to peak straightaway RPM. Another major improve-

ment was made the second year (1965) by putting small booster venturis in the main throttle bodies, and discharging the fuel into the low pressure at the venturi throat. This broke up the fuel droplets into a fine mist, assisting vaporization and speeding combustion. They lost 5—10 HP due to the booster restriction in the air passages; but fuel consumption was reduced 10—13%. It was enough economy gain to help some teams eliminate one pit stop. This more than offset the slight power loss.

Yes, Ford met all their objectives with the new four-cam engine. Maximum output on 103-octane gasoline was just about 425 HP at 8,000 rpm from an engine weighing about 395 lbs., less flywheel and exhaust pipes. 500-mile reliability was again confirmed by dynamometer cycling instead of tedious track testing. This method seemed to work as well above 8,000 rpm as it had at the lower speeds used in 1963. Several vital design changes were made in rods, bearings and valve-train parts as a result of this testing. The design was frozen and declared race-ready in April, 1964. Only relatively minor changes

were made after that. Improved camshafts boosted the power on gasoline to 440 HP at 8,400 rpm in 1965. I've already mentioned the booster venturis that improved fuel economy. Several refinements were made in the bottom end to improve reliability at crank speeds over 9,000 rpm—which some teams were turning by 1965. Oil-flow rate was increased 50% by enlarging passages, and oil-feed pressure was increased from 65 to 90 psi. Oil filtration and cooling also got attention. Rod caps and bearing shells were strengthened to reduce distortion and distribute bearing pressures more evenly. Ford engineers felt confident in extending the red line to 9,000 rpm after these changes.

I should also mention the extensive fuel tests that were run on the engine in the Ford labs in 1965. They give an accurate indication of the effect of various racing fuels on power and torque output, and fuel-consumption rates, under carefully controlled laboratory conditions. Here are HP and torque peaks for various fuel combinations, with BSFC (brake specific fuel consumption) in terms of lbs. per hour of fuel burned per HP produced.

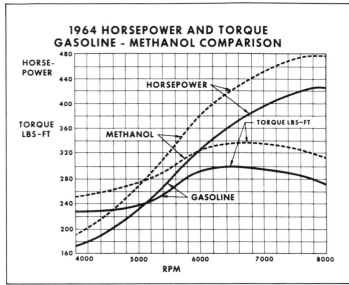

1964 HORSEPOWER AND TORQUE GASOLINE - METHANOL COMPARISON

'64 Ford 4-cam engine had excellent power (425 HP) on gasoline—about 10% more on methanol. These were the design goals. Note mid-range torque peaked about 6,500 rpm, giving strong acceleration off the corners. Most of the cars ran on gasoline in '64.

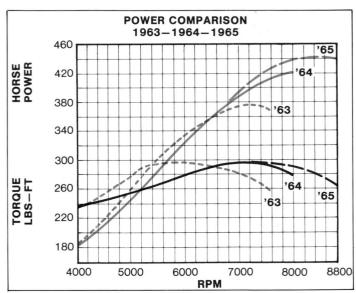

POWER COMPARISON 1963-1964-1965

Development curves for the Ford Indy engines, from '63 to '65. Note the '63 pushrod engine had much stronger low-end torque. The improvement in '65 over '64 was mostly due to camshaft design. All tests were run on 103-octane gasoline, so the curves are directly comparable.

Fuel	Max HP @ rpm	Max Torque lbs.ft. @ rpm	BSFC
103-octane gasoline	440 @ 8,400	290 @ 7,600	0.51
Methanol + 20% toluene	485 @ 8,400	325 @ 7,300	1.00
Straight methanol	495 @ 8,400	330 @ 7,300	1.31
Methanol + 10% nitro	520 @ 8,200	345 @ 7,000	1.40
Methanol + 20% nitro	545 @ 8,200	370 @ 7,000	1.45

Ford engineers developed an improved fuel-discharge nozzle in 1965 that utilized a small booster venturi—similar to that of a carburetor—to get improved fuel atomization for improved combustion. Power was reduced a little because of the booster restriction, but fuel economy improved significantly. Drawing by Erwin Acuntius.

For the academic-minded, a couple of interesting facts jump out of this test data. One, mixing a little toluene with methanol reduces fuel consumption dramatically with only a small sacrifice in power—24% less consumption with a 2% loss of power in this case. Toluene is an aromatic hydrocarbon of very high octane that has the effect of speeding up the combustion of alcohol. This helps combustion efficiency, yet it retains the cooling effect of the alcohol to increase charge density and volumetric efficiency. Toluene/methanol fuel blends became more popular in Championship racing after Ford took advantage of its benefits, at least in races where tank mileage was a factor.

Another interesting finding from the Ford tests was that the percentage increase in power from adding nitromethane to methanol is roughly 1/2 the percentage of nitro in the fuel blend. In other

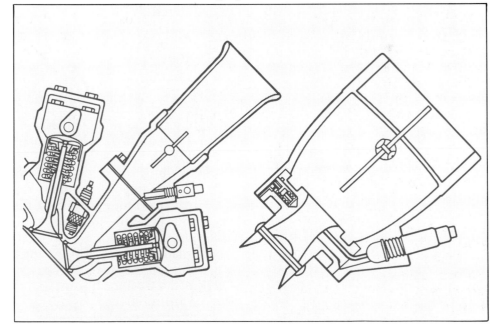

words a 10% addition of nitro to methanol should boost HP about 5%—and 20% should give about 10% more power. And of course it has long been known that methanol gives about a 10% power boost over gasoline, due mostly to

the cooling effect. So there's a potential 20—25% boost over gasoline by using methanol plus 20% nitro.

Ford's fuel findings were not wasted on the brickyard gentry, either. They say Jim Clark was

Ford hired the Wood brothers pit crew for the 1965 race. This team had a reputation on the NASCAR tracks as the fastest pit crew in racing. They helped Ford win the race. Photo courtesy of IMS.

running 30% nitro when he broke the lap record at 160.97 mph in qualifying for the 1965 race!

WINNING WITH A V-8

Let's get back to the racetrack.

The Ford people hedged their bets with the new four-cam engine in '64 by supplying them to four other teams besides Colin Chapman. These included the new Watson rear-engine car for Rodger Ward, Clark's '63 Lotus that was bought by Lindsey Hopkins for Bobby Marshman and the new Halibrand Red Ball "Shrike" for Eddie Sachs. Mickey Thompson got three engines for his Sears Specials. Plus, of course, the new Lotus cars for Jimmy Clark and Dan Gurney.

The Clark and Marshman cars were definitely the fastest of the bunch. Everyone ran straight methanol to qualify, giving them somewhere around 475 honest horses—and the Ford engineers' 8,200-rpm red line was immediately disregarded by all concerned. Jimmy Clark went out the first qualifying day and broke the lap record at 159.34 mph, turning 8,400 rpm with 4.05 gears, to win

pole position. Marshman went out a few minutes later and qualified at 157.9 mph with maximum revs of 8,600. Ward averaged 156.4 mph at a screaming 8,800 rpm. No special durability problems were encountered at the extreme revs, though Ford engineers weren't prepared for the independent ways of the Indy racer!

For the race, all the Ford teams except the Watson-Ward group followed the factory plan to run straight gasoline fuel. This slowed them down a few MPH, but made it possible to run the 500 miles on two pit stops. From the start of the race Clark and Marshman ran away from everyone, swapping the lead and breaking records right and left. Then it was all over. Marshman was forced off the track and damaged the water pump, and Clark had a tread peel from one of his Dunlop tires, bending a suspension arm in the process. A. J. Foyt went on to win the race in a Watson roadster, and Rodger Ward finished 2nd even though he made five pit stops because the fuel-injection system wasn't adjusted right for alcohol.

The innovators had to wait still

another year for success.

They made it in 1965! By then the move to rear-engined cars had progressed so fast that only four front-engine roadsters qualified for the '65 race. Ford had spread their new four-cam engine around to the right people—no less than 17 of them qualified this time. The odds were getting better.

Jimmy Clark and the Lotus team did the job. Clark qualified in the front row on a 30% nitro fuel. They used an 80/20 methanol/toluene blend to get competitive lap speeds with 3-mpg fuel economy and two pit stops in the race. Clark jumped to an early lead and won easily, leading all but 10 laps of the race. He finished almost two laps ahead of Parnelli Jones in another Lotus-Ford.

That was the last time the 4-cylinder Offys made up a substantial proportion of the starting field at Indy—until they were rejuvenated by turbocharging in the late '60s. The V-8 Ford just had too much advantage. Not only did the shorter stroke give it 1,000 to 2,000 rpm more usable crank speed, the Ford had over 50% more valve and port area for each cubic inch of displacement. These two effects together gave the Fords at least 50 HP more output on any given fuel blend. The Offys couldn't keep up.

The Meyer & Drake people, seeing their business slipping away, tried to fight the inevitable by trimming the weight of their engine so Offy-powered cars could hopefully weigh 50 to 75 lbs. less than comparable Fords. Aluminum was substituted for bronze main-bearing webs, magnesium for aluminum in the side and front covers, and the block was cast in aluminum instead of iron. They got the total engine weight down to 355 lbs., with ignition and fuel injection. A number of teams bought these new lightweight engines in the '64—'65 period. Only a few were willing to trust the aluminum block, so most ordered the original iron block, giving up about a 40-lb. weight advantage.

Actually the slight weight saving didn't make that much difference in car performance, so the Fords continued to win.

Ford Motor Co. never actually sold and serviced the four-cam V-8 engine. Once the engine was basically developed and firmly established as a winner in 1965, contracted with Louis Meyer to distribute and service it. This marked the Meyer & Drake split. Louis and "Sonny" Meyer set up shop in Indianapolis to handle the Ford engine, while Dale Drake stayed with the Offy business in Los Angeles. Ford manufactured parts at their Cleveland engine plant or jobbed them out, assembled the engines in Dearborn and shipped engines and parts to Meyer in Indy. The first year, 1966, they produced 20 complete engines to be retailed for $23,000. Apparently the 30 or 40 engines that had been produced earlier were given to the "experimental" teams for token amounts.

Even with the hefty price tags that followed, there's no question that the four-cam engine project

cost Ford a bundle of money. They say nearly $10 million. Ford engineers continued to make minor refinements and adapt tubocharging in the late '60s. Then Henry Ford II suddenly decided to pull out of all forms of racing in 1970. At this time the four-cam engine business was given over entirely to A. J. Foyt, to handle from his large shop facility in Houston, Tex. Foyt, with his engine man Howard Gilbert, had been especially innovative in developing his own stable of Ford engines in the late '60s. So the Ford brass felt he would be the ideal one to carry on the work. They gave him all the patterns and tooling to make the parts, and more than $200,000 worth of spare parts from the shelves in Dearborn and Indianapolis. Louie Meyer retired then, and Drake carried on with a growing business in turbocharged Offys in L.A.

FRONT VS. REAR ENGINE

Because the Ford V-8 engines were never used in a front-engine car at Indy, we should be careful in assessing the true performance merits of front vs. rear engine placement. That is, we should try to factor out the effect of the Ford's extra horsepower and look just at cornering and straightaway performance.

Chrondek personnel and Ford technicians ran some significant tests during practice for the 1964 race. They set up Chrondek electric-eye timing traps to clock speeds coming off turn-4, then elapsed time for the acceleration distance of 1,670 ft. to the starting line, and finally a third short trap at that point to measure peak straightaway speed. It's interesting to compare readings for three widely different types of cars through this series of time traps. See the accompanying table.

These figures seem to indicate that the rear-engine cars had no big performance advantage over the roadsters. The quicker acceleration of the roadster here would have to be attributed to the higher engine torque coming off the turn, because the peak HP of the Ford V-8 on gasoline would be about the same as the Offy on alcohol (around 425 HP). The roadster had a bit more straightaway speed because of the harder acceleration. There is no reason to believe the tiny rear-engine Lotus had a lot less wind resistance at top speed. Or if it did, it didn't have much effect on lap speed. Also look at the Novi times. The 4WD Ferguson chassis didn't have remarkably high cornering speeds, but the tremendous acceleration and high straightaway speed with the supercharged Novi made up for it in lap speed.

Clocking car speeds through turn-1 told a little different story. Here the good rear-engine cars were consistently 2—3 mph faster than the better Offy roadsters. In qualification runs for the '64 race, Jim Clark was fastest in the Lotus-Ford at 147 mph—the average for the full quarter-circle. The fastest roadsters in '64 were averaging 145 mph on the new wide tread Firestone tires.

Even the early rear-engine cars had a small lap-speed advantage over the roadsters when the two types of cars were running together. Certainly the rear-engine cars were quickly developed far beyond where front-engine cars could have been.

THE TIRE REVOLUTION

They say there's nothing that spurs technical progress like competition. This was certainly true in the case of Indianapolis tire development in the '60's. Remember that Firestone had the

Car	Off Turn	Time	Peak	Lap Av.
Lotus-Ford (gas fuel)	157	6.70	178	152.5
Watson roadster (alky)	157	6.56	184	154.4
Novi-Ferguson 4WD (660 HP)	153	6.47	194	152.5

Cause of the big tire controversy of 1963. Parnelli Jones (right) displays the special 15-in. tire Firestone made for the lightweight Lotus-Ford cars. It had 1.5-in.-wider treads than the regular 16-in. tire Jim Hurtubise has on the left. When everyone wanted the wider tires, there weren't enough 15-in. tires and magnesium wheels to go around—about half the teams got them.

Goodyear turned its eye toward Indy in 1963. First tests were with their existing NASCAR tire, shown here with the unique inner safety liner. These were available at the Speedway in '63, but no one used them.

Goodyear's interest in Indy tires sparked Firestone to prepare an entire new line of six wide-tread sizes for the 1964 race—shown here with head development engineer, Jim Thiese. Treads were nearly twice as wide as equivalent '63 sizes. Photo courtesy of Firestone.

Indy tire business pretty much to themselves since the '20s. Several tire companies had catered to the brickyard in the early days. As the performance requirements of speedway tires became more demanding, all but Firestone dropped out one by one. The others didn't want to spend the money for development and special tooling, thinking their sales could never justify the investment. Firestone was willing to write off the cost as good advertising.

In this atmosphere you could hardly blame Firestone if they were a little complacent about forced-draft technical development. Why spend the extra money for testing and tooling when no one was pushing you? Actually there was relatively little red-hot development in Firestone tires for 35 years after the Balloon-type tire was introduced at the speedway in 1925.

The break came in 1963 when Goodyear started testing special tires at the Speedway. Firestone had already made up special 15-in. tires for the rear-engine Lotus-Fords that year, as their existing

16 and 18-in. sizes were just too big and heavy for the smaller rear-engine cars. The treads on these tires were widened 1.5 inches in an attempt to maintain the "footprint" with the smaller tread diameter. Firestone engineers did this strictly to give equal tire mileage—not necessarily to help cornering speeds. When some of the roadster guys started trying the 15-in. tires, cornering speeds jumped 2—3 mph. It was obvious the wider treads gave much better lateral bite in the turns.

That started the big tire hassle of 1963. Firestone could supply enough 15-in. tires for some of the teams, but there weren't any 15-in. wheels to fit the cars . . . and the race was only three weeks away! To make a long story short, the Halibrand Engineering people, manufacturer of most of the magnesium wheels used at Indy, dropped everything. They worked night and day and turned out 300 15-in. wheels in time for the race. About half the cars used them.

They revolutionized the Indy tire scene.

In 1964 Goodyear came to the Speedway with a full line of

Many American car builders of the '60s fabricated suspension arms from steel tube, with aluminum or magnesium castings for the uprights and hub carriers.

Some Lotus cars used rather massive upper front suspension arms operating inboard coil-over shocks. Upper end of the shock is attached to the inboard end of the control arm. To keep things simple and light, the lower end is mounted to a common bolt with the lower control arm front pivot. Locating the shock unit inboard reduced aerodynamic drag and unsprung weight.

custom Indy tires. The battle was on. After hearing about the high cornering speeds Goodyear was getting in tests in the fall of '63, Firestone launched a crash program to develop a new line of wide-tread tires for the '64 race. Tire progress, followed by corner speeds and lap speeds, began skyrocketing.

Perhaps I should briefly mention some principles of racetrack tire performance right here. Cornering traction, or grip or bite, depends pretty much on three factors: (1) width of tread rubber on the track, (2) degree of softness or "stickiness" of this rubber, and (3) height/width profile ratio of the tire carcass. Consider the last factor. You can see that a tire section having a broad width in relation to its height—in other words a lower, squattier section—will have more lateral stiffness. Under cornering forces it will be less apt to distort and lose its grip on the track. This is why tires became lower while growing wider. It's to get that lower, wider-section profile that won't roll under with high side forces. This vital fact about tire performance was not known by engineers until the late

'50s. They first started doing it with European road-racing tires.

The hardness of a rubber compound can be measured with a Durometer. This device pushes a needle into the rubber and the depth of penetration for a given pressure is the Durometer *number*. Racing tires in the early '60s were about 70−75 Durometer, passenger tires a little higher.

It's interesting to compare these different numbers for an actual car/driver combination over a period of three or four years, as tire technology progressed. I have some figures for Jim Clark, (see Table below) one of the fastest cornering drivers driving various Lotus-Ford cars in the '63−'66 period. Tire technology was moving forward at a rapid rate during these years. Listed are tread widths (rear), profile ratios, Durometer readings along with the average speed through turn-1 and the lap average for the different combinations.

If you're wondering about the low Durometer reading for Clark's 1964 tires, these were basically Dunlop road racing tires. Colin Chapman wanted to introduce them to the Indy scene because Clark's turn speeds were very high with them, and he thought they would work fine. Although suited for road racing, the rubber was apparently too soft for the lack of "cool-down" time and sustained high speed at Indy. A tread peeled on the 48th lap, wrapping around a suspension arm and bending it. This put Clark out of the race.

After 1966, Durometer ratings no longer had the significance they did before. Tire engineers learned how to formulate rubber compounds that were "sticky" without being so soft that the wear rate increased radically. There was no simple way to measure this stickiness like you could the hardness. Laboratory friction-coefficient tests helped, but *stiction* varied a

Year	Tread Width (inches)	Profile Ratio	Duro-Meter	Turn Speed (mph)	Qual. Speed (mph)
1963	8.0	0.70	70	142	149.7
1964	8.5	0.65	64	147	158.8
1965	9.0	0.55	68	149	160.7
1966	10.0	0.45	65	151	164.1

Bill McCreary (left) and Jim Thiese, Firestone race-tire executives, pose with some of the special test equipment needed in the program. Firestone had a special lab for race-tire testing and spent millions of dollars through the years to supply the Indy scene. They wrote off the cost as good publicity. Photo courtesy of Firestone.

Intensive tire development during the '60s required a lot of on-track testing, too. Both Firestone and Goodyear had special mobile testing labs. Top Indy cars and drivers contracted to do months of testing on the Indy track. Photo courtesy of Goodyear.

lot with temperature and surface smoothness. Consequently the only real way to know what you were doing was to mold a tire and take it out on the track to test it.

The result of all this, once Goodyear began challenging Firestone for leadership in the racing-tire field, was the two companies were continually testing tires on the Indy track during summer and fall months. They contracted with car owners and drivers to help with the testing. At the height of the testing activity the tire companies even provided their own crew of mechanics to maintain and set up the test cars. It was big business in every sense of the term.

Progress was extremely rapid in both camps. Goodyear didn't knock Firestone out of the driver's seat overnight. There were some lean years when Goodyear had to pay plenty to get name drivers to use their tires. But they learned fast. Within three or four years about half of the teams were on Goodyears and there seemed to be no great difference in the performance of the two brands of tires. It was always necessary, though, for both companies to keep key teams under contract. Racing men are

notorious for copying the guy who is going the fastest. If they weren't bound down by contract they'd be switching tires every ten minutes on qualifying day!

By the end of this time period, 1968, the typical Indy rear tire had a tread width of 11—12 in., profile ratio of 0.40, and turn speeds of the faster cars had risen to about 158 mph. Tread-rubber compounds were much "stickier" than in the mid '60s, and yet Durometer readings were still around 65. Therefore, teams could plan on not more than two sets being needed to run 500 miles at race speeds. Tremendous progress for just five or six years.

Maybe these turn speeds will mean something if you look at it like this: Centrifugal force on the car, allowing for turn banking and groove radius, comes to something over 1.4 g. This means the tires were generating 1.4 times more side force than the force they exerted square against the track surface. This figure is known as the *traction coefficient*. With a conventional passenger-car tire on pavement, this coefficient is only about 0.8—0.9. This tells something about the progress of racing in the explosive mid '60s.

MONOCOQUE CONSTRUCTION

Any lingering doubts about the superiority of the rear-engine car were dispelled when Jim Clark and Bobby Marshman ran away from the field in their Lotus racers early in the 1964 race, before mechanical failures put them out. That year there were 24 new rear-engine cars entered for the race, 12 of them actually qualifying. The following year, 1965, saw only four front-engine cars in the race.

In this swift changeover from one basic type of car to another, it was inevitable that some construction techniques would be carried over. So it was. Where the new rear-engine cars from England used various forms of monocoque construction, most of the first American cars stuck with the familiar tubular-steel space frames that had been used for years on the roadsters. These cars used independent rear suspensions, but the "transaxle" was essentially a Halibrand quick-change center section mated to a Halibrand 2-speed gearbox. Side seals and half-shaft U-joints were fitted to the transaxle. In many ways these were roadsters with their engines relocated behind the driver. They were even offset three or four inches to the left for weight bias.

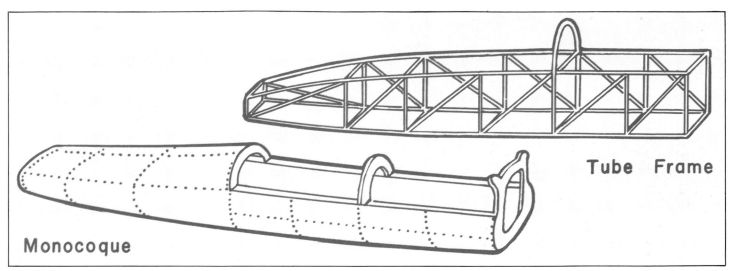

Tube Frame

Monocoque

New British rear-engine cars appeared at Indy in the early '60s with aircraft-type monocoque construction—the main body shell is the car's main structure. A monocoque "tub" is much lighter and stronger than the classic tubular space frames used on the American roadsters.

Pat Warren developed the first two-speed quick-change axle. Here Glenn Mountz assembles one of the neat Halibrand two-speed, quick-change "transaxles." Based on components from the standard Halibrand quick-change center sections, these transaxles were tooled up for American rear-engine cars. Photo courtesy of Halibrand.

Most American rear-engine cars used Guibo rubber-doughnut-type driveshaft U-joints. Light, efficient and reliable.

The English cars were more sophisticated in that they used a *monocoque* structure. The principle of this type of construction was to use the skin of the body as a stressed member, with several fabricated sheet-aluminum bulkheads to form a substructure for the shell. It was something like the construction of a ship hull or an airplane fuselage. By spreading the loads over the entire structure, particularly the outer skin, it was possible to get a better strength-to-weight ratio than when supporting most of the loads on a separate underframe with no appreciable loading of the outer skin.

One notable exception in the line-up of 1964 American cars was the "Shrike"—built by Ted Halibrand, and designed by Norman Timbs. Timbs had assisted Lou Moore with the famous Blue Crown cars back in the late '40s. He was thinking about monocoque construction even then. But he applied it in a unique way on the Shrike: Bulkheads were magnesium castings, rather than the usual fabricated sheet aluminum. The outer skin was 0.064-inch sheet magnesium. The cars only weighed 1,140 lbs. dry with the 400-lb. Ford engine. You can see the main construction was considerably lighter than the British fabricated-aluminum type of construction.

If it hadn't been for minimum car-weight limits being imposed in 1965, this type of monocoque con-

The first American rear-engine cars, like this 1964 Watson design with Don Branson behind the wheel, tended to follow construction themes of the earlier roadsters. American designers did not go to the monocoque construction at first. Photo courtesy of IMS.

Some American rear-engine cars were offset 3—5 in. to the left to achieve the left-side weight bias that seemed so effective with the roadsters. This complicated suspension design and fabrication—many suspension components were not interchangeable side-to-side.

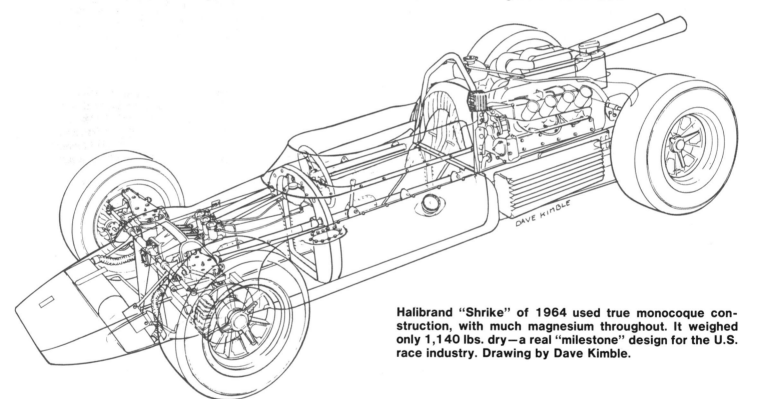

Halibrand "Shrike" of 1964 used true monocoque construction, with much magnesium throughout. It weighed only 1,140 lbs. dry—a real "milestone" design for the U.S. race industry. Drawing by Dave Kimble.

struction using cast-magnesium bulkheads might have been developed further. But once it was no longer necessary to cut out every extra ounce of weight, the builders turned to simpler and less-expensive forms of construction. The tubular space frame didn't last long. U.S. builders began to copy the British monocoque cars—primarily because they were going faster. By the late '60s, Eric Broadley's Lola cars had

become as popular at Indy as Chapman's Lotus. Both were in demand by the big-money teams because they apparently offered a better compromise between general ruggedness, crash safety and weight than many American cars. It can also be said that once our car builders got the hang of monocoque construction, they did an even better job with it than the British. Detail workmanship was always better.

By the late '60s our cars were going as fast as the Lolas and Lotuses.

EMPHASIS ON SAFETY

The firey crash in the 1964 race that claimed Dave MacDonald and Eddie Sachs triggered a quick revolution in Indy safety rules that had a big effect on car design and race strategy in the next few years.

Fuel systems got major attention. Nobody argued that the chief

Shrike front spindle-and-brake-support assembly was a magnesium casting with a pressed-in tubular steel spindle retained by a spanner nut. Brake caliper housing was also magnesium. Expensive weight saving! Photo courtesy of Halibrand.

Halibrand Shrike monocoque used unique cast-magnesium bulkheads. Four bulkheads were spaced at high-load points along the body and "skinned" with 0.064-in. sheet magnesium—extremely light, yet rigid. Photo courtesy of Halibrand.

USAC officials banned pressure fuel feed in 1965, then required all teams to use a standardized 400-gal., gravity-feed tank. Maximum tank height was 60 in. above ground.

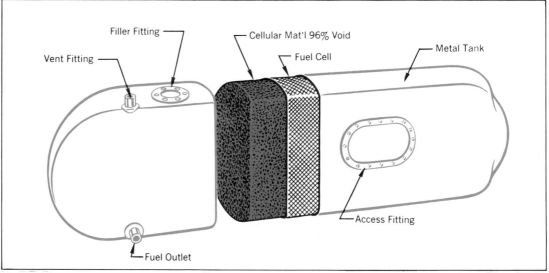

Firestone developed this "space age" fuel cell to meet 1965 fuel-tank rules. A low-density sponge-like plastic foam filled the tank, absorbing fuel as quickly as it entered. Foam controlled fuel slosh during cornering, braking and accelerating. The cell, or rubber bladder, greatly increased the rupture resistance of the fuel tank. Drawing courtesy of Firestone.

factor in the fires was the highly volatile gasoline fuel Ford was recommending for their new four-cam engine. Gasoline hadn't been used at Indy for years before that and the guys had kind of forgotten the fire hazard. Yet USAC officials didn't want to ban any viable fuel in the interests of automotive development. Their compromise was to formulate a set of rules that would encourage the use of alcohol, with emphasis on safer

handling of all types of fuel, both in the car and during pit stops.

They limited fuel-tank capacity to 75 gals. and mandated two pit stops. They included the stipulation that fuel hoses had to be hooked up on each stop, whether fuel was transferred or not. It was felt that the 75-gal. capacity would be plenty to run the race on two stops with alcohol. By requiring hoses to be inserted, it was hoped that the teams would be dis-

couraged from trying to run on gasoline with one refueling.

To make for safer fuel handling in the pits, they banned the pressurized-feed tanks that had been a fixture at Indy for years. Some of these pressurized systems were using up to 400-psi pressure on the stored fuel, and could transfer 60 gals. in 10 seconds. You can imagine what happened when a hose came loose during refueling. The new rules called for

A.J. Watson installs one of the new Firestone fuel cells. Watson has been one of the top Indy car builders and crew chiefs for a span of 15 or 20 years. More a "refiner" than an innovator, he made good designs better.

Popular with the crowds, Novi-powered 4WD Ferguson was a massive car that weighed nearly 2,000 lbs. dry. Tires had advanced so much by the mid '60s that 4-wheel traction was no longer needed. Any traction advantage was more than offset by inferior handling due to extra vehicle weight. Photo by Rowell.

gravity feed only, with a maximum tank height of 60 in. above the pit floor. The teams were free to design flow-efficient nozzle outlets and sophisticated hoses; but a tank size of 40-in. diameter by 86-in. long—400 gals.—was stipulated to prevent oversize tanks in the pits. It was felt this was enough capacity.

In-car fuel systems were even more radically changed. The goal was to prevent fuel from spilling in a crash. For instance, fuel tanks now had to be at least 0.032-in. steel or 0.062-in. aluminum, with a thick rubber bladder insert. Firestone developed these bladders in a crash program for the '65 race, along with a unique low-density plastic foam or sponge-like material that fitted inside and actually absorbed the fuel as quickly as it was fed into the tank. This material was 96% void, so there was no serious loss of capacity when it was used. But the weird stuff would absolutely prevent fuel from sloshing around— even if the tank and rubber bladder were torn apart in a crash.

Some real space-age technology at the brickyard. And much credit should go to Firestone for developing and producing the new "fuel cells," as I'm sure it cost them a bundle of money that they never recovered from the racers.

One other important rule change was to impose a minimum dry-weight limit of 1,250 lbs. on the cars; raised to 1,350 lbs. for the 1966 race. This rule change caused more controversy than any of the others. Racers said it was a step backward in technical development, that it had always been a major goal of designers to reduce unnecessary weight. Ted Halibrand had just built a magnesium-monocoque car that weighed only 1,140 lbs., and he was anxious to get on with further experiments. The new USAC rule blasted that line of endeavor overnight. The rulemakers prevailed, firm in their belief that the new weight limits would encourage stronger, more crash-resistant construction. The fact that they raised the minimum 100 lbs. after only one year is evidence of their

resolve. That brought a storm of protest from the innovators.

Protest or not, most of these safety rules stuck and were even tightened more in the following years. There is no question that they had a strong influence on the race. Cars ceased to get smaller and lighter. Frontal areas remained the same or got larger. Development in exotic, lightweight materials and construction techniques stalled. Pit-stop strategies were revised. Gasoline-based fuels disappeared overnight. A whole new technology grew up in designing tank outlets, hoses and nozzles to transfer fuel fast with a fixed gravity head. Some teams brought in professional engineers to design more efficient venturis and nozzles. They eventually got so they could transfer fuel by gravity feed almost as fast as with the 400-psi pressure! It was a fascinating time of off-track development.

And you know something? There haven't been any more crashes like that terrible holocaust in 1964.

Novi-Ferguson 4WD transmission used a gearset to offset the drive. Locking differentials controlled wheelspin. System was developed for utility vehicles, but seemed to be strong enough to handle the Novi V-8.

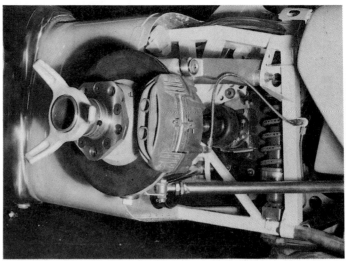

Airheart aircraft disc brakes were used on the Novi-Ferguson 4WD. They had the capacity to handle the 2,000-lb. car.

FROM FRONT DRIVE TO FOUR-WHEEL DRIVE

The idea of driving all four wheels was not new at Indy in the '60s. Racing innovators had been interested in the concept for many years—and there were several attempts to make it work. Frank Brisko led the 1934 race for many laps in a 4WD Miller. There were the 4WD Gulf Specials that Harry Miller designed in the late '30s. Never successful, but they focused attention on the unique drive concept. Then there was the radical twin-engine Fageol car Paul Russo qualified in '46. It was fairly fast, but he drove into the wall when trying to maneuver in traffic.

The all-wheel-drive concept got its greatest attention when our old friend, Andy Granatelli, took hold of it in 1963. It all started with a chance conversation between Andy and Stirling Moss, the famous British Grand Prix driver. Moss had driven an experimental Ferguson G.P. car with 4WD in the early '60s. It was not competitive on the top courses of Europe, but he was highly impressed with the traction and road-holding on tight turns and wet surfaces. He suggested to Andy that this setup might be an answer for transmitting the tremendous horsepower of the supercharged Novi engine to the Indy track.

Cockpit of the '65 Novi-Ferguson 4WD shows the gear-shift lever, instruments and padded steering wheel. They say it was a handful to drive!

That touched off the spark. By that time Andy had strong financial backing from Studebaker, and the Ferguson people in Britain were anxious to promote their patented 4WD system wherever they could. They even sent over the very race car that Moss had driven so it could be tested on the Indianapolis track. Factory driver Jack Fairman came along to demonstrate its handling characteristics. Even though powered by a tired 240-HP Climax engine, Fairman lapped the Indy track at 146 mph—and Granatelli was especially impressed that the car could run flat out all around the track. Turn speeds were only a few MPH below peak straightaway speeds, indicating unusual grip in the turns.

This was in the summer of 1963. Within a few weeks contracts had been signed and an Indy car was under construction at the Ferguson works to take the Novi V-8. The Ferguson people didn't claim to be innovative car builders as they felt the 4WD system would

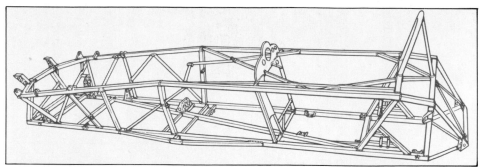

The Novi-Ferguson used this space frame fabricated from square steel tubing. It had to be very rigid and strong to take the drive forces of the 700-HP Novi engine. Drawing courtesy of AUTOCAR.

One of the first Offy turbocharger setups—No. 11 Vita-Fresh car in 1966, Bobby Unser driving. It had a shield over the top of the installation to retain exhaust heat for increased turbine efficiency. Photo by Rowell.

do the talking for them. Thus the very British chassis featured a routine tubular space frame, rack-and-pinion steering, wishbone-type suspension and inboard coil-over shocks at each wheel.

The real interest was in the *all-wheel* drive. That's the interesting part of this car. From the clutch the drive was routed through a set of spur reduction gears to offset the driveline down and to the left. This let the front-wheel driveshaft pass next to the crankcase and provided some left-side weight bias at the same time. From the reduction gear, the drive went into the main transmission. The Ferguson transmission combined four forward speeds with a unique limited-slip differential to split the torque between the front and rear wheels. This was not a torque biasing gearset; but the differential was designed with a clutch to permit some speed variation between front and rear wheels without one end spinning freely—like a conventional limited-slip unit for a rear axle. From this gearbox, driveshafts ran forward and back to conventional ring-and-pinion gearsets in magnesium housings at each end of the chassis. U-jointed half-shafts turned the wheels.

It was a sophisticated drive setup—one that had received a lot of detail engineering for commercial trucks, tractors and some

special passenger-car applications. It promised to be reasonably reliable under Indy race conditions. Handling was an unknown factor, especially as Granatelli had upped the power to 740 HP at 8,200 rpm in anticipation of additional traction. Because the car weighed nearly 2,000 lbs. dry, tire wear was another question mark.

It has to be admitted that results on the racetrack were utterly inconclusive. Granatelli assigned his top driver Bobby Unser to the car, so there's no question about driving ability. Unser did turn competitive lap speeds. He qualified for the '64 race at 154.9 mph and averaged 157.5 mph in '65. This put him well up in the starting field. But Unser could also jump into either of the rear-drive Kurtis-Novi team cars, and go just about as fast on the straights and through the corners. In both cases the cornering speeds were well below the best times turned by the lightweight rear-engine cars. In a word, the 4WD configuration just didn't show any definite advantage at Indy, even when transmitting some 600 HP coming off the corners. Obviously, the car didn't need that extra traction with the new wide-tread, sticky tires that became available in the mid '60s.

Incidentally, Unser didn't finish in '64 or '65. In '64 he was involved in the MacDonald-Sachs

crash early in the race. In '65 he dropped out on the 69th lap with an oil leak. None of the three Novi-powered cars could qualify at all in '66. It was another case of Granatelli's pet supercharged engine being left behind by chassis design.

But he still had another shot: Gas turbine engines. We'll get to that soon . . .

ADRENALIN FOR THE OFFY

Louis Meyer and Dale Drake were nothing if not adept at reading the handwriting on the wall. It didn't take a genius to see that the new four-cam Ford V-8 would put the 30-year-old Offy design out of business in a hurry unless something radical was done to zip it up. The early '60s weight-cutting program was not the answer. Lou Meyer didn't think there was an answer. He bailed out in 1966 and took over distribution of the Ford engines and parts in the new shop in Indianapolis. Dale Drake and Leo Goossen were left alone with a classic 4-cylinder engine at least 75 HP and 2,000 rpm behind the Ford.

There was really only one logical alternative: Reduce displacement under 171 cu.in. and supercharge.

This idea of supercharging the Offy engine wasn't new. I've discussed several serious attempts in the early '50s. These set-ups

Dick Jones of Champion Spark Plug did a lot of development work in the mid '60s supercharging the Offy in an effort to beat out the Autolite-equipped Fords. He worked mainly with Roots blowers and turbochargers, with turbocharging finally doing the trick. The result was an engine that couldn't be beaten off the turns, which put the Offy back in command. Photo courtesy Hugh MacInnes.

Components of the AiResearch Model TE06 turbocharger used on the Offys in the late '60s. Compressor and turbine "wheels" on a common shaft, turn at speeds up to 100,000 rpm to pump 15—20 psi boost to the engine. Lubrication was by engine oil pressure. Photo courtesy of AiResearch.

showed plenty of top-end horsepower, but mid-range torque for exiting the corners was generally weak. Engine durability for 500 miles at these higher power levels was also an unknown factor. The earlier supercharged Offys didn't last very long, so Drake and Goossen knew extensive development would be required in several areas to make an engine competitive with the strong fuel-injected Fords.

Fortunately a couple of things happened in the mid '60s that encouraged them. One was extensive development work done by Dick Jones, head of Champion Spark Plug's Racing Division. The Champion people didn't particularly like Ford engines because they used Autolite spark plugs. They were interested in promoting the Offy, even in the face of this formidable opposition.

Dick Jones saw the logic of supercharging as soon as the four-cam Fords hit the track in 1964. He had a good dynamometer available at Champion's west-coast shop, so he set out to build up a converted Offy to demonstrate the potential. He borrowed a 220-CID sprint version which could be easily sleeved down to 170 CID. It was a relative shoestring operation, so the supercharger installation consisted

Turbochargers were used on a few of the remaining front-engine roadsters in the late '60s. They were usually located outside the body on the left side.

of a GMC 4-71 Roots-type blower from a diesel engine, driven by a cog belt off the front of the crankshaft. The Hilborn two-throat fuel injector was modified from a dragster unit. There was no claim that this could be a practical Indianapolis combination; Jones just wanted to demonstrate the potential of Roots-type supercharging as applied to an Offy sized to comply with the rules.

Dynamometer performance surprised everyone, including Jones. With the blower driven at 75% of crank speed and running straight methanol fuel, a solid 545 HP appeared at 7,800 rpm on 15-psi boost. Maximum torque reading was 380 lbs.ft. at 6,500 rpm. He was especially concerned about mid-range torque because of the poor acceleration of previous supercharged Offys. He flashed the test engine to 9,000 rpm momentarily, getting slightly over 500 HP. This showed that the blower drag wasn't building up excessively at very high revs, so the combination could probably be revved safely to at least 8,500 rpm.

Jones was cautiously optimistic when he showed his test results to Dale Drake. He knew only too

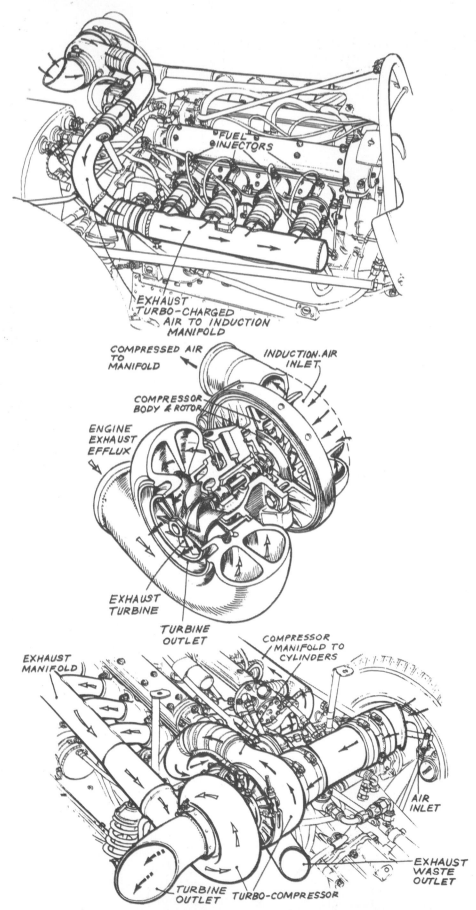

General layout of the early Offy turbocharging systems. Air was pumped to the ports, where injectors supplied the fuel. Turbocharger cutaway shows turbine and nozzle, bearings, compressor wheel, etc. The system added 200—300 HP. Drawing courtesy of AUTOCAR.

well that track and dynamometer performance didn't always correlate well—and that a lot of engineering and expensive tooling would be required to adapt supercharging to the Offy to make a track-practical installation.

Just in the nick of time Drake and Goossen got a push from another direction that made them even more convinced that supercharging might be the answer for the Offy's future. This resulted from experimental work with turbocharging by a brilliant three-man team of Stuart Hilborn, the fuel-injection expert, master mechanic Herb Porter, and a turbocharger engineer from Garrett's Air Research Division, Bob DeBisschop. These three men had long been interested in the possibility of applying turbocharging to the Offy. When the four-cam Ford engine appeared they suddenly saw it as a necessity. They rigged up a crude turbocharger installation on one of Porter's spare Offys in the summer of 1965. Just a few quick dyno runs confirmed that well over 600 HP was available with off-the-shelf components. It looked much more practical than a mechanically driven Roots supercharger.

Perhaps I should pause here and briefly review how a turbocharger works. Essentially it's a tiny centrifugal supercharger or compressor that's driven by an engine's exhaust gases through a radial-inflow turbine. The supercharger impeller and turbine are mounted on opposite ends of a common shaft. These impellers are contained in their own housings that include inducer and diffuser sections for the impeller, collector and nozzle ring for the turbine, and the necessary bearings, seals and lubrication for the shaft. The whole assembly only weighed 15—20 lbs. The impeller and turbine wheels turn at extreme speeds of 100,000 to 120,000 rpm, and the supercharger side can develop boost pressures as high as 30 to 40 psi.

The obvious advantage is this is relatively "free horsepower." In other words the turbocharger generates no drag on an engine where a mechanically driven Roots blower requires 50 to 75 HP at high revs. It's only partly true to say the turbocharger generates no drag. The restriction of the nozzle and turbine generate a back-pressure in the exhaust manifold that the engine's pistons have to push against on the exhaust stroke. This would theoretically subtract some power. However if the intake-manifold boost pressure is equal to, or higher than, the exhaust-manifold back pressure—obviously there would be no loss, because the boost pressure would push down on the pistons on the inlet stroke. So the designer has to fashion his complete inlet/outlet system carefully to keep exhaust pressures below intake pressures.

Another advantage of turbocharging is you can select an oversize turbo that has the capacity to pump your desired maximum-boost pressure at medium engine speed and by-pass part of the exhaust gas at higher engine speeds to maintain that constant boost up to peak revs. This is what a *waste gate* does. It's a diaphragm-operated valve on the exhaust manifold, usually sensitive to intake boost pressure. It begins to by-pass exhaust when boost reaches a predetermined level. They usually select the turbo/waste-gate combination to develop full boost at medium speeds coming off the turns.

Probably the worst disadvantage of a turbocharger is the slight "turbo lag" coming off the corners. When the driver lets off the throttle entering a corner, the turbine slows down. It takes a second or so to build up full boost again when he gets on it coming out—when he wants maximum power. Remember there's no direct connection between car speed and turbocharger speed like there is with a gear- or belt-driven blower. The

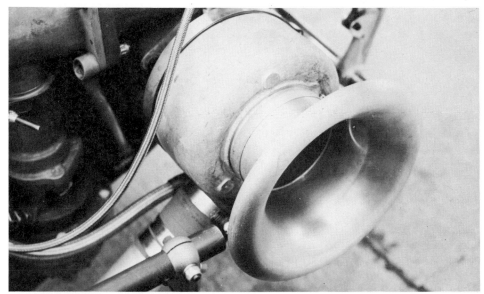

Most Indy turbos use an air horn of some sort on the compressor inlet to smooth intake airflow.

The first Ford turbocharger installations in 1968 used reflective metallic blankets over the exhaust manifold. Optimum turbine efficiency requires maximum gas temperatures into the turbine. Ford also used massive air cleaners to protect the compressor wheel. Photo by Rowell.

best ways to fight this lag effect is to design the impeller and turbine wheels extremely light, so they can accelerate quickly. Also it helps to squirt in a little extra fuel on throttle tip-in, so you get a sudden surge of extra exhaust gas to spin the turbine. These little refinements didn't occur overnight, needless to say. The first turbocharged Offys were pretty crude compared to units three or four years later.

Hilborn, Porter and DeBisschop firmly established the practicality

of the idea in 1965—just when Dick Jones was experimenting with Roots supercharging in another part of Los Angeles. When both groups came to Dale Drake that summer, asking for a downsized Offy for developing their new supercharging ideas, he really could not turn them down. It was supercharging or die for the 30-year-old Offy design.

Leo Goossen went to work immediately on the redesign. The key factor here was a radical shortening of the stroke. Offys had

Dale Drake introduced a Roots-supercharged Offy at the same time the turbo Offys appeared in 1966. It developed 540 HP at 7,800 rpm on 15-psi boost. In fact, the Roots-blown cars were faster than the turbos in '66.

always been noted for "long-stroke torque" and it had been proved many times that quick acceleration off the corners with a high-torque engine was a big factor in lap speed. Goossen also knew that they were somehow going to have to be able to rev the Offy to 8,500—9,000 rpm to compete with the V-8 Fords, even with the extra boost of supercharging or turbocharging. A much shorter stroke was the obvious route. He laid out the first factory Offy ever to have an oversquare bore/stroke ratio—4-1/8 in. bore x 3-1/8 in. stroke for 168 CID.

There was a lot more to it than just sticking in a short-stroke crankshaft. To retain a reasonable ratio of stroke length to rod length, the rods were shortened radically from 7.50 in. to 5.67 in. center-to-center. Then the cylinder block was too high, so they recast the block/head with a whopping 2-5/8 in. taken off the bottom. Goossen had to completely redesign the cam drive to the lower height. He reduced the number of gears in the train from 13 to 10 in the process and redesigned the front magneto drive. While they were at it they decided to cast the block in aluminum, using siamesed cylinders with dry sleeves and valve-seat inserts. They wanted to cut

weight as much as possible so the complete engine-turbocharger or supercharger assembly wouldn't weigh much more than an unblown 252-CID Offy. They came close. Both the Roots and turbo installations weighed 40—50 lbs. more than the unblown 252, giving a 425—450-lb. total engine-package weight. It took a sizable investment in new patterns and tooling to bring this off.

The original plan was to offer the new 168-CID short-stroke engine as a bare package, for the buyer to build up his own blower system. The Roots blower drive proved so complex that Goossen designed a gear take-off from the back of the crankshaft, with an enclosed magnesium housing to take a gear train to the blower mounted on the left side of the engine. A Hilborn two-barrel injector fed the fuel. This package was priced at $17,000, still $6,000 less than a four-cam Ford engine.

Drake never did offer complete turbocharger installations for the 168 engine. Stu Hilborn handled this demand. His 1966 installations were cobbled from existing components, using AiResearch TEO6 diesel turbochargers. By the following year he had a beautiful bolt-on package for the 168 Offy. It included the turbocharger assembly, necessary brackets, complete

fuel-injection system with cast-magnesium manifolds, plus the exhaust waste-gate valve. For $3,500 you could make a winner out of a 168-CID Offy.

In their original 1966 form the new 168-CID Offys delivered about 540 HP at 7,800 rpm on 15-psi boost with the Roots setup—and 625 HP at 8,000 rpm on 17 psi with Hilborn's turbo. The turbocharged engine could develop more HP by increasing the spring load against the waste-gate valve to increase boost to 20—25 psi. But 625 HP at 17 psi was considered the maximum safe limit for the engine. Incidently, note that the difference between the 540 HP of the Roots-blown version and the 625 HP of the turbo—just about the power required to drive the Roots, plus the difference between 15- and 17- psi boost.

SUPERCHARGED OFFYS ON THE TRACK

It would make a good story to say the new supercharged Offys beat the nasty old Fords the first time on the track—and everyone lived happily ever after. Victory didn't come that easily, believe me. Six of the new engines qualified for the 1966 race, three turbocharged and three Roots-blown. Fastest of the bunch was

Parnelli Jones' Roots-blown Agajanian Spl., qualifying in the 2nd row at 162.5 mph. He finished 8th in the race. None of the others finished.

Everyone expected the turbocharged Offys to be faster. But they had to be detuned about 100 HP to keep them running. When they hit the track they immediately began having problems from excessive internal heat due to their fuel-injection systems not being adapted for use with turbocharging. Exhaust temperatures probably reached 2,000°F. Exhaust valves burned, valve seats warped, cylinder sleeves worked loose— even the magnetos didn't have enough voltage to give reliable ignition with the high cylinder heat and pressure. It was necessary to back off the waste-gate adjustment to 12—15-psi boost to keep running at all.

It was back to the drawing board for Leo Goossen. Valve-seat and cylinder-sleeve problems were cured easily by going back to iron blocks. This added 30 lbs., but everyone considered it a necessary move at the moment. Goossen modified the block-casting cores to provide additional water jacketing around the exhaust-valve seats. Finally Joe Hunt increased the output of his bolt-on Offy magneto to give reliable ignition to at least 9,000 rpm. As a little extra insurance, water flow was increased 20% to help cooling. Some engines were made with compression ratio reduced from 8-to-1 to 7-to-1. The same AiResearch turbocharger unit was used, so boost stayed at 17 psi and rated output was still 625 HP at 8,000 rpm.

It was immediately obvious in 1967 the turbo Offys were stronger. Lloyd Ruby qualified one in the 4th row at 165.2 mph and finished 7th. The turbos still had no appreciable performance advantage over the stronger unblown Fords; but they were gradually creeping up. They still weren't using the full 17-psi boost,

Bobby Unser was first to win an Indy race with a turbocharged engine in 1968. This is the installation. Crew chief Jud Phillips purposely restricted boost to 15 psi and 580 HP for reliability. It paid off. Francis photo, courtesy of IMS.

even in '67. The mechanics remained wary. No one had yet even scratched the performance potential of this mysterious little device. They didn't want to chance blowing up $20,000 engines. It seemed like the boys were even more afraid of turbos than they were of nitro fuels 15 years earlier. Even when Bobby Unser won the first race with a turbocharged Offy in 1968, he was using only 590 HP at 15-psi boost. That's what they dyno-tested in California before coming to Indy. The potential had barely been touched.

Perhaps the most clinching evidence that turbocharging was truly the wave of the future at Indianapolis was Ford engineers quietly went to work turbocharging the four-cam V-8 shortly after the '67 race—even before a turbo Offy had been in the winner's circle. Again, the handwriting was on the wall, but this time Ford's engine was in trouble!

The Ford people used several different ideas with their turbocharging project—perhaps just to be different from the Offy than to be better. They used a specially designed Schwitzer 3MD turbocharger unit, slightly larger than the AiResearch used on the Offy.

A modified Bendix aircraft fuel-injection system used a venturi-type air meter on the blower inlet to measure mass air flow. A portion of the fuel was introduced at the blower inlet—the rest at the eight individual ports. The mass-flow metering system gave much closer air/flow-ratio control than Hilborn's mechanical-injection system on the Offy. The complex inlet manifolding on the V-8 caused all kinds of fuel-distribution problems. Ford engineers worked with various manifold designs right up to two weeks before the 1968 race; but the turbocharged Fords never ran clean that year.

However the potential was there. The turbo Ford actually developed more power than the Offy at constant speed on the dyno—about 650 HP at 9,000 rpm on 25-psi boost. The cars had tremendous acceleration off the turns—which surprised everyone because of the Ford's extremely short 1.90-in. stroke. This acceleration boosted one test car to a peak straightaway speed of 214 mph! But they couldn't get the various race cars to run consistently clean over a full lap. When they tried over-rich fuel mixtures to

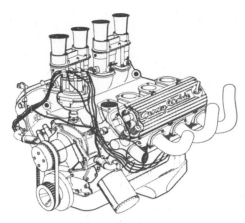

Dan Gurney used special Weslake cylinder heads on a 302 Ford small-block V-8 to build a very competitive stock-block car in 1968. Vertical intake ports were venturi shaped for a broad torque curve. Lucas fuel injection used slide throttles—Weber carburetors are shown. Well over 500 HP available on alky, with revs safe to 7,500 rpm. Drawing courtesy of HOT ROD Magazine.

Gurney ran exhaustive dyno tests to prove the reliability of this '68 Gurney-Weslake Ford stock-block. It paid off with 2nd place money.

cure flat spots in the acceleration, mileage dropped as low as 1.7 mpg. This would require two extra pit stops in the 500 miles. With reasonable fuel mixtures and 2.5 mpg, throttle response was erratic.

Mario Andretti did well to qualify in the 2nd row at 167.7 mph for the '68 race. But it was hopeless. He, and all the rest running turbo Fords, dropped out early with various engine troubles. Bobby Unser went on to win at record speed with a turbo Offy.

Ford started their turbocharger development two years too late!

STILL MORE STOCK-BLOCK ATTEMPTS

USAC officials have traditionally tried to encourage inexpensive stock-block engines in Championship racing every few years. The urge comes in cycles. They did it again in 1966 by raising the displacement limit for stock-block pushrod engines to 5 liters, or 305 cubic inches. Previously they had the same limit of 256 CID as unsupercharged overhead-cam engines. It was felt a little edge of about 50 CID might encourage the "hot rod" brotherhood, which by then had developed some truly sophisticated equipment for Detroit V-8 engines.

Actually only one really significant stock-block project came

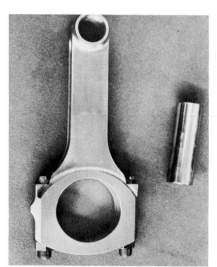

Carrillo billet-steel rods and ForgedTrue pistons were vital ingredients in all competitive stock-block engines in the '60s. In fact many Offy mechanics used them, too. Practically bulletproof when correctly used.

along in the next few years: Dan Gurney's modified 289-CID small-block Ford with specially designed Weslake cylinder heads. The way it happened, Gurney had contracted with the well-known British engine designer, Harry Weslake, to create a set of aluminum heads that would bolt on the Ford block. Its valves were to be operated through pushrods from the center camshaft. Gurney hoped Weslake's legendary airflow expertise would result in at

least 1.5 HP per CID on gasoline—with a broad torque curve. His intention was to sell the heads to low-budget racers for everything from drag racing to ski boats.

Harry Weslake did a great job. He kept port and valve sizes moderate to maintain high gas velocities for mid-range torque. By reducing curvature of the ports and giving them a slight venturi shape, they flowed twice as much air at high valve lifts as the stock Ford wedge heads. Lucas fuel

Workmanship on the 1968 STP-Lotus gas-turbine cars was exquisite. The cars were literally designed around the P&W gas turbine, with construction rugged enough to take the 500-mile pounding. It's tough to design for strength and minimum weight at the same time. Photo by Rowell.

Jack Adams' under-developed gas-turbine car in 1966 really started the "Granatelli" turbine era that took off the following year. The car never turned any fast laps, due to poor braking and throttle response. It was the car's acceleration that impressed Granatelli. Photo by Rowell.

injection with slide-throttle valves also helped the flow. Then the bottom end had to be beefed up to take sustained 8,000-rpm speeds. Gurney used all the accepted hot-rod goodies: ForgedTrue pistons, Carrillo billet rods, billet crank, dry-sump lubrication, etc. Dan admitted to $14,000 in the engine. It met his performance goals, giving 535 horses at 7,800 rpm on 10% nitro for qualifying and slightly over 500 HP on straight alky for the race. That was equal to the better four-cam unblown Fords. By gearing to run under 7,500 rpm in the race, Dan was optimistic that the package could be competitive.

It was. Gurney surprised even himself by qualifying his Weslake-powered Eagle in the 4th row at 166.5 mph for the 1968 race—continuing to finish 2nd, running on the same lap with Bobby Unser at the end. It was certainly the most successful stock-block attempt at Indy for many, many years. It encouraged USAC officials to raise

the stock-block displacement limit another notch to 320 cubic inches for the '69 race. They could foresee a flood of $5,000 engines that would draw a whole new element into Championship racing. But it never happened. By 1969 the turbo Offys and Fords were improved enough so even 320-cube stock-blocks didn't have a chance.

Gurney's Weslake star rose and fell in six months.

INVASION OF THE TURBINES

The idea of running a gas-turbine engine at Indianapolis didn't originate with Andy Granatelli. In the mid '50s a group of Boeing engineers installed one of their 175-HP gas turbines in a Kurtis race car and tested it briefly on the Indy track. In 1962 John Zink sponsored another Boeing-powered car at Indy. No less than Dan Gurney took it around for a few cautious laps with not much speed to show. Four years later Jack Adams took another shot with a General Electric turbine in a

Demler chassis, with Bill Cheesbourg driving. That car was eventually ruled unsafe by USAC officials. Owner Norm Demler claimed he was banned because the car was showing too much speed potential—up to 260 mph on the straights—and track officials felt there would be a hassle with other car owners if the car qualified. I don't know. The car never showed much lap-speed potential and cornering was erratic.

At any rate the Jack Adams Spl. started USAC officials thinking about how they would handle an invasion of gas-turbine engines. Up to then they never had any clause covering them in the rulebook. It was obvious that the logical way to limit a gas-turbine-type engine would be to restrict the air-inlet area because this type of engine burns a very lean air/fuel mixture, so lean that the majority of air passing through it never combines with fuel. They studied the G.E. turbine engine in the Adams car and noted it had an air-inlet area of 32 sq.in. It seemed

Andy Granatelli decided this Pratt & Whitney Model ST6 gas-turbine engine was ideal for an Indy car. It developed 550 HP at 6,200 rpm output speed and weighed 260 lbs. It was designed originally for helicopters and cost $100,000! Photo courtesy of STP.

logical that an arbitrary reduction of the area to, say, 25 sq.in. would at least get a handle on the gas-turbine thing for the 1967 race. And so it was.

Enter Andy Granatell. He was down after the '66 race—couldn't even get his 800-HP Novi-powered cars qualified that year. Chassis development had again left the mighty Novi engine in the dust. Andy needed a completely new type of power plant. He had watched the Adams-Demler project with great interest. Maybe a gas turbine was the answer for utilizing the superior traction of the Ferguson 4WD system.

Consider how a gas turbine engine works. Essentially there is some form of high-capacity rotary compressor—usually a centrifugal or axial-flow type—which takes in air and compresses it to a very high pressure of 100 to 150 psi. The fuel is sprayed into a series of burner cans where it is ignited by a plug for starting. Once started, ignition is continuous until the fuel supply is shut off. This combustion causes a tremendous expansion of heat and pressure. Hot gas expands through turbine discs to turn compressor and the wheels of the car through a reduction gear—the compressor and

turbine have to rotate at extreme speeds to work. That's about all there is to a gas-turbine engine. It's really quite simple.

There are several important advantages for a race car. One, the engine is very small and light in relation to the amount of power produced. Two, it has a rising torque curve—in fact, maximum torque of a conventional two-spool turbine occurs with the output shaft stalled. Neither a clutch or transmission is required. This rising torque curve means tremendous acceleration coming off the corners. One final advantage is a gas turbine burns petroleum-base fuels with high heat value (BTU's) per pound having potentially better fuel economy than low-heat alcohol fuels.

No wonder Granatelli was intrigued by the idea of using a gas-turbine engine in conjunction with four-wheel drive. One bug was that commercial gas turbines of the size needed cost over $100,000 at the time. He never could have swung a project on his own. But by that time Andy was an executive of the Studebaker Corp., and had their full financial backing. The die was finally cast when Andy located a Pratt & Whitney Model ST6 two-spool

engine, originally designed for helicopters. It had an air-inlet area of 21.9 sq.in.—well within the new 25-sq.in. limit. The engine weighed only 260 lbs. and was rated 550 HP at 6,230 rpm! It looked ideal for an Indianapolis car.

This was in the fall of 1966. There was never any thought of trying to install the gas-turbine engine in one of Andy's Kurtis cars—or even the big Ferguson. The engine was too long. An all-new car would have to be literally built around the engine. For this job Andy brought Ken Wallis over from England. Wallis was an experienced car builder. He was excited about the idea of combining the gas turbine with the traction and handling potential of 4WD. Due to the length of the engine, Wallis placed it on one side of the car, near the center. The driver would be seated opposite with a "backbone" type of frame going down the center of the car supporting engine, suspension and so forth. It was a unique idea which solved the engine-size problem very easily. It made for a very wide body, with lots of frontal area. But the light weight of the engine made it possible to hold overall dry weight to 1,400 lbs.

Granatelli's first gas-turbine car in 1967 used a massive "backbone" frame, with the driver seated on one side and the gas-turbine engine on the other. This was necessitated by the long engine length. Ken Wallis designed the car, using the Ferguson 4WD system. Photo courtesy of STP.

Gearbox transfer case, which then used a Morse chain—more efficient than gears. Photo courtesy of STP.

The open area in the center of the chassis provided convenient space to package the elaborate transmission and fore-and-aft driveline.

Accompanying pictures show some chassis details. The backbone frame was fabricated from sheet aluminum. Front and rear independent suspension was by double wishbones and inboard coil-over shock-absorber units in the British tradition. The Ferguson transmission was updated with a 3-inch Morse chain to offset the drive to one side—rather than the gears used in '64. The differential now incorporated torque-split gearing that could proportion the engine torque to front and rear wheels in any desired ratio. This was to assure maximum tractive thrust with varying front-rear weight distribution. Very little was known about the concept at that time, and as far as I know they ran with a 50/50 torque split in 1967. The locking feature of the differential was retained.

It's difficult to evaluate the true potential of this new STP turbine car—for the simple reason that Granatelli didn't want to let its full potential be shown for fear of

Instrument panel of the 1967 STP turbine car had elaborate gas-turbine speed, pressure and temperature monitoring. Photo courtesy of STP.

further USAC restrictions on future turbine cars. Word around the garage area was Granatelli's driver, Parnelli Jones, was instructed not to use any more performance than necessary to get comfortably into the starting field, and to win the race—go fast, but not *too* fast. This would seem to be confirmed by his 2nd-row qualifying average of 166.1 mph, and his modest 153-mph turn speeds—on a par with many of the better Offy-powered rear-engine cars. That was competitive, but not outstand-

ing performance.

As soon as the race started it was obvious that Jones had performance he hadn't used yet. He accelerated past the first two rows of cars on the back stretch of the first lap and started pulling away. From that point he completely dominated the race, losing the lead only shortly on his two fuel stops. He was leading 2nd-place A. J. Foyt by 43 seconds on the 197th lap when failure of the infamous $6 transmission bearing put him out of the race.

'68 STP-Lotus turbine cars were relatively long, with a general wedge shape for low drag and high-speed stability. Graham Hill, famed European Formula-1 driver, handled No.70. Photo courtesy of STP.

1968 Lotus-built STP turbine car had a different layout than the '67. Moving the driver far forward and extending car length allowed placing engine on center in the rear. Photo courtesy of STP.

The cars for 1968 were completely different and probably inherently faster. Colin Chapman was commissioned to build three new cars using the Ferguson 4WD system, but with the engine placed behind the driver and on center in the chassis to allow a more streamlined wedge shape. The combination seemed very well suited to the Indy track. Cornering was improved by running large tires on the front as well as the rear—rear-drive cars traditionally use much smaller tires on the front. Using the larger tires on the front was the obvious thing to do. The front end was more heavily loaded, both from engine, driver and driveline placement and tractive force from the engine, than the then-conventional rear-drive car. At any rate, driver Joe Leonard was clocked at a record 159 mph through turn-1 while setting a new lap record of 171.95 mph. The new STP-Lotus turbocars were definitely the most controversial and fastest cars on the track in 1968.

Incidentally, the other five turbocars entered in the '68 race didn't materialize. Three Shelby-sponsored cars built by Ken Wallis had 4WD and used GE T-58 turbines that were squeezed down from 32 sq.in. inlet area. It was discovered these engines were fitted with inlets that could be opened remotely. Track officials "requested" that the cars be removed from the track. The Jack Adams team used Allison turbines with only 12.5 sq.in. in original form. But HP was less than 400 and the cars were not even brought to the speedway.

Meanwhile the three new STP-Lotus cars were getting a lot of attention, and after high qualifying speeds by the other two drivers—Graham Hill and Art Pollard—it was generally concluded that they would win the bulk of the prize money. In fact the rest of the brotherhood raised quite a stink about this entirely new type of engine. The general feeling was gas turbines should not race against piston engines at all. It was obvious that USAC was in trouble regardless of how the race turned out.

Gas-turbine power had arrived at Indianapolis. In the next year there was an explosion of development activity. Nine gas-turbine-powered cars were entered in the 1968 race—in the face of another radical reduction of air-inlet area to 16 sq.in. by USAC officials. They figured their arbitrary figure of 25 sq.in. set in 1967 gave a gas turbine too much advantage over a 170-CID supercharged piston engine. Not so much on top-end horsepower, but on mid-range torque. It was obvious that Parnelli Jones' big advantage in the '67 race was in superior acceleration off the turns and in traffic. Restricting the air-inlet area another 40% or so was a frantic attempt to keep the piston-engine owners happy without completely killing the new gas-turbine contingent that was generating so much valuable public interest.

Meanwhile Granatelli was so steamed about the new air-inlet limit he brought a court suit against USAC for obsoleting his Pratt & Whitney engine after only one year of service. He couldn't make it stick. The court ruled that USAC had the right to make their own rules for their own racing circuit. Granatelli gave in—tapped the Studebaker bank account again—and commissioned P&W engineers to modify the ST6 engine to operate efficiently at 15.9 sq.in. of air-inlet area. They say this work on the four engines that were bought for the '68 STP turbocars cost over $200,000. Compressor-blade angles had to be changed, the inlet annulus necked down, and the turbine had to be recalibrated to operate with less gas flow. Granatelli said considerable horsepower was lost with

1968 STP Lotus front- and rear-suspension, brake and drive components could be interchanged front-to-back. Note the hub carriers and upper control arms. A link from the upper control arm to the hub carrier replaced the steering linkage when the two assemblies were used at the rear (right). Photo courtesy of STP.

the reduced inlet area—how much he never said. But the performance of the cars didn't confirm this. They were *faster*!

Well, a gas turbine didn't win the race. Two dropped out with fuel-pump failure and Graham Hill hit the wall. Furthermore, the performance superiority of gas-turbine cars over the best piston-engine cars was not as clearcut in 1968 as it might have been in '67. The 16-sq.in. inlet-area limit apparently was somewhere near being fair. Joe Leonard was leading the race when his fuel pump failed, but the lead was swapped several times during the race and he didn't seem to have any clear performance edge over piston-engine drivers like Bobby Unser, Dan Gurney, Lloyd Ruby, etc.

It came out later how the cars were able to turn such high qualifying speeds. The trick was to screw up the fuel valve so the turbine engines "idled" at 80% of full speed. This gave them a much quicker, stronger jump when the throttle was opened coming off the turns. You have to realize that the power output of a turbine engine falls off roughly as the cube of RPM. Thus a 20% reduction from maximum RPM—in this case from 37,000-rpm turbine speed to about 30,000 rpm—reduced power by about half. This high-rpm idle meant entering the turns with the

Joe Leonard set a new Indy lap record of 171.95 mph in the '68 STP-Lotus No.60 turbocar, clocking 159 mph through the number-1 turn. He had the fastest combination on the track that year. Photo courtesy of STP.

engine still putting 200—250 HP to the wheels. Doing this was possible by having the driver lift early and get on the brakes hard approaching the turns. Of course this was *very* hard on the brakes. The disc-brake pads lasted only a few laps and it was necessary to circulate the brake fluid through a special radiator. A tremendous amount of heat was generated throughout the car.

But you can see what the trick did for lap averages. Big tires all around—plus 4WD—allowed very high turn speeds. Then response

was instantaneous when the driver would hit the throttle off the turns—and this surge carried through to peak speeds well over 200 mph on the long straights. Then scrub off your speed with the brakes, into another turn, off the brakes . . .

Gas-turbine cars were exciting at Indianapolis, but they were never meant to be. Under intense pressure from the piston-engine contingent, the USAC Contest Board voted another reduction in gas-turbine inlet area to 12 sq.in. for the 1969 season. That did it.

Nobody felt any commercially available gas-turbine engine could be made competitive under those restrictions. Granatelli first screamed, then sulked. His were the last gas-turbine-powered cars to compete on the "bricks."

PEAK PERFORMANCE

At the end of this time period being analyzed, 1968, it becomes apparent that the STP-Lotus turbocars were the fastest Indy cars yet—at least with the engine-idle setting at 80% of maximum speed. Under these conditions both Leonard and Graham Hill lapped in the high 171-mph bracket with turn speeds at 158—159 mph and peak straightaway speeds a little over 200. They could maintain this pace for only a few laps until the brake pads wore down. Meanwhile the faster turbocharged Offys and Fords seemed 1—2 mph slower on both lap average and turn speed, though they were just as fast on the straights. When an Offy would come off a corner beside one of the Lotus turbocars, the gas turbine would out-accelerate the Offy for a few-hundred feet—but then the Offy would gain a few car lengths at the peak of the power curve, just before shutting off for the next turn. The net effect over one full lap would put the turbocar ahead by several lengths.

Under race conditions there wasn't that much difference in performance. That is, the gas turbines had to be adjusted back to idle settings of 20—40% of maximum speed to save the brakes. Off-the-turn acceleration was still potentially better than the piston cars. But with the inherent gas-turbine *lag*—the time necessary to speed up the compressor after the throttle was opened—there wasn't any big gain for the first few-hundred feet of the straight. The driver could compensate somewhat by punching the throttle early, before he wanted the extra power. But this took a lot of practice and inherent skill. It would have been interesting to see how

MG Liquid Suspension Special of the mid '60s, built by Joe Huffaker, used unique gas-liquid springs from the MG Mini passenger car. The spring cushioning and fluid damping were combined in one unit—heavier, more complex and tougher to package than the coil-over shocks.

"Ducktail" body was popular in the mid '60s, before we got down to serious aerodynamic development. Swept-up tail acted as a little spoiler, increasing rear-wheel loading. Electrical cord exiting the right of the transaxle is supplying power to an oil-sump heater—oil is warmed before the engine is fired. Photo by Rowell.

different drivers might have adapted to driving gas-turbine cars. With their brief showing at Indy, only a handful of drivers were ever privileged to even try out gas-turbine power. Who knows what Foyt or an Unser or Johncock might have done with one??

Four-wheel-drive, in itself, did not show any conclusive performance advantage in the 1960's. Its good showing on the turbine cars did encourage several teams to build 4WD piston-engine cars in the late '60s. Eric Broadley built several 4WD Lola cars, and Colin Chapman built a new 4WD Lotus design for STP after the gas-turbine cars were ruled out. These

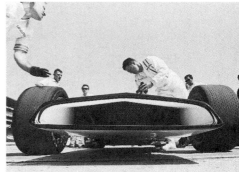

Although gas turbines were effectively banned after '68 by USAC's maximum 12-sq.in. intake-area rule, Granatelli didn't give up on the 4WD Lotus chassis. Here's Vince overlooking the installation of a stock-block Chrysler in the Lotus chassis—it didn't work out. Note the crates of retired gas turbines stacked against the wall in the background. Photo courtesy of STP.

Noses came in all shapes. The wedge-shaped body was the plan in the late '60s, trying to get aerodynamic downforce with minimum drag. Chapman's STP Lotus turbocars in 1968 were prime examples.

4WD cars never showed any really measurable lap-speed improvement over comparable rear-drive cars. Tire traction had been improved so much by then that there was no need for the extra traction to transmit 600 or 700 HP. Then there is the additional weight, driveline power loss and inertia, and complexity of a 4WD system to consider.

It's interesting to study the remarkable improvements in lap performance and race-car technology during this short six-year span in the mid '60s. We made the transition to rear-engine cars, four-wheel independent suspension and more advanced high-traction tires. Then there was the effect of increased engine power and torque with turbocharging. Compare the figures in this table for a typical Offy-powered car at the beginning and end of the '63—'68 period:

Year	HP	Wt (lbs.)	Lap	MPH Turn	Straight
1963	400	1600	149	140	160
1968	650	1400	169	156	200

This was more performance progress in a six-year period than Indianapolis history had ever seen. And this was just a warmup for the development of the '70's . . .

8
TURBOS, TIRES AND TUNNELS THE ROARING '70s

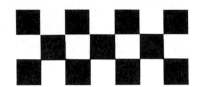

'79 Chaparral 2K exemplifies the developments of the '70s; wings, ground effects, engineered chassis and turbocharged Cosworths. Photo by Ed Ingalls.

I'll begin my analysis of the 1970's in 1969 because a couple of rule changes in '69 had considerable influence on later developments. One was a reduction in the maximum-allowable engine displacement for supercharged overhead-cam engines from 2.8 to 2.65 liters, or about 171 to 162 cubic inches, respectively. The idea was to give the less-costly unsupercharged engines a better chance against the turbochargers without requiring radical changes in existing turbocharged engines. The rule did not accomplish its purpose. Turbocharged engines were still 100 to 200 hp stronger, even though their larger unblown cousins had up to 256 cubes. What the rule did accomplish was to encourage a rethink on bore/ stroke ratios of the Ford and Offy turbo engines, eventually leading to extended rev ranges and improved durability.

The other important rule change was an increase in allowable wheel-rim width from the old 9.5-in. standard front and rear rim width to 10 in. front and 14 in. rear. This was done at the request of the tire companies. They were pretty well stymied in tire development with the 9.5-in. rims. Tread-width increases of 1 to 2 in. by both Firestone and Goodyear in 1968 failed to improve lap speeds or turn speeds appreciably on comparable cars. It was obvious to everyone they had reached the point of diminishing returns on increasing tread width with the 9.5-in rim width. When USAC officials agreed to the big jump in rim width for the '69 race, both Firestone and Goodyear tire engineers promised substantial improvements in grip, wear, cornering stability and maneuverability in traffic.

It is interesting to note USAC banned 4WD cars after the '69 race. They had been under development for five years and hadn't really shown any con-clusive advantages in cornering or straightaway grip, or traffic maneuverability. It was generally agreed that swift improvements in tire grip during the '60s eliminated the advantage of 4WD. Besides, the complex driveline was extremely costly. Because USAC officials considered it a technological blind alley, they simply removed the temptation to experiment!

Indy race officials have often been criticized for this kind of thinking. There's no question that they've killed a lot of interesting technical development down through the years, usually in the interests of safety or lower costs for the little guys. I haven't liked everything they've done. But the fact remains—the Indianapolis 500 is the most famous and successful auto race in the world. The guys who ran it must have been doing something right!

Now let's look at how the boys went faster and faster in the 70's . . .

1971 M16 McLaren was a "milestone" in every sense of the term. A lot of attention was paid to aerodynamics. The turbocharger packaged low and the rear wing was separated from the body to get maximum "clean" airflow under as well as over it. Twin radiators positioned in side pods allowed for a wedge-shaped nose. Front-suspension coil-over shock absorbers were mounted inboard to further drag reduction. Peter Revson and the M16 were the fastest combination on the track that year.

Author Roger Huntington (left) talks with Dan Gurney prior to the '71 race. I've been at the track each year for the last 30 years, gathering material and pictures for magazine articles and this book.

A BREAKTHROUGH IN CHASSIS DESIGN

There hadn't been anything really earthshaking in Indy chassis design after Britishers Colin Chapman and Eric Broadley introduced the rear-engine monocoque car to the American scene in the mid '60s. Our top car builders quickly duplicated the concept—Rolla Vollstedt, Fred Gerhardt, A. J. Watson, Joe Huffaker, Dan Gurney—and improved on it in some respects. It was mentioned in the last chapter that our rear-engine monocoque cars generally performed as good as the British examples—once our builders got the hang of the construction. In fact, with the design assistance of Phil Remington, Dan Gurney's Eagle cars were in as much demand as the British Lotus and Lola in the late '60s.

Admittedly, it was another British designer/builder team—Gordon Coppuck and Bruce McLaren—that must be credited with the next major breakthrough in Indy chassis design. This was the 1971 McLaren M16. No car in Indianapolis history ever had such a wide margin of performance over its opponents. With drivers

Mark Donohue, Peter Revson and Denny Hulme, the cars were 3—4 mph faster than their immediate opposition and 8—9 mph faster than the best hardware in 1970. Donohue broke the 180-mph barrier practicing for the '71 race and was clocked at 163 mph through turn-1. That was 4 mph faster than any previous car. Furthermore the car's good aerodynamics allowed him to accelerate to nearly 220 mph on the straights on his record laps. No one else was close.

Several new design features contributed to the sudden surge of performance. It was then thought that the key was grouping the major masses of the car more closely around CG than previous rear-engine designs. By extending the wheelbase to 104 in. it was possible to position the driver forward 10 in. and the engine forward 4 in. Putting most of the fuel tankage in the center of the car near the CG meant there was little change in front/rear weight distribution as fuel was used. Also the nose-mounted radiator was replaced by two smaller radiators in pods on each side of the car. This not only moved a major weight mass toward the center, it helped

streamlining by giving the body a general wedge contour as viewed from the top or side.

I've mentioned before this business of reducing the polar moment—or "flywheel effect"—of a car by grouping the major masses closer together. This makes a car more responsive, or less resistant to changes in direction. The German Auto-Unions of the '30s were low-polar-moment cars, but were very skittish. Modern chassis, high-grip tires and relatively smooth tracks changed this. Responsiveness of the rear-engine cars of the '60s with their major masses located closer together improved considerably over conventional front-engine, rear-drive cars. So reducing polar moment was a major objective in the early '70s. This trend reversed somewhat in the late '70s because the cars became "twitchy"—too responsive. Rear weight bias also underworked the front tires. But advancements in all areas were being made—particularly aerodynamics. Engine and chassis improvements continued. The 1971 McLaren M16 seemed to have everything right—its handling outclassed everything.

First aerodynamic restrictions in 1969 limited total front wingspan to 9 in. A few cars used these rudimentary wings with adjustable pitch for front-end downforce.

Evolution in aerodynamics. Shown are the 1971, 1972 and 1973 front rows (top to bottom). Note the change in wings and other aerodynamic improvements. Pole speed increased from 178.7 mph to 198.4 mph during this period. The big increase was from '71 to '72. Speeds jumped from 178.7 to 195.9 mph because of the rear-wing location— higher and farther to the rear. At no other period of Indianapolis history has there been that much performance increase so quickly.

Bruce McLaren and Gordon Coppuck were the toast of the Speedway in '71—not to mention their stature in Formula-1 and Can-Am road racing. The little British company was flooded with orders for cars for the '72 season. They had to set up shop in the Detroit area to keep up with their multiple racing endeavors. Also, because of its overwhelming success, the McLaren M16 became the general pattern for the top Indy cars used by all the builders for the next four or five years.

It's interesting to note that Indy chassis design was gradually slipping out of the hands of car builders and into the hands of engineers and design specialists. The engineered designs introduced by the British required a working knowledge of technical concepts such as roll centers, roll rates, bump steer, scrub radius, polar moment, lever ratios, etc.

You couldn't just weld up a combination of tubes and joints and expect to be successful against the competition. It might, but more than likely it wouldn't. The investment was too much to risk. So the car builders brought in specialists to tell them what to build. The names might not be familiar to you: Roman Slobodynsky, Phil Remington, Bob Riley, Maurice Phillippe, Geoffrey Ferris and Gordon Coppuck. I can assure you these men and others had more influence on Indy-car design in the '70s than the men who did the welding and cutting.

PUTTING AERODYNAMICS TO WORK

The idea of using air flowing over a moving car to force it down against the track to improve cornering did not originate at Indianapolis. The first rudimentary airfoils—inverted wings—

were seen on Formula-1 and Can-Am cars in the '60s. Texan Jim Hall went a step further on his Can-Am car by rigging two engine-driven blowers to create a vacuum under the car, sealed by side skirts that touched the ground. The arrangement was very effective, both for braking as well as cornering and acceleration. So effective, in fact, that it was quickly banned!

It was inevitable that aerodynamic downforce would be used at the brickyard. Colin Chapman's wedge-shaped STP-Lotus turbine cars in 1968 were an attempt to create a small amount of downforce with minimum drag at high speeds. The first rudimentary front wings appeared the following year—with the general wedge-shaped body then well established. By 1970 we saw the first hints of crude rear wings on the upper part of the body.

Riley-designed '73 Coyote wind-tunnel-test scale model, track testing at Phoenix, and A.J. Foyt with finished product. Note slight changes between model and final car: front-wheel fairings, side-mounted radiator-housing shape and added engine cover. Extreme effort was made to reduce height of monocoque structure, or "tub," to reduce drag and increase airflow to rear wing. The Ford's relatively large front profile—particularly the induction system—limited what could be done in this respect. Note beginnings of ground effects here—small skirts on the sides of the tub and air intake under the nose. Photos courtesy of Bob Riley.

At first USAC officials tried to discourage this type of aerodynamic development, feeling it might lead to unpredictable lift and instability at 200-mph speeds. Their first attempt to control it by rule in 1969 limited total body height, including any aerodynamic devices, to 28-in. above the track surface. Overall span of front airfoils was limited to 9 in. on each side, and not to extend past the tire center. It was felt that these limitations would require any wings to be incorporated as part of the body shell, not separate add-on devices.

The milestone M16 of 1971 was designed to meet these rules. Designer Gordon Coppuck achieved a greater aerodynamic effect within the framework of the rules than USAC officials ever thought possible. The "secret" was a rear-mounted wing with the turbocharger system and body work designed to allow maximum airflow under it. The rear wing was integrated within the body design, as the rules intended, but set up in such a way that would more than double downforce on the rear tires. All previous cars were just directing the air over the top of the wing. They were more spoilers than wings. A spoiler gets its downforce by merely deflecting or daming air. A true airfoil, or wing, depends on suction, or low pressure, on the side of the desired direction of "lift."

Firestone engineers instrumented one of the M16 cars following the '71 race and measured a total aerodynamic downforce of 600—700 lbs. at 200 mph—nearly half the car weight! There's no question that this extra tire loading against the track was the major factor in Mark Donohue's higher turn speeds when qualifying in '71. His average in turn-1 jumped from the previous high of 159 mph to 163 mph. Because aerodynamic forces vary as the square of speed, his downforce at 163 mph should have been about 450 lbs. This would just about account for the increased lateral grip necessary to go 4—5 mph faster through the turn—without any increase in static tire grip.

Designer Maurice Phillippe tried auxiliary diagonal front wings in addition to the usual horizontal airfoils on Parnelli Jones' 1972 cars. No conclusive aerodynamic benefit was proved then, but one feature picked up later was the tips of the "structural" diagonal wings acted as upper control-arm inner-pivot mounts. This divorced the body cross-section or frontal area from the upper-control arm mounts—an important feature later when more room was needed between tire and body for air flow to side-mounted radiator and ground-effects ducts.

Phillippe/Parnelli car used large midship-mounted diagonal wings which also housed the oil coolers. The plan was to eliminate the conventional rear wing to lower overall drag. An empty wing mounting hole (below the e in Samsonite), remounted oil cooler below it and added conventional wing (not pictured) testify to the effectiveness of these "different" wings. Low-drag NACA type air duct, developed for high-speed aircraft, was widely used at Indy in the early '70s.

Let me explain this. The centrifugal force the tires have to resist in a flat turn depends on car weight. The maximum grip a given set of tires can develop depends on the force pressing them against the track—and this, in turn, depends on the weight of the car *plus or minus* the vertical aerodynamic forces—they can be down or up. This is why a car corners faster by just adding wings to increase downforce, without any improvement in tire grip. Without areodynamics, wings in this case, the only way you can go faster is to improve the tires. When you improve tires and aerodynamics at the same time, as they were doing at Indy in the early '70s, lap averages increase dramatically.

We saw another big breakthrough in 1972 when USAC opened up the rules on wings. They no longer tried to ban separate wings, but limited their size and placement. Rear-wing height was limited to 32 in. above the bottom of the main body. Its width could not exceed the car's rear track width—distance between the centers of the two rear tires. Its rear edge could not be more than 42 in. behind the rear-wheel cen-

terline and overall car length could not exceed 180 in. It was felt that these liberalized rules would give the guys room to experiment without encouraging freakish and possibly unstable cars.

Under these new '72 rules, Dan Gurney's Eagle suddenly emerged as the car to beat. His designers—Roman Slobodynsky, Dick Lindhurst and Gary Wheeler—took full advantage of the rules by using the full 180 in. of permitted length. They put the front and rear wings at the extreme ends of the 15-ft. span, with the rear wheel positioned to put the trailing edge of the rear wing 42 in. aft of the wheel center. This gave both front and rear wings more leverage to apply downforce to the wheels at each end of the car.

To explain: Assume the center of pressure on the rear wing was 36 in. behind the rear-wheel center. With a wheelbase of 108 in., a rear-wing downforce of 500 lbs. would apply an additional load of about 670 lbs. on the rear tires due to the leverage effect of the 36-in. moment arm. It also lifts 170 lbs. off the front wheels—which was restored by the smaller front wings. Although the front

Restrictions on aerodynamic devices were relaxed in 1972, and the "wing era" started. Dan Gurney used a large outrigger rear wing—end plates and all—on his Eagles that year. They were the fastest cars on the track. With the wing in "clean" air and the leverage effect of its positioning, increased downforce on the rear wheels made the Eagle a superior cornering car.

wings would in turn unload the rear tires a small amount, the net effect was about a 2-to-1 proportioning of rear-to-front downforce.

No extensive wind tunnel tests were made on the '72 Eagle, so we don't know exactly how front and rear aerodynamic forces were distributed. It was estimated that the total downforce at 200 mph was nearly equal to the dry weight of the car, or nearly 1,500 lbs. This is entirely conceivable with inverted

Gurney also increased aerodynamic benefit at the front of his '72 Eagle by extending the nose, then mounting front wings of full-allowed span—to the center of the front tires. Total downforce at 200 mph was nearly equal to car weight.

In the mid '70s there was a trend toward the "sports-car nose" to get downforce with less drag. This resulted in massive shovel-like noses like the one on this Lola. Photo courtesy of Goodyear.

Rear-wing structure cantilevered off the transaxle of Mark Donohue's McLaren. Wings were rigged so pitch could be easily adjusted in the pits.

high-lift airfoils in relatively clean air. Less turbulence from the body resulted in smooth air flow both over and under the wing. The Eagle had about 6.5 sq.ft. of wing area in back and 2.5—3.0 sq.ft. in front. With a modest lift (or downforce) coefficient of 1.5 for the air-foil section, this much wing area could provide 1,400—1,500 lbs. of downforce at 200 mph.

With these kinds of downforces at work, cornering speeds jumped radically in 1972. In fact Dan Gurney's top driver, Bobby Unser, was clocked at an astonishing 183 mph through turn-1 when setting the new lap record of 196.68 mph! That was a full 20 mph faster than Donohue had gone the previous year in the M16 McLaren. The increase was almost entirely due to the additional downforce from the more effective wings on chassis that took full advantage of them. If you determine the tire grip necessary to go through the turn at 183 mph— allowing for the additional downforce—it comes out almost the same as Donohue required to go 163 mph with less than half the downforce in '71.

Donohue could have increased his lap speed 15 mph with the same wing used by Unser—by just taking advantage of the additional wing loading!

Any time lift is generated, *induced drag* is also generated. It simply "comes with the farm." How much drag a wing has is determined by its *drag coefficient.* For instance, a wing with a 0.05 drag coefficient will have 50 lbs. of drag when it is generating 1,000 lbs. of lift. Drag coefficient multiplied by lift gives drag. This means maximum straightaway speed is not going to be as fast with the same amount of horsepower. Unser could only hit a peak of 206 mph on his record laps, compared with 217 mph for Donohue in '71. Here was the strange situation of a car lapping 15 mph faster while peaking 10 mph slower down the straights. Like this:

	Turn	MPH Straight	Avg.
Donohue, '71	163	217	179
Unser, '72	183	206	196

It proved dramatically what every Indianapolis mechanic had known for years: Getting through the turns fast helps the lap average more than a high peak speed on the straights.

Some interesting aerodynamic tests were reported on the Bryant team car Rolla Vollstedt built to the '72 rules. The airfoils were tested in the Boeing wind tunnel in Seattle, Wash. At 200-mph air speed the rear wing produced 860 lbs. downforce with 48 lbs. drag— while the two front foils totalled 305-lbs. and 19-lbs. Vollstedt's car wasn't as aerodynamically efficient as Gurney's Eagles; but these figures give you some idea of how the forces were distributed front and rear. You can see they were proportioned roughly 2/3rds rear and 1/3rd front.

Also notice the total drag figure of 67 lbs. Theoretically that would

'72 Antares Manta. The plan was to duct the radiators so the expanding heated air gave a "jet assist." According to calculations, the car was capable of 200-mph laps, but after extensive modifications Roger McCluskey could only manage 182.7 mph for qualifying. Bobby Unser won the pole at 195.9 mph. Photo by Rowell.

McLaren took full advantage of the relaxed wing rules in 1972 to develop a very fast car around their new "low-polar-moment" theme. Gary Bettenhausen qualified this one in the 2nd row at 188.9 mph. Photo by Rowell.

Evidence of the streamlining trend in the mid '70s was modifying the Offy induction system to put the main intake-manifold plenum above the engine, with the individual port stacks sweeping down in a curve. This permitted a smaller body fairing behind the driver to enclose the plumbing. Photo by Rowell.

Maximum allowable rear wingspan was cut to 36 inches in 1974 in an attempt to restrict speeds. 200-mph lap averages were making Speedway officials uneasy. As suspected, the cars showed up with a more effective wing; the Liebeck airfoil, or "banana wing." Its high lift coefficient and large end plates made up for the loss in real wingspan. Photo by Rowell.

'74 version of the '73 Coyote. A.J. Foyt caused no end of consternation around the garages when he covered the air duct in the nose and radiators at the sides of his car. Everyone wondered what he was hiding—nothing more than a "psych job." Regardless, he was 2 mph faster than anyone else that year. Photo by Rowell.

More aerodynamics of the mid '70s: Narrow cockpit and engine cover. Roman Slobodynski designed this car for Lindsey Hopkins—Roger McCluskey driving. Photo by Rowell.

When the '69 rules allowed 14-in. rear-wheel rim widths, tire treads quickly reached the same width. Goodyear introduced this 15-in.-wide rear tire in 1972, but it was not widely used. Most teams felt they got the best traction/handling compromise with 14-in. tires on the back and 10-in. at the front. Photo courtesy of Goodyear.

Ultimate expression of the "shovel-nose" theme. Small wing above the nose gave additional downforce, and made it possible to "tune" handling by adjusting wing angle. This is the Bob Riley-designed, Bignotti-built '78 Wildcat driven by Gordon Johncock. Photo by Rowell.

take 36 HP to push through the air at 200 mph. This explains why these elaborate wings reduced car speed on the straights.

As it turned out, this type of aerodynamic development reached a quick peak in the '72–'74 period. There were some refinements after the initial surge of "big wings" in '72: airfoil contours, wingtip plates, adjustable flaps, slots, trailing-edge lips, etc. It wasn't possible to get large increases in aerodynamic forces without more wing area—not permitted by the rules. USAC almost immediately acted to squeeze down rear-wing size when they realized what tremendous forces were being developed. In 1974 they stipulated a 36-in. maximum rear-wing width—almost 20 in. narrower than some of the big wings used in '72–'73.

Cornering speeds peaked temporarily in the 186–188-mph range in 1973. They fell off a little when the smaller wings came in '74—later tire, chassis and other aerodynamic developments offset this. These speeds came back up

into the 185–190 mph range in 1980 on the fastest cars.

You can see the concept of aerodynamic downforce had a quick and violent evolution at Indianapolis. I think it's safe to say no single development before or since had such a potent effect on lap average. Putting air to work proved to be dramatic. You can't help but compare this concept with the idea of reducing aerodynamic drag, which had such a miserable evolution in the mid '50s.

TIRES FOR THE JOB

I mentioned earlier that a major rule change in 1969 increased maximum wheel-rim width from 9.5 in. to 10 in. for front wheels and to 14 in. for rears. This gave the tire companies a whole new lease on life for increasing tread widths and improving grip.

The immediate result was a general increase of 1 to 2 in. in tire-section and tread widths and another reduction of profile ratios from around 0.40 to 0.35 or less. The most popular Firestone and Goodyear tire sizes in '69 had

front tread widths of about 10 in. and rears about 14 in. Firestone offered a wider 15-in. rear tread that year, but few teams tried it. They seemed satisfied with the handling of the 14-in. size. Ever since the revolution in tire widths and profile ratios in the early '60s, racing men seemed to prefer tread widths roughly equal to the wheel-rim width. It was an easy rule of thumb to follow and tires seemed to work well in that relationship— especially with ratios below 0.50.

This extra 1 to 2 in. of rubber on the track helped cornering speeds. The faster Offys in 1968 were hitting around 155 mph in turn-1 with 9 and 12-in. treads front and rear. In '69 they increased this to 157–158 mph with 10 and 14-in. treads—with no other significant changes. That may not seem like much in comparison with the 5 and 10-mph speed increases achieved with wings in later years, but this slight increase indicated a tire-grip improvement of about 0.10—a very satisfactory annual improvement factor to a tire engineer.

Section of typical mid '70s Indy tire showing the extremely flat, squatty contour. The aspect ratio, or height-to-width ratio, was about 0.35 when mounted and inflated.

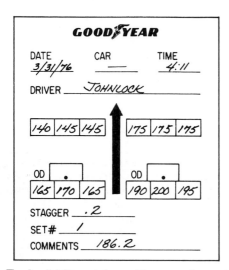

GOODYEAR

DATE	CAR	TIME
3/31/76	—	4:11

DRIVER _JOHNLOCK_

| 140 | 145 | 145 | | 175 | 175 | 175 |

| OD | . | | | OD | . | |
| 165 | 170 | 165 | | 190 | 200 | 195 |

STAGGER .2

SET# 1

COMMENTS 186.2

Typical data card used to record tread temperatures immediately after a run to assist in setting up a chassis. Temperatures are measured at three points across the width of the tire. Because the right-rear tire is loaded the most, it usually runs hottest as shown here. Conversely, the left-front runs coolest.

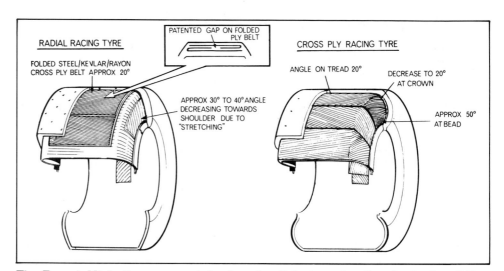

The French Michelin company introduced radial-ply racing tires in the late '70s. They used a patented fold-ply belt construction. This may be the next major change in Indy tires as Michelin had success with it in Formula 1—even though Alan Jones won the 1980 World Championship on non-radial Goodyears!

From the early '70s on, there weren't any significant changes in Indy-tire sizes, tread widths and profile ratios. When the widths again stabilized at 10 and 14 in. front and rear, there was no place to go on further tread width increases for improved performance. Grip improvements after that were achieved through general inflation-pressure reductions from the 30-psi range to 20—26 psi. Softer carcass constructions were also used to get the tire to "work" more and rubber compounds were made "stickier" by using more oil and resins in the mix. It was possible to do this after maximum fuel-tank capacity was lowered to 40 gal. and the cars had to make six or eight pit stops in the 500 miles. Tire wear was no longer a factor and the companies could

use very sticky compounds that would only last 100—200 miles. This improved tire grip more than the last 2 in. of tread-width increase!

Relating all this in terms of effective grip, coefficients increased from about 1.35 at the start of the tire revolution in the mid '60s to a peak of maybe 1.55 in the late '70s. This latter coefficient is required for 188-mph cornering with the downforces of 1980 aerodynamics.

Admittedly tire development has slowed down in recent years. Firestone pulled out of the Indy scene in 1975, after fighting the good fight for more than 55 years. The hassle of battling Goodyear was getting too expensive, especially weighed against the tighter economic conditions expe-

rienced by the tire industry due to rising gas prices and slumping car sales.

Don't you know, once Goodyear had the Indy scene to themselves, tire development slowed. Same deal as when Firestone had it to themselves in the '40s and '50s. When there's no competition there's little incentive to move forward. Goodyear is supplying good, safe, long-wearing, efficient tires today, but they aren't changing much from year to year. The next big change will undoubtedly be a switch from bias-ply to radial construction—just as happened in Formula 1 following Goodyear's departure.

SCREWING UP THE BOOST

I mentioned earlier that reducing the displacement of

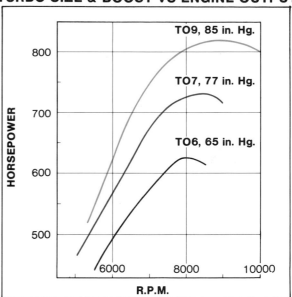

By the early '70s, the Hilborn fuel-injection system for turbocharged Offys had been updated to inject fuel on both sides of the throttle butterfly. Also a large-volume "plenum" was used on the intake stacks to damp air surge. These changes improved throttle response off the corners.

Turbocharger design had a tremendous influence on performance. These curves show the increase in Offy power with three AiResearch turbos used in the late '60s and early '70s.

supercharged overhead-cam race engines by 9 CID in 1969 had no effect in giving unsupercharged engines a better chance. In fact, the output of the turbocharged Offy was increased substantially at that time by using the larger Series TEO67 AiResearch turbocharger unit. It had approximately 3/8-in. larger impeller and turbine diameters and more turbine-nozzle area than the TEO6. It could pump 15—20% more air at 80,000 rpm instead of 100,000. The reduction in rotor-tip speed gave better compression efficiency and less exhaust back pressure. Result: Power up from 625 HP at 8,000 rpm on 17-psi boost to 730 HP at 8,500 rpm on 23 psi. This was with the Offy's cylinder bore reduced to 4.030 in. to arrive at 159 CID.

What they did was to provide a better "match" between the turbocharger and engine. This is a vital factor in turbocharger work, whether it's on a race car or a diesel tractor. Compressor- and turbine-flow parameters must be carefully matched to engine flow, or a monstrosity results. The compressor must not be allowed to get

into a "surge" or "stall" condition within the engine operating range, and the turbine nozzle must be sized to get quick mid-range response without excessive top-end back-pressure. It's even possible for a turbine to "choke" at the top end—where nozzle velocity reaches sonic, and you can't get any more gas through the turbine regardless of the pressure differential. All kinds of weird gas-flow situations can occur with a mismatched turbocharger.

In this case, obviously the original Series TEO6 turbocharger was a marginal match on the 168-CID Offy. When engine revs and manifold pressures were increased just a little, it went into a very inefficient operating range. The larger Series TEO67 gave another 100 HP with only a small increase in boost. Maximum-boost potential with the TEO67 was at least 30 psi. The 23 psi quoted above was the rating point of this particular turbocharger model: 80 lbs. of air per minute at 80,000 rpm at 77 *inches of mercury* discharge pressure.

Perhaps I should start right now to refer to boost pressure in terms

of inches of mercury (in.Hg.) *absolute pressure*. Normal atmospheric pressure at sea level will support a column of mercury 29.92 in. high, or roughly 30 in. This is equivalent to the standard 14.7-psi atmospheric pressure. 1-psi equals roughly 2 in.Hg. pressure. When I speak of manifold "boost pressure" it's normally understood to mean the positive pressure *above atmospheric*. But when I use the inches-of-mercury scale we generally state the total pressure above zero pressure, or the absolute pressure. Thus to convert absolute pressure in inches to boost in psi, subtract 30 in. first, then divide by two. For instance 70 in.Hg. absolute manifold pressure would be 70 in.Hg.—30 in.Hg. = 40 in.Hg., divided by 2 = 20-psi boost.

From now on I'll refer to it correctly as 70 in. manifold absolute pressure, or MAP. It's not 70 in. boost. It would be 40 in. boost, or 20 psi. Confusing?

One characteristic of turbocharger performance must be thoroughly understood before attempting to analyze the output

Some teams tried to utilize the velocity energy of exhaust gases to improve turbine efficiency by routing individual exhaust pipes to the turbine. Dyno tests showed some benefit.

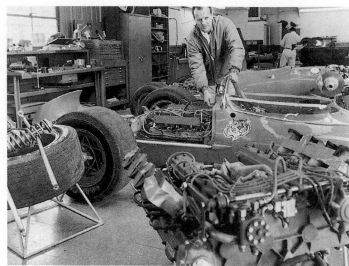

A.J. Foyt took over the Ford Indy engine parts and service business in 1970 after Ford dropped out of racing. His Ford-powered cars were top performers when boost and fuel-consumption restrictions came into force in the mid '70s.

of these race engines. The usual practice in selecting a specific turbocharger model and size was to get one that would deliver a strong boost pressure at medium engine speed—5,000—6,000 rpm—then use some type of waste gate to by-pass exhaust gas for holding more or less constant boost at higher speeds. This assured good torque coming off the turns without blowing the engine apart on the straightaways.

Engine power at high speeds could be readily increased by merely adjusting the spring load on the waste-gate valve so it would allow a higher boost before opening and by-passing the exhaust. It could be done in a few seconds by just turning a screw on top of the waste-gate valve. Some cars even had a cable mechanism so the driver could adjust the boost on the track. This is what I mean by the term, "screwing up the boost." It was somewhat akin to "tipping the can" when nitro fuels were popular 20 years earlier.

Just like nitro, there was a sharp limit to how much power could be obtained by merely turning the waste-gate screw. Any given turbocharger will operate most efficiently at some specific air-flow rate, rpm and discharge pressure. When you get out of this range— as you can when increasing tur-

bocharger boost—you get into all kinds of bad things like excessive compression-heat buildup, excessive exhaust back pressure, higher exhaust temperatures, etc. If you were to run an engine at constant rpm and measure the horsepower as you screwed up boost pressure, you might get dyno figures like this:

Boost in. Hg.	HP
65	640
75	730
85	780
95	800
105	790

The obvious answer to get still more power would be to get a larger turbocharger with more air-flow capacity. Then the compressor and turbine would be operating within their high-efficiency "envelope" with the higher air-flow rates. Higher boost pressures could be delivered with a moderate amount of exhaust back pressure and temperature

buildup. Assuming, of course, the engine can handle the extra boost without blowing apart. This wasn't always the case.

In another sense, though, a larger turbocharger is going to hurt you on an oval racetrack. That is, the larger impeller and turbine will have more inertia or "flywheel effect," so there is less throttle response coming off the corners. In this sense you would want to use the *smallest* turbocharger that will give the desired air flow and boost. This is a tough compromise that each engine builder must deal with.

Development of the turbocharged Offy quickly progressed through three sizes of AiResearch turbochargers in the late '60s and early '70s as air flow and boost pressures were gradually increased. Here are typical HP and torque figures for these three turbos on a good-running Offy—with average race-setup output and all-out qualifying horsepower:

Year	Turbo	HP @ rpm	Torque lbs. ft. @ rpm	in.Hg.	Max.HP @ in.Hg.
1966	TO6	625 @ 8,000	430 @ 6,000	65	680 HP @ 72
1969	TO7	730 @ 8,500	510 @ 7,000	77	850 HP @ 90
1972	TO9	820 @ 9,000	560 @ 7,000	85	1,050 HP @ 110

Getting even air distribution to all cylinders was a major problem with turbocharged Ford V-8s. As can be seen here on Foyt's Coyote, intake manifolding was tucked in as tight as possible to reduce airflow restriction to the rear wing. All kinds of unusual manifold arrangements were seen.

I don't want to imply that all it took was to bolt on a larger turbocharger to achieve these tremendous outputs from the 4-cylinder Offy. It also required a lot of work on pistons and valves to withstand the higher exhaust pressures and temperatures. A lot of development was done initially when the engine was first converted for supercharging in the '66—'67 period, but this work had to continue as boosts were increased.

Also major bottom-end changes were necessary to handle the higher loads which came with 9,000—9,500-rpm crankshaft speeds. In 1970 the Offy's stroke was further shortened from 3-1/8 to 2-3/4 in., with a corresponding increase in bore. Connecting-rod length was increased from 5.67 to 5.86 in. to utilize the same cylinder block. The object was to permit higher revs without increasing piston speed. Some private teams later had special cranks made with strokes as short as 2.60 in., searching for the optimum stroke/rod length ratio. It might also be mentioned that a number of teams abandoned the classic Offy tubular connecting rods during this period, opting for Carrillo rods machined from a flat steel plate.

These had been proving themselves in all types of stock-block racing. Tests showed they were stronger—if not lighter—than the standard-Offy tubular rods.

At any rate the strongest Offys were apparently capable of 9,600—9,800 rpm in qualifying by the mid '70s—and 9,000 rpm for 500 miles—with a reasonable degree of reliability.

A.J. AND THE FORD

For some obscure reason the four-cam Ford V-8 engine never seemed to be as comfortable with turbocharging as the Offy. They never could use more than 80—85-in. manifold pressure without burning or warping the pistons. The problem was even so critical that boost had to be reduced a few inches on a hot day. Ford engineers used to run a temperature probe in the intake manifold to measure mixture temperatures. As long as this temp didn't go above 180°F it was OK, but if it went even 15—20° higher "you might as well hang it up." They eventually learned to control manifold-mixture temperatures by richening the air/fuel ratio at the injector by-pass to use the cooling effect of raw alcohol. This wasn't without compromise. 80-in.

manifold pressure could be run on a hot day if 1.6-mpg was acceptable. If air temperature cooled they could run just as fast with 2.0 mpg by leaning the mixture.

Some of these problems might have been solved if Ford hadn't pulled completely out of racing in 1970. A. J. Foyt took over the four-cam engine business, but he didn't have the resources or facilities to do the extensive kind of development needed to sort things out. He did the best he could. A. J. and his engine man, Howard Gilbert, experimented with several piston designs and ring combinations. He even tried to increase turbulence and speed up combustion by inserting sleeves in the intake ports to increase gas velocities entering the cylinders. With all this, Foyt was never able to use more than 80—85-in. manifold pressure for any length of time. The engine would develop about 825 HP at 9,600 rpm at this boost.

Some have speculated that the basic problem with the Ford was the location of the intake ports between the camshafts—which required complex manifolding to distribute the air/fuel mixture from a turbocharger. Fuel distribution was uneven at best, and

157

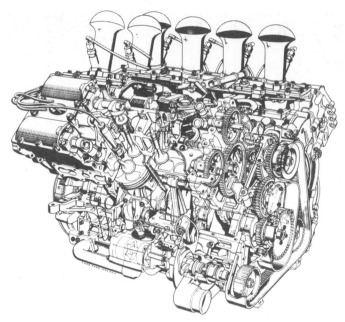

DFV Cosworth V-8, adopted from the Formula-1 scene and rechristened DFX in Indy-car trim, was unlike any previous Indy engine. It featured dual-downdraft intake ports, narrow valve angles, Lucas timed fuel injection, dual water pumps, external oil pumps, and a very rigid crankcase structure—a very complex, expensive engine. Drawing courtesy of Ford of England.

External appearance of the Formula-1 DFV Cosworth is essentially the same as its Indy-car DFX counterpart, except for the absence of turbocharging. Photo courtesy of Ford of England.

this was the root of all the other problems.

Under these conditions it's not surprising that Foyt wasn't competitive in qualifying for the race in 1972 and '73 when the top Offys were running 10-, 20- and 30-in. higher manifold pressures. His qualifying speeds were down 7—10 mph and he couldn't keep up in race traffic either. When he tried screwing up the boost without richening the fuel mixture, the engine would fail. If he ran rich enough to save his pistons, he lost time making extra pit stops. The Ford engine just wasn't in it in the early '70s.

This situation was reversed in 1974 when USAC went to an 80-in. manifold-pressure limit for qualifying and put a cap of 280 gals. on total fuel consumption for the race. The boost limit was an attempt to slow the cars down a little for safety reasons. The fuel limit was nothing more than a public relations gesture during the infamous Arab oil embargo.

The new rules gave the Ford engine a new lease on life. With twice the valve and port area per cubic inch of displacement of the Offy, the Ford developed about 50 HP more at a given manifold pressure. USAC officials rigged up modified jet-engine bleed valves with flanges that could be bolted to an intake manifold. The valve would bleed off excess air when manifold pressure reached 80 in. The little valves proved to be great performance-equalizers at the Speedway. Cars would accelerate up to the 80-in. pressure, then just hang there. Dyno testing with the valves showed the 8-cylinder Fords were 40—50 HP stronger than the 4-cylinder Offys. Foyt reported 820 HP at 9,600 rpm for his Ford at 80-in. boost. A typical Offy was good for 770 HP at 9,000 with the big TEO691 turbo at 80 in.Hg manifold pressure.

Sure enough, Foyt's qualifying speeds were suddenly 2—3 mph faster than his opposition. He sat on the pole in '74 and '75, and was 2nd row in '76 and '77. Just as important, the large breathing area of the Ford was an advantage when fuel supply was limited. Foyt

could maintain race speeds with less boost, and thus get better mileage. He finished in 2nd and 3rd places in '75 and '76. He won in '77.

It was a perfect example of one particular type of engine being helped by a change in the rules. It's happened many times in racing. In fact A. J. Foyt's unusual handle on things in the mid '70s encouraged several other teams to dust off their Ford V-8 engines. They were common on the Championship trail in '76 and '77. The trend might have gone further if the British Ford Cosworth V-8—also a four-cammer—hadn't appeared about that time. It was a better engine in most ways than the Ford.

RISE OF THE COSWORTH

As part of Ford Motor Co.'s worldwide racing program in the mid '60s, they decided to back the development of a 3-liter V-8 that could be a potential world-beater in Formula 1. It was to parallel the development of the four-cam V-8 for Indianapolis. Rather than

Cosworth V-8's massive wet-sleeved aluminum block, O-ringed deck, and a water pump for each cylinder bank driven by a cog belt housed at front. Designed basically for unblown operation on gasoline, it adapted well to turbocharging and alcohol.

Al Unser going out for 1976 practice in his backup turbo-Cosworth-powered Parnelli—the Indy-car version of Mario Andretti's Formula-1 Parnelli. He qualified in the second row at 186.2 mph. Aerodynamics, sophisticated chassis and turbocharged Cosworths all played a significant roll in the late '70s. Photo by Tom Monroe.

involve factory engineers and facilities this time, the entire development and tooling program was contracted to a private engineering firm in England—Mike Costin's and Keith Duckworth's "Cosworth" company. They had developed modified-production Ford engines for racing and rally work, so their abilities were well established. They had the facilities, the experience and the personnel. Costin and Duckworth started this Formula-1 project in late 1965. A competitive engine was turned out in probably half the time and cost than it could have been done in the restrictive Ford organization. It was the world-beater Ford wanted.

This is the basic engine that eventually drifted over to Indianapolis in the mid '70s, after being honed to a high stage of performance and reliability during 10 years of Formula-1 road racing. The team of Parnelli Jones and Vel Melitich was the first to experiment with a de-stroked Cosworth in 1975. They could see the success Foyt was having with his engine under the new fuel and boost restrictions. They also felt that the basic Ford Cosworth design was better suited to Indy than the four-cam Ford.

For one thing the Cosworth ports were sized to give a theoretical gas velocity of over 300 ft./sec. at peak power. This helped give a broad, flat torque curve. The Ford ports were always too big for anything below 9,000 rpm. Remember Foyt's attempt at sleeving the ports down in size to get higher mixture velocities into the combustion chambers. Along this same line, the Cosworth engine used a British Lucas fuel-injection system which injected the fuel in timed spurts rather than in a constant stream. This permitted more precise air/fuel-ratio control over a broad range of speeds and loads. Parnelli Jones felt this would allow finer tuning for fuel economy.

The Cosworth also had some advantages in the bottom end. Cooling was especially effective because the *wet* cylinder sleeves were in contact with engine coolant—and the coolant was pumped in at the lower center of each of side of the cylinder block, using dual water pumps. The built-in dry-sump-lubrication system was just as sophisticated. A unique lower crankcase section and oil sump combined the main-bearing caps in a single casting secured by long through-bolts which threaded into the main cylinder-block webs.

This gave an extremely rigid engine assembly. In fact the whole idea was to make the engine strong and rigid enough to allow use as a main chassis structural member. In Formula 1 cars the monocoque structure, or tub, was attached to the front of the engine, and the rear suspension was bolted to the back! This resulted in a more rigid car weighing 50 lbs. less.

I'm sure this feature didn't go unnoticed by Mr. Jones.

Another advantage the Cosworth had over the 4-cam Ford was its small profile as viewed from the front, particularly with the intake manifolding fitted. Ford's intake-manifold fitted the intake ports between the cams on top of each cylinder head. They stuck out in the airstream, interfering with air flow to the rear wing. This not only increased drag, turbulent air generated by the manifold reduced the rear wing's effectiveness. On the other hand, more compact Cosworth intake manifolding tucks in on top of the engine between the cylinder heads. The Cosworth engine package could be shrouded completely under smooth body panels without presenting any more frontal area than the profile of the

Turbocharged Cosworths seemed to perform best with a very large intake plenum above the individual port stacks. This seemed to help throttle response off the turns a lot. Note USAC boost-pressure blowoff valve on top of plenum. Photo by Rowell.

driver and his cockpit. This was basically free horsepower and additional rear-tire loading due to reduced drag and improved air flow to the rear wing.

The F-1 Cosworth appeared to be fairly simple to convert to Indianapolis conditions. Its 182 cubic-inch displacement was close enough to the 161-CID Indy limit for turbocharged engines that existing cylinder sleeves and forged-crankshaft billets could be machined to the necessary bore and stroke. They could also use the original rods, valves, gears, accessories, etc. It was mostly a matter of adapting the turbocharger to the engine, converting the Lucas fuel system to pressure induction, lowering the compression ratio to 8.5-to-1 and tailoring the valve timing to allow for the high exhaust back pressure and pressurized induction.

Early dynamometer tests were very encouraging. It looked like a well-tuned Cosworth might be 50 HP stronger than the Ford—as much as 100 HP stronger than a typical Offy at the 80-in. manifold-pressure limit introduced in 1974. One reliable test showed 885 HP at 9,200 rpm on 80 in. using the large AiResearch TEO691 turbo. Others showed 850 to 870 HP at 9,000 rpm, depending on cam timing. The torque curve was broad and

flat as predicted. Fuel consumption was a pleasant surprise at 1.1 lbs. per HP-hour. Very importantly, the engine seemed reasonably reliable up to 10,500 rpm, a speed which might easily be reached in the heat of qualifying.

The Cosworth came on very quickly at Indy. The Jones-Melitich team first started experimenting with the engine in 1975, though no attempt was made to qualify a car. The following year Al Unser qualified the first Cosworth 2 mph slower than the pole car starting in the 2nd row. By 1978 nearly half the starting field was using Cosworths and Al Unser won the race with one. It's also important that Tom Sneva's all-time lap record of 203.62 mph was set with a Cosworth in '78, running 80-in. manifold pressure. The engine obviously was considerably stronger than the Offys at that time. Just as important, its fuel consumption was not excessive. In this department it had the same advantage over the Offy as the Ford: It could develop the same power as the Offy on considerably less boost pressure—thus less fuel consumption. This gave the Cosworth an extra edge under the tight fuel restrictions USAC imposed in the late '70s.

There weren't a lot of bugs in the Cosworth design, although

considerable development work was done to make it suitable for Indy racing. For instance, McLaren used Carrillo connecting rods and Nicholson pistons in the process of destroking the crankshaft to 2.256 inches to reduce displacement. Dearborn Crankshaft machined the Cosworth crankshaft billets. The most serious problem was inadequate cooling around the exhaust valves. McLaren cured this problem by circulating more oil above the exhaust valves and increasing water-pump flow. Cosworth followed this by recoring the heads for larger water passages and upgrading the valve-seat-insert alloy. Valve-train parts were surprisingly troublefree, perhaps because these Cosworth engines were being revved to 11,000 rpm in Formula-1 competition. The engine gave little trouble when turbocharging doubled output.

A superb engine design! Teams winced at over-$30,000 price, but the car owners dug into their wallets. Before long, some two-car teams had three or four spare engines!

UPDATING THE OFFY

Poor Dale Drake. He no sooner got his classic Offy outperforming the turbocharged Ford V-8 in the early '70s than another 8-cylinder

Sparks-Goossen-Drake (SGD) version of the Offy had the angle between valves reduced from 72° to 44°, a lower piston dome, and ports for the 16 valves split. Output increased 40—50 HP with a concurrent reduction in fuel consumption.

Late Drake-Offy, introduced in 1976, was usually identified by the name cast on the cam covers—but not always. This version had valve angle reduced to 38°, flat-top pistons, and ports were again siamesed. Another boost in power and fuel economy.

menace came along—the Cosworth. Just one crisis after another for the basically obsolete 45-year-old engine. This time the handwriting on the wall was bigger and bolder than even before. There just weren't that many promising tricks or radical modifications left to upgrade the Offy's performance to catch up to Cosworth's 100-HP superiority at a given manifold pressure. Death was nigh.

It's ironic that the first serious attempt to upgrade Offy performance in the '70s came, not from the Drake organization, but from an old innovator from the '30's—Art Sparks. Remember, he was the force behind the fabled 6-cylinder Thorne cars of the '30s and '40s. He was still figuring and cogitating 40 years later.

So the story goes, Sparks traveled to Germany in the early '70s to confer with the famous Mahle piston manufacturers on problems with forged pistons for the Offy. Sparks had been producing them for several years. During his visit he was also exposed to a lot of German combustion-chamber, valve-train and port-arrangement technology. When he came back he had an idea for improving Offy performance with relatively simple changes in the cylinder-block design. Believe it or not, he patterned the combustion chamber

and port arrangement after the huge 12-cylinder Daimler-Benz engine that was used to power German Messerschmitt fighter planes during World War II!

Essentially what he wanted to do was to narrow the angle between the valves from the original 72° to 44°, making a much flatter combustion chamber. This promised to help breathing by reducing the curvature of the port. It also improved combustion by allowing a flatter dome on the piston to increase turbulence and flame speed. The Daimler engine also had individual port passages for each of the four valves per cylinder. Sparks thought this might also help the Offy, as the huge siamesed ports were too big for the small bores and strokes that were being used in the '70s. His ports were completely split on the exhaust side. On the intake side they were split out to about 1/2 in. from the flange face—so it might be called "semi-siamesed."

Actually Art Sparks never commissioned such an engine to be built. He passed along the idea to Dale Drake—more or less one racer to another. Drake was interested enough to assign Leo Goossen the job of converting the idea into working drawings. This was in 1973, before the Cosworth

challenge surfaced. Unfortunately Goossen never lived to finish those drawings. Over 70, his health was failing. He died with the drawings half-finished.

The story might have ended there but for the increasing competition from the Ford engine under the new fuel and boost limits in 1974. Sparks had run across a clever young draftsman in Germany, named Hans Hermann. After Dale Drake died in 1972, his son John and widow Eve hired Hermann to complete the Sparks-Goossen redesign. They financed it by selling the idea to millionaire car owner Pat Patrick. Patrick, a staunch Offy devotee, was desperately looking for a way to keep up with the Fords under the new rules. This brought Patrick's crew chief, George Bignotti, into the picture with his intuitive sixth sense on "right and wrong" in engine design. Bignotti's input proved invaluable in the later stages of the redesign. In return Drake promised the team six engines in time for the 1975 Indy race—plus exclusive use of the design for one year.

Patrick and Bignotti were tickled with their new secret weapon. The seemingly minor changes in the combustion chambers and ports were good for another 40—50 HP at 80-in. manifold pressure, with

Late Drake-Offy had a raised intake-port face, tilted back at the top to reduce port curvature. Fuel-injector throats came down from above, giving a straighter shot into the cylinders. Fuel was injected from two atomizing nozzles below the throttle valve.

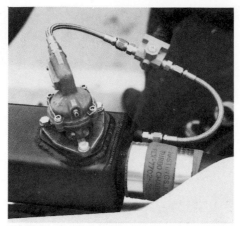

USAC's first boost-pressure blowoff valve, used in 1974 to limit boost pressure for qualifying. It was basically a jet-engine pressure-bleed valve made by Allison. It was calibrated by an orifice valve in the signal line.

an improvement in fuel economy as bonus. They were able to run less spark advance, indicating faster combustion. There was also an improvement in throttle response off the turns with the large TEO691 turbocharger.

Things worked out on the track, too. Driver Gordon Johncock qualified at 191.6 mph, right next to Foyt in the front row—2 mph slower than Foyt's Ford, but 1/2-mph faster than any of the conventional Offys. Although the other Patrick car driven by Wally Dallenbach couldn't qualify the first day, he was also faster than most of the Offys. In the race Johncock dropped out early with mechanical failure; but Dallenbach moved quickly to the front from his 7th-row starting spot. He lead the race by 41 secs. at one time—with fuel consumption well under control. Then he hit some debris from the Sneva crash in turn-1, damaging the suspension enough to put him out of contention.

Those convincing performances assured the success of the "narrow-angle" Offy. Everyone wanted one for the '76 race and Dale Drake was ready and willing to oblige. But not with Sparks' "ideal" 44° valve angle. Drake figured if the Offy could get that much improvement from that

modest change in angle, why not go as far as possible with the basic block/crankcase configuration? He huddled with Hans Hermann and they worked out an included angle of 38° as being just about the minimum valve angle that could fit. This narrower angle permitted a flat-top piston for optimum flame travel, plus they were able to get almost a straight intake port. This was done by raising the port opening on the block and tilting the intake-flange face back against the valve angle. Injector throttle tubes were then brought down from above, so there was very little curvature all the way to the cylinder. Exhaust ports exited horizontally on the opposite side. The ports were again siamesed, which appeared to work better with turbocharging. Note also that the intake-port passages were made considerably smaller than the Sparks redesign. This increased mixture velocities and helped throttle response and fuel economy with the limited boost.

Indy historians will want to be clear on these two distinct Offy configurations. The design initiated by Art Sparks, with the 44° valve angle, was known as the "Sparks-Goossen-Drake," or SGD, engine. It had plain cam covers like the older Offy. There

were eight individual exhaust ports on the left—with nearly split intakes on the right. Fewer than 15 of these engines were made.

The later Drake-Offy with the 38° valve angle and siamesed intake and exhaust ports can be readily identified by the different port-flange angles on each side. The intake was put on the right because it best fit the average rear-engine configuration. The 38° version introduced in 1976 has been known as the "Drake Offy" It has DRAKE cast on the cam covers. I understand between 20 and 30 of these engines have been built. They have been more widely used than the SGD version.

Did the 38° valve angle perform measurably better than the 44° angle? They say the difference was too small to show up conclusively in track performance. There was less than 20 HP difference on the dyno. Also the Drake Offy was never extensively developed. Just about the time it was introduced, the Cosworth V-8 was starting to come on. Within one year all the top teams were using the Cosworth. Only the teams with less financing used the Drake—these people didn't have the resources to do much development on their own.

It was a case of too little too late. The 4-cylinder configuration had definitely reached the end of the line. Doom was sealed when USAC went to the 280-gal. fuel limit for the 500-mile race. This required considerable fuel-mixture leaning, meaning higher combustion-chamber temperatures. The big-diameter Offy pistons just couldn't dissipate heat as efficiently as the Cosworth's small pistons. The Offy was more competitive with the Ford V-8 because of some inherent cooling problem the Fords always seemed to have, plus its higher cost and larger overall size. The Cosworth was another story. It did everything a V-8 should do.

The Drakes made one last drive to stay in business in 1977 by designing an all-new four-cam V-8 with a unique cog-belt drive for the overhead cams. They obtained financing from several sources. Several prototype engines for dyno and track testing were built. Pat Patrick was one of the backers, and crew chief Bignotti planned to run at least one Drake V-8 in the '78 race. Early dyno tests even suggested output within 20 HP of a good Cosworth.

It wasn't to be. For one thing, the cam drive belt gave problems. Bignotti was determined, so another $10,000 of Patrick's money went toward developing a gear drive and housing for the cams. Then there were bugs in the rods and lubrication system. Bignotti gave it the old college try, but after a few more months of cutting and testing, cutting and testing, he decided it was easier to just buy a Cosworth and join the crowd.

The Drake shop was locked up for the last time shortly after the 1979 race, thus ending certainly the longest and most fascinating engineering story in auto-racing history. Offys are still running in 1981—and will be for a long time to come. There are enough parts around to supply the limited needs to those Offy die-hards who would never use another engine. Unfortunately, the only ones you'll eventually see at Indianapolis will be in the museum.

SCIENTIFIC SLOWING

Increasing boost pressures, stickier tires and aerodynamic devices had USAC and Indy track officials biting their nails in the early '70s. They felt a need to slow the cars for safety reasons. However, their dilemma was they didn't know how to do it effectively without making everyone mad by obsoleting a lot of expensive hardware. Not to mention the ever-present danger that the "greatest spectacle in racing" would become a boring parade of pretty cars.

After a lot of soul-searching, the powers that be came up with three

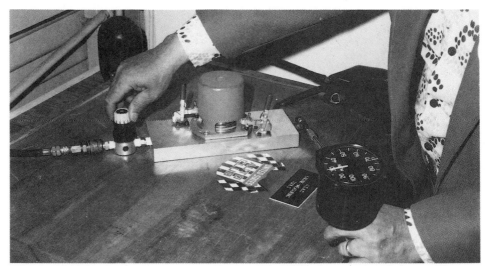

USAC officials did their best to calibrate blowoff valves accurately so all cars were handicapped equally. They claimed the valves were accurate to within 0.5-in.Hg pressure. But some of the racers claimed they were off as much as 3—4-in.

ideas to be implemented all at once or in stages:
1. Simply limit the total amount of fuel that could be used for the 500 miles. By squeezing down the fuel allotment they could force the teams to detune engines and reduce power to almost any degree the officials wished without actually obsoleting any basic equipment. This de-tuning could be done with boost pressure, cam timing, gearing, fuel mixtures, etc.
2. Reduce the car's fuel capacity, beneficial from a safety standpoint. Another plus would be a potentially more exciting race with the additional pit stops. Pit action had always been of great crowd interest at Indy. By requiring as many as six or eight fuel stops, pit work could easily be the winning factor for a given car and team. Race officials were pretty sure the racers wouldn't like a deal like this— maybe the fans would eat it up . . . maybe.
3. Boost-pressure limitation with a bleed-off valve on the intake manifold. In other words, a calibrated spring-loaded valve that would open and relieve pressure at some predetermined boost level. Very simple and *seemingly* foolproof.

To make a long story short, USAC eventually used all three

tricks to slow the Indy cars. In 1972, the first fuel allotment since the '30's was declared. It was first set at 325 gals., still too much to cause any serious fuel shortage problems. It didn't slow any one down. You can't help but contrast this with the fuel limits of 60, 45 and 37.5 gals. imposed in the mid '30s. Dramatic proof that it takes lots of fuel to make lots of horsepower.

In 1974 the Arab oil embargo gave USAC a perfect excuse to shoot the works on fuel and boost limits. There was a lot of public feeling at the time against auto racing as being a gross waster of precious petroleum. There was even some fear that all long-distance auto races would be temporarily shut off by presidential decree. The fact that the Indy cars used alcohol-based fuel made from natural gas, wood or grain didn't seem to occur to the press. That a pro football team on a coast-to-coast jet trip used many times more fuel than all the cars in an Indy race completely escaped the critics. It was a time of public hysteria, so race officials had to tread lightly.

USAC did the natural thing by clamping the lid tight for the '74 race: (1) Manifold pressures of 80 in.Hg for qualifying, limited by a

163

George Bignotti tried to "trick" the blowoff valve in 1974 by using this oversize AiResearch T18 turbocharger. His idea was to pump more air than the valve could bleed off so manifold pressure would be higher. It worked during qualifying—but officials made him run it in the race.

Later USAC blowoff valves were designed to pass so much air that officials figured there was no way the racers could trick it. We've heard that before! Valve is set to bleed air at 48 in. Hg as indicated by the 48" on top.

calibrated bleed valve installed and sealed by USAC; (2) fuel allotment of 280 gals. per car for the full 500 miles; and (3) onboard fuel capacity limited to 40 gals.— all to the left of car center—away from the wall-side of the car.

The new rules did slow the cars down—without hurting the spectacle of the race one bit. For instance, just by changing gearing, the average car turned 500-rpm less down the straights and picked up 0.2 mpg in fuel economy, losing only 1 mph in lap speed. It was a good tradeoff.

If maximum horsepower wasn't a consideration, there wasn't really that much improvement needed to be made in fuel economy. When the 280-gal. allotment was announced in 1974 most of the turbocharged cars were getting 1.5 mpg at race speeds. This mileage needed to be increased 0.3 mpg to 1.8 mpg, or 20% better to go 500 miles on 280 gals. This assumed the engine inhaled the last drop of fuel the instant it completed the 500 miles. It wasn't any big deal with modifications to cam timing, fuel mixtures, etc.

The real problem was tuning for the "ragged edge"—using just as much boost and pulling just as much horsepower as possible without falling under the 1.8-mpg limit. One of the neater tricks

some teams used was installing a temperature probe in the turbocharger turbine inlet to monitor exhaust-gas temperature—leaner fuel mixture means higher exhaust temperature. Turbine wheels could take about 1,750°F for up to 30 minutes without falling apart and they could handle 1,650° all day. So a driver had more to do than the classic driving job, he also had one eye on the turbine-temperature gage and one hand on the boost regulator. Some cars were even fitted with a fuel-mixture-adjustment knob for the driver. He could control the turbine-temperature by turning the boost and mixture-control knobs.

This was racing at Indianapolis in the mid '70s—drivers watching gages and adjusting knobs and crews counting gallons and monitoring lap speeds in the pits. With minute-by-minute instructions by two-way radio, the drivers hardly had time to do any racing.

There were frustrations too! In the 1978 race, for instance, Penske's team planned lap speeds of 188 mph at 72-in. manifold pressure and six pit stops. Tom Sneva figured to win the race easily from his pole starting position. Something went wrong with the fuel system. Sneva could run no faster than 184 mph at 60 in. without dropping below the 1.8-mpg

minimum fuel mileage. He had no choice but to drive at this speed and hope for the best. He almost made it. Sneva was running in 2nd place, 31 secs. behind Al Unser, when Unser bent a front wing during a pit stop. With his car out of trim, Unser had to slow in the turns keep the car under control, dropping his lap averages below 180 mph. Sneva started closing rapidly at his steady speed of 184 mph, but he was helpless and couldn't speed up as his fuel was disappearing fast. He gritted his teeth, drove his speed, and finished 8.3 secs. behind Unser. A few gallons of fuel cost him $170,000 in prize money!

Didn't the crowd love the excitement! It was good, clean fun. Coping with the boost regulation was another ball game. The racers didn't take this lying down. The more resourceful ones felt there just might be some way of squeezing out a tiny advantage with the small-capacity USAC bleed valves on the manifolds.

It didn't take long for the first serious attempt to surface. Even before the boost limitation was imposed in 1974, the Penske team had been experimenting with a great big AiResearch T18 turbocharger. The idea was to use it for qualifying, pumping 120—130-in. pressure and a lot of volume.

The T18 was considerably larger than the popular TEO691 unit and gave less exhaust back pressure, plus more air flow and pressure. Roger Penske finally decided not to run it in 1973 when told by USAC that he would have to run the same turbo in the race that was on the car during qualifications. He knew acceleration off the turns would be more sluggish with the larger turbine—and fuel consumption would certainly be higher.

When the 80-in.-pressure limitation was announced for '74, Penske had another idea: Why not utilize the higher air flow of the big T18 turbo to literally overpower the flow capacity of the little USAC bleed valve? Perhaps the valve couldn't bleed off enough air being pumped and manifold pressure would continue building above the 80-in. limit—with horsepower going up proportionately. Penske mechanics dyno-tested an Offy with the USAC bleed valve, first with the regular TEO691 turbo and then with the big T18. Sure enough, manifold pressure jumped up to 92 in. and the power jumped 106 HP with the T18. Voila! The little USAC valve didn't flow enough to do the job the officials had intended

It was predictable Penske would never use the big turbo. He had already been told by race officials he would have to race with the same turbo he qualified with. He had already made the decision not to try to race with the T18. He was really just playing around with it on the dyno. When things went so beautifully, the secret quickly leaked out—as it always does in racing. The story goes that a T18 turbocharger found its way to George Bignotti's shop in Indianapolis a few weeks before May, 1974.

George was just the man to do a number with it. He was never one to ask first. His motto was to try it first—and maybe get away with it! He first dynoed the T18, getting similar results. To George it looked like an easy way to go fast

during qualifying—as simple as that. Without hesitation he installed the big turbo on Wally Dallenbach's Wildcat. The car gained 7 mph overnight and Wally put it on the front row.

Then the trouble started: Bignotti proceeded to switch back to the more fuel efficient TEO691 for the race, but word got out. USAC officials descended on him—with a lot of support from the other Offy teams. Officials used the rule that says a car must race "in the same configuration" used to qualify. Turbochargers weren't specifically mentioned, but USAC bore down with a firm hand. Bignotti had no choice but to leave the big turbo on Dallenbach's car. As it turned out, the car dropped out of the race early with mechanical failure. It's quite probable the engine would have consumed too much fuel at race speeds to complete 500 miles.

Good try anyway.

An even more bizarre attempt to beat the boost rule came in 1979 after the Cosworth engines were cut radically from 80 to 50 in. of manifold pressure. Theoretically, this should have chopped off about 300 HP and 15 mph of lap speed. But the top cars were down only 8—10 mph during qualifications. Nothing much was said. On the second weekend of qualifying, when the starting field was almost filled, the roof caved in. Word leaked out that most of the teams were increasing boost by restricting the dump tubes on the wastegate valves. They were using various tricks—using a smaller pipe diameter, crimping the pipes, partially plugging the pipe by inserting orifice plates. It all had the effect of forcing most of the exhaust through the turbine at high speeds, rather than out the dump pipe. This increased the speed of the compressor wheel so it pumped more air than the blowoff valve could handle. USAC was using a bigger blowoff valve at that time—but it couldn't handle compressor speeds over 100,000

rpm. Manifold pressures must have been 10—15 in. over the legal 50 in. It was essentially the same thing Bignotti had tried in '74 with the big turbo. This was a more sophisticated attempt to increase boost using methods that were harder to detect!

There's no question that this cutie triggered the bitterest hassle ever to hit the brickyard. USAC officials were caught in an impossible situation. It was immediately obvious that most of the qualified cars had been running higher-than-legal boost—no one could prove which ones did and which didn't. It was easy enough to check the cars yet remaining to be qualified when they knew what to look for. Was this fair to the unqualified cars? USAC ended up declaring a quickie rule requiring dump pipes with a 1.47-in. unrestricted inside diameter and checking all remaining cars carefully.

Needless to say the curses flew. Lawsuits were filed. Some cars were withdrawn. Everyone was mad. USAC managed to weather the storm without being hit by court judgments, fielding a full 33-car field for the '79 race. No qualified cars were thrown out. Really, no one but crews—and maybe some drivers—ever knew what manifold pressures were used to qualify. My calculator suggests 60—65 in. for some of the Cosworths. Furthermore there is reason to believe some of the teams still managed to override the USAC blowoff valves during the race. For instance Mike Mosley turned the fastest official race lap at 193.22 mph as he battled Foyt for 2nd place in the late going. Could he have gone that fast with 50-in. manifold pressure—7 mph faster than he qualified? Not likely!

It was easy enough for USAC to take care of the boost problem in 1980. They simply went to a radically larger blowoff valve with twice the air-flow capacity. It had enough capacity to gulp all the air

165

Another streamlining trick of the late '70s was to tuck the turbocharger in behind the engine, above the transaxle. Exhaust exited straight back and the air-intake duct was flush with the engine-cover. Note flanges and Dzus fasteners for fastening the engine cover to the duct. Nothing protruded beyond the body side panels. Photo by Rowell.

Major rule changes for 1978 gave stock-block engines a better chance. American Motors officials were excited enough to supply car owner Warner Hodgdon with special aluminum blocks and heads for the AMC V-8, saving 250 lbs. over the standard engine. He had reasonable success with it.

an overspeeding compressor might deliver.

Wounds from the 1979 fiasco didn't heal that easily. Future race historians may very well trace USAC's downfall from the great boost controversy of '79. About that time several top Indy teams got together and formed "CART"—Championship Auto Racing Teams, Inc. They set out to sanction and administer a series of Indy-car races around the country in the traditional USAC Championship-circuit style. Because car owners were the motivating force behind CART, control was in the hands of the car owners rather than outside parties, as USAC had long been criticized for. In 1981 Championship racing was still being batted around between the two organizations, much to the detriment of the sport.

It's not my intention to take sides. I'm just reporting that the boost controversy of 1979 may have been the straw that triggered it all. A little cheating can perhaps be winked at, but in this case the race officials completely lost control of the situation. How harshly they should be judged is for history to decide.

ANOTHER BOOST FOR STOCK-BLOCKS

Prior to 1979, Indy rules allowed 320 CID for unsupercharged stock-block engines and 209 CID for those with superchargers. These limits were some 50 CID more than allowed for overhead-cam racing engines and it was felt this would be enough edge to give a well-built stock-block a fighting chance.

The car builders felt differently as there were only sporadic—and not very serious—attempts to compete with stock-block equipment in the early and mid '70s. Dan Gurney's 2nd place in 1968 with a Weslake-Ford was the last impressive performance by a stock-block. Equipment manufacturer Fred Carrillo managed to qualify a turbocharged American Motors V-8 in 1976 and '77 at reasonably competitive speeds. The AMC people became interested enough to supply special aluminum blocks and cylinder heads for an all-out attempt in '78. Exact copies of the iron parts, these aluminum pieces were quickly certified by USAC officials as "stock." They brought engine weight within 50—75 lbs.

of the Cosworths and Offys. At this point Carrillo got cold feet, feeling he didn't have the finances to give the AMC people a fair shake. He sold his equipment to wealthy Warner Hodgdon, along with the services of mechanic Dennis McCormack. In '76 and '77 McCormack set up the successful AMC engines in the strongest stock-block effort since Gurney's project. Hodgdon had a new car built and hired veteran Roger McCluskey to drive it.

The project attracted a lot of attention around the garages that year. The modified AMC engine was said to develop 875 horses at 8,500 rpm on 80-in. manifold pressure—equal to most of the Cosworths. McCluskey qualified it in the 4th row at 192.2 mph despite his weight handicap. He was running strong in the race and moving up when gearbox failure put him out on the 82nd lap. The transaxle had been sized for a Cosworth engine and couldn't handle the extra torque of the larger-displacement turbocharged AMC. Until then no one knew the gearbox was stressed that close to the ragged edge.

The AMC's good showing did

Turbocharged AMC stock-block used fairly long individual intake stacks between the plenum and cylinder-head ports. Good response and power. Note blowoff valve on the turbocharger-to-plenum pipe. Photo by Rowell.

Hurst-Airheart and Lockheed disc brakes are seen more and more on many late cars, replacing traditional Halibrands.

not go unnoticed by USAC officials. They saw visions of a new era of $10,000 stock-block engines competing on even terms with $35,000 Cosworths, bringing a whole new element of young grassroots racers into Championship racing. Giving them just the right incentive without alienating the established big-money teams was going to be the trick. They gave a lot of thought and discussion to major engine revisions for 1979.

First off, the displacement limit for unsupercharged stock-block engines was raised radically from 320 to 355 CID. This figure was chosen to fall in the same area as the current NASCAR limit of 358 CID. Championship racers always looked down their noses at the crude two-ton NASCAR "stockers" that had been bashing fenders on southern speedways for years. They knew all too well the stock-block pushrod engines in these cars were really quite sophisticated, both from a standpoint of performance and rugged durability. Some of them produced over 600 HP from 358 cubes on gasoline and a single 4-barrel carburetor! The better ones could run

500 miles at 7,000 rpm without spitting out connecting rods. So USAC officials figured the Indy mechanics could get well over 600 HP with fuel injection and alcohol.

The major reason for matching the NASCAR displacement limit was to take advantage of the huge choice of factory and aftermarket engine performance equipment available for that size engine. Big-port cylinder heads, high-strength iron and aluminum blocks, titanium rods, billet cranks, gear cam drives, needle-bearing rocker arms, dry-sump lubrication systems, roller-cams, lightweight valves, etc. The largest segment of American auto racing for the last 30 years had been based on the stock-block pushrod engine. Here all this equipment was just waiting to help the stock engine get a foothold in Championship racing. A clever mechanic could conceivably build a competitive Indy engine using off-the-shelf parts!

One more key rule for '79 helped put stock-blocks on the map: The displacement for supercharged stock-blocks was kept at 209 CID—but they were given an 8-in. manifold-pressure advantage over the turbocharged

Cosworths. That limited Cosworths to 50 in., while allowing 58 in. for the stock-blocks. This was the first time USAC had tried this sort of thing. Turbocharged Offys were allowed 60 in. The idea of selectively "adjusting" manifold-pressure limits for different types of engines proved an effective, if controversial, method of evening up Indy competition. I didn't like to see them do it, as it always leads to a lot of problems, but it worked out quite well as of 1981.

Anyway, it's now history how the '79 rules change triggered the strongest surge of stock-block competition at Indy since the early '30s. The first year two cars qualified. Grant King built a 355-CID fuel-injected Chevrolet small-block V-8 and Phil Threshie qualified it in the 10th row at 185.8 mph. Warner Hodgdon was back with his turbocharged-AMC aluminum engine, reduced to 650 HP because of the boost limitation. Jerry Sneva put this one in the field at 184 mph. Both cars dropped out early with mechanical problems, but all involved seemed excited about future possibilities.

In 1980 no less than 18 stock-block cars entered, most of them

Dan Gurney's 355-CID stock-block Chevrolet qualified nicely for the 1980 race, using the Donovan aluminum block and new factory aluminum heads. It developed over 600 HP on alcohol. He admits to $14,000 in the engine—a lot less than a Cosworth.

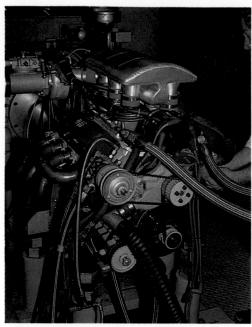

209 CID Chevy V-6 stock block undergoing development on Ryan Falconer's dynamometer. Lindsey Hopkin's team ran this engine which developed 600-plus HP and 450-plus lbs.ft. torque in the 1980 race. Photo by Bill Howell.

unblown 355-CID Chevys. Three 355's managed to qualify. Roger Rager had the best speed of 186.4 mph, using a relatively low-budget cast-iron engine in a 4-year-old Wildcat chassis. He was running strong in the race until a car spun in front of him on the 58th lap. Dan Gurney had a much more exotic Chevy engine in his Eagle chassis for Mike Mosley. He used the new Donovan aftermarket aluminum block with newly released factory aluminum cylinder-head castings featuring recontoured ports and water passages. Gurney's car was 150 lbs. lighter than Rager's Wildcat. Several Chevy teams switched back to iron cylinder blocks after experiencing bottom-end problems. The NASCAR guys wouldn't touch aluminum blocks for long-distance racing! In fact Chevy's special siamese-bore NASCAR block, introduced in the late '70s, was 30 lbs. heavier than the standard iron block. However, engine weight isn't as critical in a 3,700-lb. Grand National car as in an Indy car. And the light Indy cars didn't impose the tremendous bottom-end stresses on an engine when "backing off" for a corner.

Probably the most interesting stock-block engine in 1980 was Lindsey Hopkin's turbocharged Chevy V-6 in Hurley Haywood's No. 99 Lightning. Chevrolet was interested in promoting their new 90° V-6—made on small-block V-8 tooling—in various types of racing and youth/performance applications. To make it attractive to the racers they developed a high-strength nickel-iron block with splayed outer bolts on the main caps, and special aluminum heads using the large port and valve sizes of the V-8 heads. The heads weighed just 12 lbs. each. Ryan Falconer, noted California race-engine builder, did a beautiful job on the buildup, even to a $2,000 billet crankshaft with offset crankpins to give more even firing similar to the passenger-car version. The car showed instances of superior speed, but the team was plagued by rocker-arm breakage. A fuel leak put the car out of the race.

The stock-blocks certainly weren't world-beaters under the new '79 rules. As a class, they were more competitive in Championship racing than they had been for many years—and they did meet the goal of costing only a fraction of the price of the typical overhead-cam race engine. We haven't seen the last of stock-block engines at Indy.

PEAK PERFORMANCE

It's interesting that the highest speeds ever achieved at Indianapolis were not with the unlimited 1,000-HP engines and huge wings of the '72—'73 period—but with 80-in. blowoff

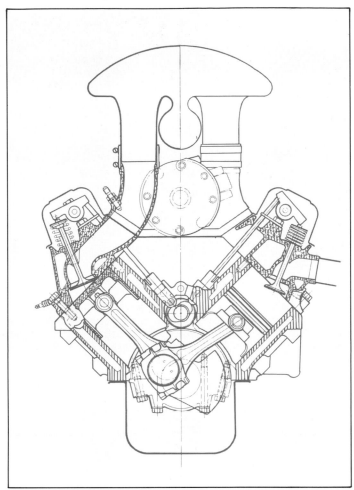

Fastest car ever at Indy: Tom Sneva's Penske PC-6 of 1978. This combination still holds the all-time lap record of 203.62 mph. With the chassis and aerodynamic improvements since then, it makes one wonder what today's cars could do with 1978 boost restrictions. Matthews drawing, courtesy of Penske.

Chevrolet was interested enough in promoting their new 90° V-6 that they made up special big-port aluminum heads and a high-strength siamesed-bore block. Those are big-block Chevy rods they're using! Drawing courtesy of Chevrolet.

valves and 36-in. wings at the peak of their development in 1978. Under these restrictions Tom Sneva turned the all-time lap record of 203.62 mph in the Penske PC-6—hitting 191 mph in turn-1 and 220 mph on the straights. He was using 850—900 HP in a 1,550-lb. car.

There are a couple of simple reasons for this seeming contradiction. One, the Indy track was completely repaved in 1977 to give a surface that improved traction and allowed higher overall speeds. They used an asphalt made from a very fine No.14 sand, leveling it to a tolerance of 1/4-in. per ten feet or better. The track was like a billiard table for the '78 racers. They say the track alone was good for 2—3-mph improvement in lap average.

The other major factor in the impressive '78 performance was tires. There was no particular technical breakthrough that year. Tire development was a gradual evolutionary thing that happened to reach a peak at the same time the track was repaved. Result: Record lap speeds. The key to it all, as alluded to before, was the 40-gal. onboard fuel-capacity limit. This required at least five pit stops, thus immediately relieving the tire engineers of any consideration of wear in their development. As long as blistering could be controlled, they could make the tires as soft and as sticky as they wanted, even if they lasted only 100—150 miles. This made all the difference in the world in grip.

So even though the '78 cars may not have achieved as much aerodynamic downforce as the big-winged cars of the '72—'73 period, the smoother track and stickier tires more than offset it. The later cars were 3—4-mph faster through the corners. The smaller wings reduced aerodynamic drag enough so they were 10—15-mph faster down the straights. It all added up to 3—4-mph higher lap averages. This was another example where brute horsepower alone doesn't always create fast lap times.

FLAT-OUT TO GLORY

The very low boost restrictions in '79—'81—only 50 and 48 in. manifold pressure for Cosworths—led to a unique situation where the drivers could go flat out all the way around the track. With outputs down around 600 HP for all engines in 1980, there wasn't enough acceleration off the corners to build up much additional speed down the straights. The cars quickly reached a "terminal" speed—and just hung there. A little speed was "scrubbed off" in the corners . . . then it gradually increased 5 or 10 mph and the car hung there at that speed. Meanwhile the driver just kept his foot hard down and steered.

To put it into numbers, a typical

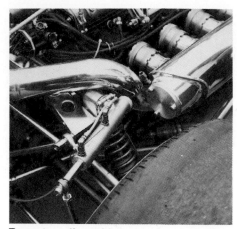

Remote adjustable sway bar from the late '70s. The driver could pump this hydraulic piston in or out to increase or decrease front- or rear-suspension roll stiffness. This was a handy gadget to compensate for fuel-load and track-condition changes from the cockpit—assuming the driver knew what he was doing.

Hydraulics was dropped in favor of cable-operated sway-bar adjusters. This was done by rotating one or two rectangular sway-bar lever arms to get the desired roll stiffness. Lever arms in this installation extend back through the front bulkhead and are linked to the inner upper-control-arm ends. Arms on edge gave maximum stiffness—reduced as they were rotated toward being flat. Link tying the two lever arms together is above the sway bar. Adjuster cable is routed above the clutch and brake master cylinders. Photo by Tom Monroe.

Weismann transaxle has become popular on Indy cars. This one uses the ring and pinion from the Chevrolet Camaro 12-bolt rear axle—less expensive and stronger than the British Hewland gearbox.

On-board radios and electronic monitoring equipment means most Indy cars are equipped with batteries today.

well-tuned and well-set-up 1980 Indy car running a Cosworth at 48-in.-maximum manifold pressure would go through the corners at 190 mph, hit 197 mph peak on the straights and average 193 mph for the lap. Exciting?

Such is life with 48-in. manifold pressure and modern-day grip! If this 48-in. pressure were combined with a rule limiting tire-tread width to 8 or 10 in., there'd be excitement again, but probably less-safe racing.

GROUND EFFECTS: BLACK MAGIC OF THE 70s

When race officials all over the world began restricting the size and placement of wings in the mid '70s, it was inevitable that car designers would find other and possibly better ways of developing aerodynamic downforce—and with less drag.

The aerodynamic principle used starting in the mid '70s is known as *ground effects*. As the term implies, this concept uses the track surface, or ground, as one surface of the car's aerodynamic system to generate downforce. Large air ducts are designed into the two body pods at the sides. Their undersides are contoured so the bottom half forms a venturi throat near the car's center of gravity. The track surface forms one side of the venturi. The theory is, the air flowing through this duct system—due to the forward motion of the car—accelerates to a higher velocity at the venturi

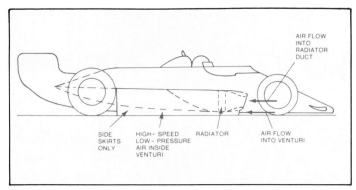

Ground-effects cars utilize the venturi principle to produce downforce by creating a lower-than-atmospheric pressure under the car at speed. Side skirts extending to the track surface prevent outside air from "leaking" into this low-pressure area. Radiator air is ducted separately from the undercar air.

Side skirts for the '80-vintage ground-effects cars were carbon-fiber reinforced plastic with separate aluminum rub blocks to control wear. Articulated skirts that slide against the track like this were banned for 1981. Photo by Tom Monroe.

Jim Hall's 1979 2K Chaparral was a prime example of the modern "ground-effects" car. It had the full venturi tunnels which extended just past the transaxle, with deep side skirting. Details under the skin: engine as a major structural member; compact packaging of the turbocharger system behind the engine for maximum streamlining and ground-effects ducting to the rear; structural fuel tank between engine and driver. Photo by Mark Mitchell.

throat, generating low pressure under the car. This is in accordance with the Bernoulli principle of velocity and pressure changes in a flowing fluid. As fluid—air in this instance—flows faster, it generates low pressure. The same law is used to generate low pressure in a carburetor throat to suck fuel through the nozzle. The above drawing shows this effect.

You can also see that the sides of the body—in effect the sides of the venturi-shaped ducts—must be very close to the track surface for maximum effect. In fact, they should theoretically contact the track surface so there is no

appreciable air leakage into the low-pressure area created in the duct. This led to the development of various types of skirt devices that extend down from the main body to the track surface. Initially these skirts were made from flexible polycarbonate, an extremely tough plastic that actually rubbed against the track with no great amount of drag on the car—or excessively fast wear of the skirt. First the skirts were fixed in place, however the more effective rigid carbon-fiber-reinforced-plastic skirts were located in guides and suspended on hinge linkages, with light spring loading to hold them

lightly against the track. Aluminum rub blocks fitted to their bottom edges kept abrasion wear to a minimum. These are known as *articulated skirt systems*.

Admittedly, there has been a lot of controversy surrounding these various skirt devices. Some claim skirt systems which keep the skirt against the track leave a fine powdery residue from the plastic material. They say this makes the track slippery after a few laps, constituting a safety hazard. The official feeling on both sides of the Atlantic seems to be against these articulated-skirt systems. They have been banned at Indianapolis

Side pods of the 2K Chaparral contain the venturi tunnels and radiator ducts. Fixed side skirts extend down from the outer edges of the side pods, adjusted so they barely touch the track when running. The '80 2K Chaparral skirts were spring loaded firmly against the track for positive sealing. Photo by Rowell.

Large radiator opening with ground-effects venturi directly below. Note how the Chaparral's suspension and its mountings are designed to give the air a "straight shot" at the radiator and venturi openings. As with any successful design, an Indy car must work as a system. A good example of everything working together: suspension, engine, structure, body, aerodynamics, etc. Photo by Tom Monroe.

for '81, and in Formula 1.

It's not possible to ensure that skirts won't touch the track. Even fixed skirts will be drawn down against the track when the car moves up and down on its suspension from track irregularities or by downforce from the wings or suction under the car. Some '79 and '80 ground-effects cars were so efficient that you could see them draw down closer to the track as speed increased.

I hasten to add that there were good ground-effects cars and not-so-good ones. There seems little doubt that Formula-1 cars were initially much more advanced in this area than Indy machinery of the mid '70s. They were four or five years ahead in development. The first true Indy-type ground-effects cars were seen at Indy in 1979—the Pennzoil Chaparral for Al Unser and the Penske PC-7 that Bobby Unser qualified. Penske's other driver Rick Mears tried a PC-7 and decided to qualify the non-ground-effects '78 car, ending up fastest of the three. By 1980, most of the cars in the first four rows were using the ground-effects principle. The concept caught on very quickly.

If you study the design of these cars you will see that only one— Jim Hall's Pennzoil Chaparral— really utilized full ground-effects construction. It is the only one to carry the side ductwork all the way to the back of the car. Notice the side "tunnels" carry back behind the rear axles and transmission. The other cars terminate the side ducts just behind the venturi

Rear venturi-tunnel exits are large diffusing cones that control the expansion of the air from the venturi throat—help give minimum air drag with maximum downforce. Photo by Tom Monroe.

Body being waxed and oil heated—note electric heater probe in oil tank—in preparation for race start. Central fuel-tank of Gordon Johncock's '80 Phoenix accomplished several things: left side pods free to house ground-effects and radiator ducting; improved safety from reduced vulnerablility; increased polar moment of inertia—driver forward, distributing car weight farther from its CG. This also put more weight on the under-utilized front tires. Just as low polar moment of inertia increases maneuverability, high polar moment increases stability—an Indy car needs stability. Photo by Tom Monroe.

throat. How much did this hurt the downforce effect? I don't know, but the Chaparral equaled or bettered the Formula-1 cars, which were admittedly more efficient in this respect at first. In fact, the more advanced F-1 cars started using narrower transaxles so the duct exits could be wider. That gave expanding cones behind the center venturi to draw even more air through the tunnels for increased downforce.

I don't know whether the 1980 ground-effects cars developed appreciably more total downforce at a given speed than the most efficient wing cars of 1978—or even the big-wing cars of '72–'73. Wind-tunnel test data was not available when this book was published in 1981. Turn speeds give a clue, but these are slightly colored by the low boost limits of recent years. Tom Sneva hit 191 mph in turn-1 during his record 203-mph lap in 1978, with a non-ground-effects car. I don't know of any one exceeding that through 1980. Of course we know that 1980 tires

were stickier than those of the '72–'73 period, which could account for the 3—4 mph higher turn speeds in 1980. It wouldn't take any improvement in aerodynamic downforce in the last eight years to account for 1980 turn speeds.

There is one other factor—aerodynamic drag. They say a good ground-effects car has less drag in relation to downforce than one with elaborate external wings. This would help lap speeds slightly by allowing higher peak straightaway speeds with the same horsepower. So far we haven't seen much benefit here with engines effectively limited to around 600 HP by boost restrictions. Very few of them could manage 200 mph on the straights in 1980. With the latest 14-in.-wide tires and aerodynamic downforce technology, they don't have to slow down for the corners.

Maybe this is a good place to leave off our technical history of the Indianapolis race car. From the early high-wheeled monsters that

barely had enough horsepower to accelerate from turn speeds to 1980's power-restricted cars that can go through the same turns flat out at nearly 200 mph. You certainly couldn't say that the Indy track has been a big, bad challenge that has defeated the best racing minds in the world. I would say the big, bad cars have defeated the track!

For right now anyway . . .

Chaparral rear wing is supported by large end plates that help high-speed stability. Car is more airplane than car—designed for "flying on the ground." Compare smaller wings of ground-effects cars to those prior to ground effects. Wings are used mainly to "trim" the ground-effects car rather than provide downforce, especially at the Speedway. Photo by Rowell.

Jet Engineering Eagle, first new car built to 1982 rules requiring stock-block engines. Cast-iron block and Jet titanium connecting rods are used. Titanium wheel spindles and structural members are used throughout the car. Photo by Tom Monroe.

Gordon Johncock going out for practice in one of Pat Patrick's '81 Phoenix cars at Phoenix International Raceway. Designed to the '81 rules banning moveable skirts. Photo by Tom Monroe.

INDEX

D-12.22518632753